AF552414

OSI EXPLAINED
End-to-End Computer Communication Standards
Second Edition

ELLIS HORWOOD SERIES IN COMPUTERS AND THEIR APPLICATIONS

Series Editor: IAN CHIVERS, Senior Analyst, The Computer Centre, King's College, London, and formerly Senior Programmer and Analyst, Imperial College of Science and Technology, University of London

Computer Communications and Networking

Currie, W.S.	LANS EXPLAINED
Deasington, R.J.	A PRACTICAL GUIDE TO COMPUTER COMMUNICATIONS AND NETWORKING, 2nd Edition
Deasington, R.J.	X.25 EXPLAINED, 2nd Edition
Henshall, J. & Shaw, S.	OSI EXPLAINED, 2nd Edition
Kauffels, F.-J.	PRACTICAL LANS ANALYSED
Kauffels, F.-J.	UNDERSTANDING DATA COMMUNICATIONS
Muftic, S.	SECURITY MECHANISMS FOR COMPUTER NETWORKS

Computers and their Applications

Abramsky, S. & Hankin, C.J.	ABSTRACT INTERPRETATION OF DECLARATIVE LANGUAGES
Alexander, H.	FORMALLY-BASED TOOLS AND TECHNIQUES FOR HUMAN–COMPUTER DIALOGUES
Atherton, R.	STRUCTURED PROGRAMMING WITH BBC BASIC
Atherton, R.	STRUCTURED PROGRAMMING WITH COMAL
Baeza-Yates, R.A.	TEXT SEARCHING ALGORITHMS
Bailey, R.	FUNCTIONAL PROGRAMMING WITH HOPE
Barrett, R., Ramsay, A. & Sloman, A.	POP-11
Berztiss, A.	PROGRAMMING WITH GENERATORS
Bharath, R.	COMPUTERS AND GRAPH THEORY
Bishop, P.	FIFTH GENERATION COMPUTERS
Bullinger, H.-J. & Gunzenhauser, H.	SOFTWARE ERGONOMICS
Burns, A.	NEW INFORMATION TECHNOLOGY
Carberry, J.C.	COBOL
Carlini, U. & Villano, U.	TRANSPUTERS AND PARALLEL ARCHITECTURES
Chivers, I.D.	AN INTRODUCTION TO STANDARD PASCAL
Chivers, I.D.	MODULA 2
Chivers, I.D. & Sleightone, J.	INTERACTIVE FORTRAN 77
Clark, M.W.	PC-PORTABLE FORTRAN
Clark, M.W.	TEX
Colomb, R.	IMPLEMENTING PERSISTENT PROLOG
Cope, T.	COMPUTING USING BASIC
Curth, M.A. & Edelmann, H.	APL
Dahlstrand, I	SOFTWARE PORTABILITY AND STANDARDS
Dongarra, J., Duff, I., Guffney, P., & McKee, S.	VECTOR AND PARALLEL COMPUTING
Duan-Zheng, X.	COMPUTERS IN SEQUENTIAL MEDICAL TRIALS
Dunne, P.E.	COMPUTABILITY THEORY
Eastlake, J.J.	A STRUCTURED APPROACH TO COMPUTER STRATEGY
Eisenbach, S.	FUNCTIONAL PROGRAMMING
Ellis, D.	MEDICAL COMPUTING AND APPLICATIONS
Ennals, J.R.	ARTIFICIAL INTELLIGENCE
Ennals, J.R	BEGINNING MICRO-PROLOG
Ennals, J.R., *et al.*	INFORMATION TECHNOLOGY AND EDUCATION
Filipič, B.	PROLOG USER'S HANDBOOK
Ford, N.	COMPUTER PROGRAMMING LANGUAGES
Guariso, G. & Werthner, H.	ENVIRONMENTAL DECISION SUPPORT SYSTEMS
Harland, D.M.	CONCURRENCY AND PROGRAMMING LANGUAGES
Harland, D.M.	POLYMORPHIC PROGRAMMING LANGUAGES
Harland, D.M.	REKURSIV
Harris, D.J.	DEVELOPING DEDICATED DBASE SYSTEMS
Hepburn, P.H.	FURTHER PROGRAMMING IN PROLOG
Hepburn, P.H.	PROGRAMMING IN MICRO-PROLOG MADE SIMPLE
Hill, I.D. & Meek, B.L.	PROGRAMMING LANGUAGE STANDARDISATION
Hirschheim, R., Smithson, S. & Whitehouse, D.	MICROCOMPUTERS AND THE HUMANITIES: Survey and Recommendations
Hutchins, W.J.	MACHINE TRANSLATION
Hutchison, D.	FUNDAMENTALS OF COMPUTER LOGIC
Hutchison, D. & Silvester, P.	COMPUTER LOGIC
Koopman, P.	STACK COMPUTERS
Koskimies, K. & Paaki, J.	AUTOMATING LANGUAGE IMPLEMENTATION
Koster, C.H.A.	TOP-DOWN PROGRAMMING WITH ELAN
Last, R.	ARTIFICIAL INTELLIGENCE TECHNIQUES IN LANGUAGE LEARNING
Lester, C.	A PRACTICAL APPROACH TO DATA STRUCTURES
Lucas, R.	DATABASE APPLICATIONS USING PROLOG
Lucas, A.	DESKTOP PUBLISHING
Maddix, F. & Morgan, G.	SYSTEMS SOFTWARE

Series continued at back of book

OSI EXPLAINED

End-to-End Computer Communication Standards

Second Edition

JOHN HENSHALL B.Sc., F.S.A. Scot.
SANDY SHAW B.Sc., M.Sc.
both Senior Computing Officers
Edinburgh University Computing Service

ELLIS HORWOOD
NEW YORK LONDON TORONTO SYDNEY TOKYO SINGAPORE

This edition first published in 1990 by
ELLIS HORWOOD LIMITED
Market Cross House, Cooper Street,
Chichester, West Sussex, PO19 1EB, England

A division of
Simon & Schuster International Group

Typeset in Times by Ellis Horwood Limited
Printed and bound in Great Britain
by Hartnolls, Bodmin, Cornwall

British Library Cataloguing in Publication Data

Henshall, John *1953—*
OSI explained: end-to-end computer communication standards. — 2nd Edn. —
(Ellis Horwood series in computer communications and networking).
1. Computer systems. Communication networks. International standards. Open systems interconnection
I. Title II. Shaw, Sandy *1950–*
004.62
ISBN 0–13–639451–5

Library of Congress Cataloging-in-Publication Data

Henshall, John, 1953–
OSI explained: end-to-end computer communication standards / John Henshall, Sandy Shaw. — 2nd ed.
p. cm. — (Ellis Horwood series in computer communications and networking)
ISBN 0–13–639451–5
1. Computer networks — Standards. 2. Data transmission systems — Standards. I. Shaw, Sandy, 1950– . II. Title. III. Series: Ellis Horwood books in computers and their applications. Series in computer communications and networking.
TK5105.5.H47 1990
004.6–dc20 90–41329
CIP

Contents

Preface

> Owl explained about the Necessary Dorsal Muscles. He has explained this to Pooh and Christopher Robin once before, and had been waiting ever since for a chance to do it again, because it is a thing which you can easily explain twice before anybody knows what you are talking about.
>
> A. A. Milne, *The House at Pooh Corner*

The purpose of this book is to explain the nature and capabilities of the standards for Open Systems Interconnection (OSI) which have been defined by the International Standards Organization (ISO). OSI has had a long period of gestation; its conception can be traced to 1977 when ISO began work on a Reference Model for OSI. The goal of OSI is to equip differing computer systems with the ability to interwork, and so provide the end-user with a variety of communications-based services. We shall show how OSI makes this possible, regardless of the diversity of the computer systems involved.

Special attention is paid to services which are particularly visible to end-users — file transfer (FTAM) and electronic mail (MHS/X.400) — but all the subordinate end-to-end communication services that make interworking possible are also examined.

The Appendix of relevant ISO documents gives an indication of just how many standards have been produced. Clearly, it is not possible to describe every aspect of these standards; the ISO documents themselves constitute the comprehensive definition. However we have attempted to present the essence of OSI in a form palatable to the computer-literate reader, offering more than just a basic understanding of the subject. The grounding in OSI principles, and detailed review of the higher layer OSI standards will be sufficient for the purposes of most readers. However, the book will enable the committed reader to progress to a study of the standards documents themselves.

This edition is correct with respect to the developing standards available at the time of publishing; these are not expected to change significantly during their progression to full International Standard status.

When one of my (JH) young nieces discovered from her mother that I was writing a book she immediately responded 'Is it about witches?' OSI certainly does have an air of mystique and it has been our main purpose to dispel this and explain how OSI actually works. In presenting this explanation, we received help and advice from many friends and colleagues, and would like to thank Bill Byers, Brian Gilmore,

Adam Hamilton, George Howat, Andrew McKendrick, Graham Rule, and Ackroyd.

Particular thanks go to Norman MacCaig for his kind permission to reproduce 'Power dive' (from: *Collected Poems*, Chatto and Windus, London, 1985), the closing poem.

David Stewart-Robinson laboured long and hard to produce the diagrams from our hasty sketches and we are indebted to him for that, especially since he did not once lose his cool as we changed specification in mid-flight.

Special thanks must be accorded to two people: John Murison gave many hours of his time to provide us with numerous valuable suggestions and constructive criticism. The statement 'I think I prefer Vogon poetry' (see Adams 1979) sums up how Chris Henshall felt about the content of the book as she attempted, patiently, to steer the book's technical tutorial progress clear of ravines. For this, and for her forbearance during the long period of research and writing, I (JH) am deeply grateful.

Finally we extend thanks to several organizations:

Extracts from British Standards are reproduced by permission of the British Standards Institute. Complete copies can be obtained from them at Linford Wood, Milton Keynes, MK14 6LE.

There are quotations throughout the book taken from two works, *Winnie-The-Pooh* and *The House at Pooh Corner*, both by A. A. Milne. They are used by the kind permission of the publishers, Methuen Childrens Books, London.

Extracts from *Winnie-The-Pooh* and *The House at Pooh Corner*, both by A. A. Milne are used by permission of the Canadian Publishers, McClelland and Stewart, Toronto.

Extracts from *Winnie-The-Pooh* by A. A. Milne. Copyright 1926 by E. P. Dutton, renewed 1954 by A. A. Milne. Reprinted by permission of the publisher, E. P. Dutton, a division of NAL Penguin Inc.

Extracts from *The House at Pooh Corner* by A. A. Milne. Copyright 1928 by E. P. Dutton, renewed 1956 by A. A. Milne. Reprinted by permission of the publisher, E.P.Dutton, a division of NAL Penguin Inc.

NOTE TO THE SECOND EDITION

In this second edition we have **updated** all sections in line with standards development — in particular adding a substantial section on **filestore management** to the chapter on FTAM. The chapter introducing the application layer has been substantially enhanced to look in depth at the **internal architecture** of that layer, and the chapter introducing functional standards now has an example. A new chapter has been added to cover **Directory services (X.500)**, and a tutorial on **ASN.1** has been included as a new appendix.

John Henshall
Sandy Shaw

Edinburgh
June 1990

ELECTRONIC MAIL

The authors can be contacted using the following electronic mail addresses:

NRS: S. Shaw@uk.ac.edinburgh
INTERNET: S. Shaw@edinburgh.ac.uk
or S. Shaw%edinburgh.ac.uk@nss.cs.ucl.ac.uk
BITNET: S. Shaw%uk.ac.edinburgh@ukacrl
UUCP: . . . !uunet!ed!S. Shaw
X.400: C=GB; ADMD=' '; PRMD=uk.ac;
O=Edinburgh; I=S; S=SHAW

The authors have also developed a one day seminar that is a complete introduction to OSI and the upper layers. Details are available from Computer International Ltd, 10 Farmbrough Close, Stocklake, Aylesbury, Buckinghamshire HP20 1DQ. Tel: 0296 434911, Fax: 0296 436965.

1

Introducing the ISO reference model

The aim of Open Systems Interconnection, OSI, is to provide communications-based user services that operate between computer systems which may be located in different countries and supplied by different manufacturers. The current state of such user services is bounded by severe limitations: generally, one manufacturer's products can interwork only with equipment of similar origin. Some organizations have dealt with this problem by procuring all their equipment from a single supplier, or by implementing private standards of operation on all their installed equipment. These options are not always open to smaller organizations who must live with the fact that they can only function in a localized 'closed' environment. Many research and development organizations have addressed the problems of bridging dissimilar systems with a plethora of experimental interim solutions.

International Standards Organization (ISO) is responsible for developing standards, by international agreement, over a wide range of technical areas, and has adopted the title OSI for the set of standards concerned with computer communications. The goal of OSI, the provision of communications-based services between computer systems of different origin, will remove two constraints from the end-user: the first is commercial, by reducing the dependency on a single supplier; the second has much wider implications, raising the possibility that the users of any two computer systems may:

— exchange files,
— exchange electronic messages,
— log on to the other's system,
— submit jobs to the other's system.

Thus the isolated systems and 'closed' groups of interworking systems will be opened to each other as OSI products become widely available. The series of standards developed by ISO define the rules and procedures which must be implemented on every computer system which intends to participate in OSI.

An impressive demonstration of the user services made possible by standards of this kind, though of a rather older vintage, is provided by the international telephone system. Subscribers in different countries can make direct calls to one another as a matter of course. This is made possible by the existence of international standards, agreed in this case between telecommunications administrations. For OSI, ISO has attempted to devise standards which will enable a wide range of communication-based services to be sustained amongst a global community of computer systems.

As a basis for the development of these standards, ISO developed a reference model (ISORM), to partition the problem into discrete *layers*, and provide a conceptual framework for understanding the complex processes involved in computer communication. The ISORM has seven layers, as shown in Figure 1.1.

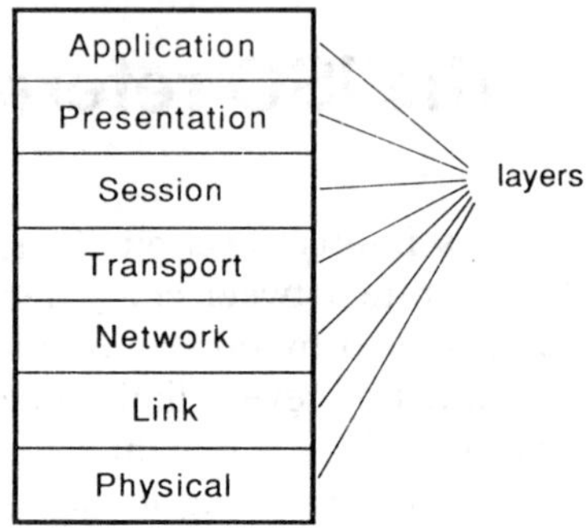

Fig. 1.1 — The seven layers of the ISORM.

The ISORM specifies the functionality of each layer, the interfaces between adjacent layers and the method of achieving layer-specific functionality between cooperating computer systems, over real physical media. The communications functions associated with each layer are now examined in turn.

"There are seven verses in it."
"Seven?" said Piglet carelessly as he could.
"You don't often get *seven* verses in a Hum, do you, Pooh?"
"Never," said Pooh. "I don't suppose it's *ever* been heard of before"

A. A. Milne, *The House at Pooh Corner*

1.1 LAYER FUNCTIONALITY

1.1.1 The application layer

The goal of OSI is realized at the application layer, since it is this layer that provides the communication-based service to the end-users. The subordinate layers of the model exist to support, and make possible, the activities that take place at the application layer.

In this layer all 'high-level' system-independent applications activity is performed. Such activity is managed by an entity embedded in a local operating system which interfaces the system-independent nature of the ISORM to the specific nature of the computer system. We shall refer to this entity as an *application agent*. An application agent may operate purely as a service provision for *remote* user access to local computer system resources (such as a filestore). Alternatively, it may provide a *local* client (a program or human user) with an interface to an OSI application.

As the uppermost layer of the ISORM, the application layer differs from the other six in that it makes OSI services available to the users of the computer system on which it resides. The layer embodies a wide range of system-independent application functions, some of which are well recognized and are therefore standardized by ISO. These include:

— file transfer and file directory operations (delete, rename, etc.),
— message handling services (e.g. electronic mail),
— job transfer and remote job management.

In a *standardized* application, the way in which its functionality is achieved, and the services offered by it, are defined by an ISO Standard. Any product marketed as conforming to an International Standard (IS) is guaranteed to conform to a defined set of rules, which enable it to interwork with all other conforming products.

Thus the application layer is concerned with providing services, covering a range of applications, to an end-user. Application layer activity involves the transfer of *information* over OSI between distinct cooperating computer systems. Given that the representation of information within computer systems differs from one system to another, an understanding of the syntax and encoding of the information that is to be transferred must be established between the cooperating systems. This is the function of the next layer of the model.

1.1.2 The presentation layer

The function of the presentation layer is to provide a common representation of application information whilst it is in transit between two cooperating computer systems. As an example of the differences that must be bridged, we can consider character representation. It may be that two computer systems use the same local storage technique for character files, say, the character encoding defined by ASCII. In this case, little need be done by the presentation layer other than to establish that this common encoding applies. If, on the other hand, one of the systems uses the EBCDIC character encoding, then the presentation layer must ensure that appropriate transformations are performed on the information. To do this it establishes, by negotiation between the two computer systems, a common representational form for character information for use whilst such information is in transit between them.

The application layer offers high-level system-independent activity over OSI between two cooperating computer systems, and the presentation layer ensures that any information exchanged between the systems, as a result of application layer activity, is in a commonly understood form. As yet we have not seen any activity associated with the establishment and control of data communication between computer systems. This is provided by the next lower layer, the *session* layer.

1.1.3 The session layer

The session layer occupies the area between the application-oriented upper layers and the 'real-time' data communication environment. It provides services for the management and control of data flow between two computer systems.

DATA communication service user	application	application INFORMATION exchanged
	presentation	application INFORMATION representational issues resolved
DATA communication services provided	session	application INFORMATION handled as transparent DATA

Fig. 1.2 — The three upper layers.

For example, session allows for insertion of synchronization points in the flow of application information between computer systems. This permits the application to identify specific points in the flow of information so that, should the data flow be interrupted, with the possible loss of information in transit, it can be restarted at some recognized point, thus avoiding a (wasteful) rerun of the whole transaction.

Session layer activity management services allow activities to be started, halted, abandoned or restarted under the (indirect) instruction of the application layer. Use of these services allows an application to order and manage its work. An activity may perhaps be halted to permit a more urgent activity to be undertaken, and then restarted at some later time.

The lower layers of the ISORM provide a *full-duplex* communications service which may or may not be required by the application layer for the application in question. Session provides both a full-duplex and a *half-duplex* capability to the upper layers. It also provides a *token* scheme, for controlling 'turns' at data transmission in a half-duplex service.

The 'real-time' communications environment begins at the *transport* layer, layer 4.

1.1.4 Transport and the lower layers

The lowest three layers of the ISORM — *network* (3), *data link* (2) and *physical* (1) — are concerned with the provision of data transmission. The network layer provides data transmission services to the layer above, the transport layer. Reliable data transmission services between computer systems, that is *end-to-end*, are assumed by the session layer. What does the transport layer add to the network layer services?

The lower layers deal with data transmission over a real physical medium (such as coaxial cable), and so model a communications technique for data transmission over a particular physical medium between two attached computer systems. Communications media differ in fundamental ways, as do the data transmission techniques used over them. Many standards have already been defined to govern data communication over various types of medium (we shall refer to the pairing of a real physical medium with a specific communications technique as a *sub-network*). The result is that, although each sub-network conforms to the principles of the ISORM in the provision of data transmission services by the network layer, the quality of the service offered differs between one sub-network and another.

Quality of service is an important factor of sub-network capability and a major aspect of this is the detection and correction of errors in data transmission. Some sub-networks are designed to offer services with comprehensive detection and correction while others offer little. Communications technology is such that, in order to achieve high speed data transmission over a sub-network, error related facilities are either minimal or non-existent. It follows that, in high speed data environments, data exchange over a sub-network cannot be assumed to be 'reliable'. An important function of the transport layer is to perform error handling on data transmitted across sub-networks which are not designed for reliable data exchange. Hence the transport layer provides session with a reliable data transmission service, irrespective of the nature of the underlying sub-network.

Sub-networks fall into two categories, *connection-oriented* and *connectionless*. Connection-oriented sub-networks operate by establishing *connections* (examined in Chapter 3) and exchanging data in discrete 'packets'. One or more intermediate specialized computers, known as switches, may be used in conveying each data packet from its origin to its destination. Connection-oriented sub-networks tend to operate at low speeds, typically up to 64 000 bits per second, but can operate over any distance. They can be seen as representing the 'wide area network' environment (WAN) and are operated throughout the world by PTTs as public switched data networks.

By contrast, connectionless sub-networks are often capable of transmitting data at very high speeds, typically up to 10 million bits per second. This is made possible by the nature of the physical medium which can be installed between systems in close proximity. For this reason high speed connectionless sub-networks are only available within localized geographical areas. Such localized environments are known as local area networks (LANs).

The ISORM defines the manner in which high-level application activity can be performed between two computer systems, regardless of the type of sub-network to which they are attached. Indeed, a variety of sub-networks may be traversed in a route between the computer systems.

Independence from the type, quality and number of sub-networks involved in communication between computer systems is inherent in the services offered by the transport layer.

Lower layer summary

The physical layer models the interface of a computer system to the physical medium for the provision of data bit transmission. It includes such aspects as physical connectors from the computer system to the medium and the voltage level to be used in data bit transmission.

The data link layer provides a framework around data for transmission by the physical layer; detection and correction of errors may be performed in this layer.

The network layer makes use of the underlying data link services to provide data transmission services across sub-networks. It is particularly concerned with *routing*, that is establishing a route between the two computer systems, and *relaying*, the use of intermediate computer systems to provide a data flow from one sub-network to another (possibly dissimilar) sub-network, which may be necessary on the chosen route. In this way data transmission services between two computer systems can be

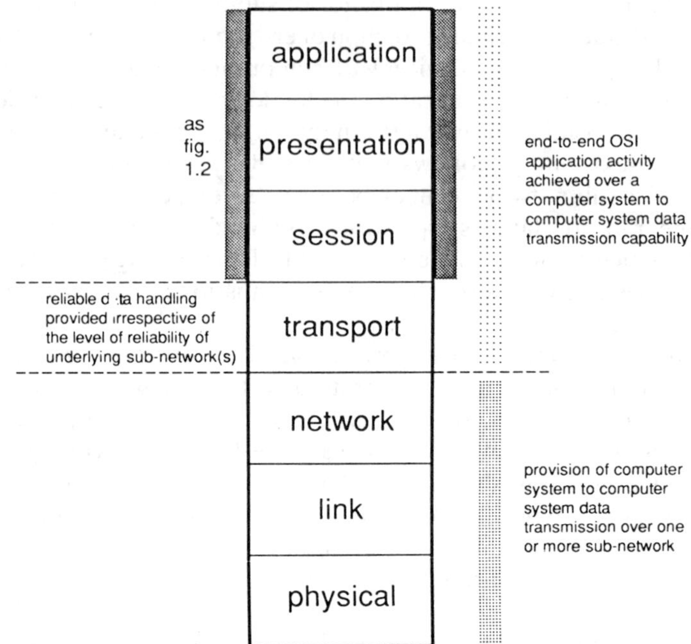

Fig. 1.3 — Role of transport layer.

provided to the transport layer even when the two systems are not attached to the same sub-network. The services offered by the network layer to the transport layer conceal from it the numbers and types of sub-network that may be involved in the communication. The transport layer is said to operate *end-to-end* between two computer systems, that is without explicit involvement in any intermediate computer system that may be used for relaying between sub-networks.

For the rest of this book we shall use the word *network* to mean the network as seen by the transport layer, though it may be composed of more than one sub-network. There are many books that discuss the lower three layers of the model and the various ways of constructing a network service (in particular we refer the reader to Currie (1988), Deasington (1986), Tanenbaum A. S. (1988)). Here we concentrate on the end-to-end communication issues: the upper four layers of the ISORM.

1.2 LAYER COOPERATION

When two computer systems, or *end-systems*, are involved in OSI communication, they do so by obeying the rules, or *standards*, associated with each layer of the ISORM. The standards dictate how the functionality of a layer can be achieved by the cooperation of two implementations of a layer standard, one on each end-system. An implementation of a layer standard must be capable of understanding and acting on messages exchanged with an implementation of the same layer standard on another cooperating end-system.

When such an implementation is 'invoked', that is involved in an OSI communication, it is known as a *layer entity*. We can consider a layer as being split across the two end-systems and represented on each by a layer entity (Figure 1.4). These two

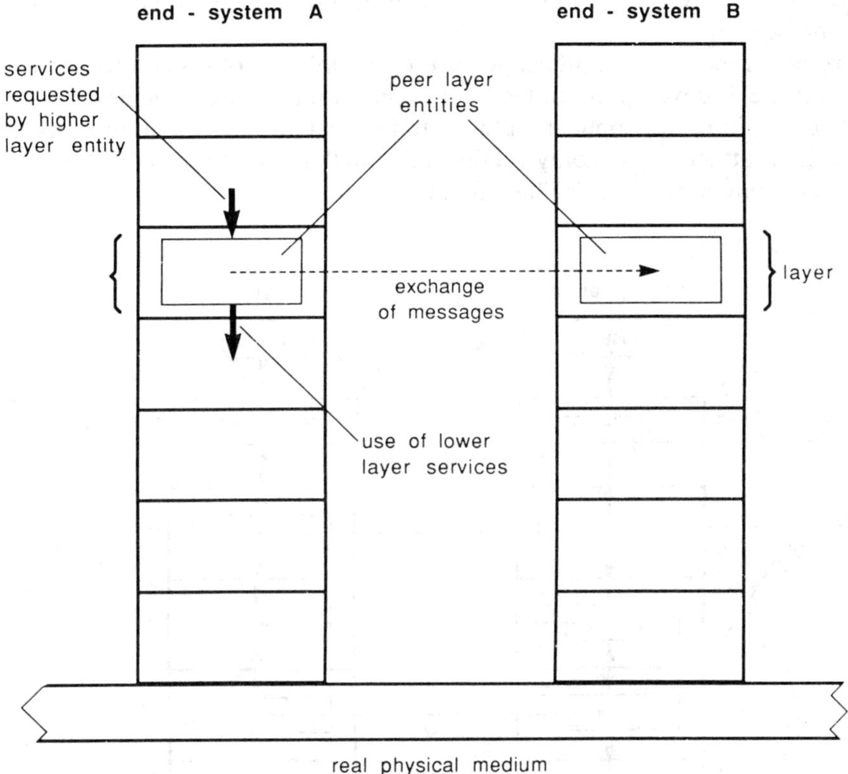

Fig. 1.4 — Layer activity achieved by cooperation.

entities, *peer* entities, will perform a layer function by the exchange of messages in a coordinated manner, as defined by the standard associated with that layer.

The application layer provides high-level services, for instance opening and reading a file on a remote end-system. These functions are achieved by the exchange of messages between peer application entities, resulting in a flow of file information between application entities and hence between file and 'user'. The representation of information in a common form over an OSI communication is the responsibility of the presentation layer, so in order to achieve information transfer the application layer must make use of the services of the presentation layer. The process begins with an application layer 'user' requesting a service of an application entity. The entity will perform the function by the exchange of messages with a peer application entity on the remote end-system in question. The initiating application entity will bring about this exchange by requesting a service from a presentation entity. The presentation entity will in turn initiate the required function by the exchange of messages with a peer presentation entity.

(Notice that in Figure 1.4 we have used two bold 'curly brackets' to enclose two entities and attached a label to that enclosure, in this case 'layer'. This form of labelling, which may enclose elements on several end-systems, will be used throughout the book.)

If we now repeat this sequence for presentation's use of session we start to see that a 'cascade' is developing. Indeed, OSI application activity is achieved by such a cascade down from the application 'user' to the real physical medium to which the end-system is attached. It is only via this medium that a real exchange between two end-systems can occur. This is illustrated in Figure 1.5.

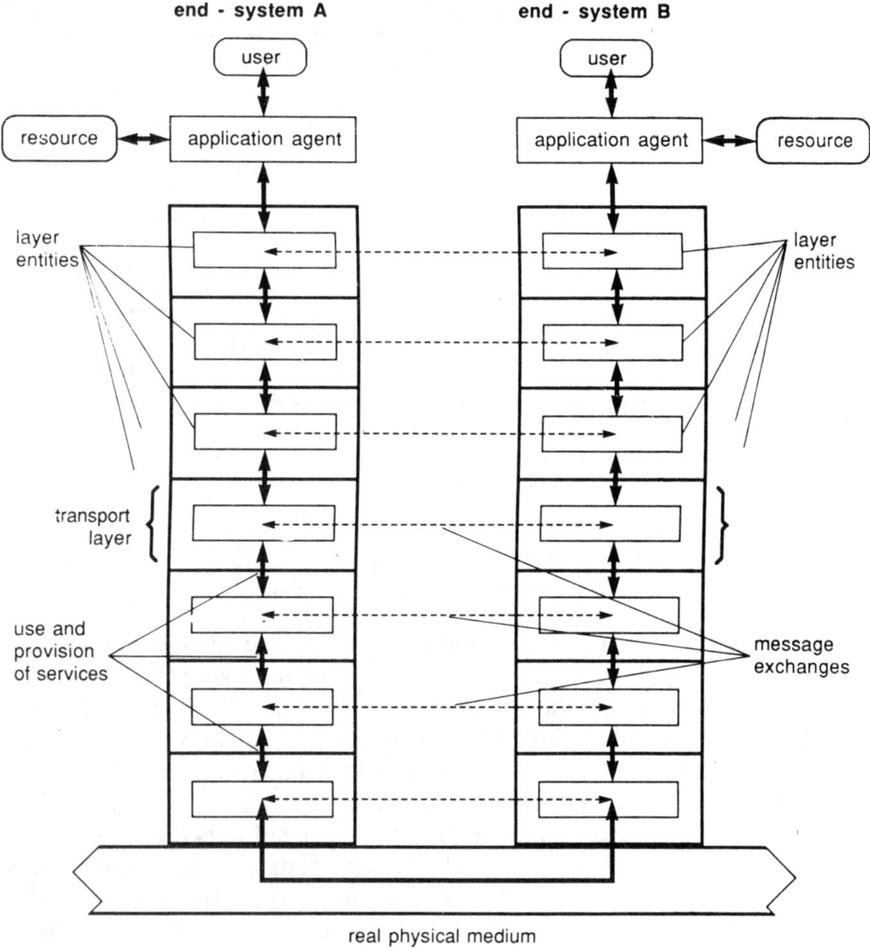

Fig. 1.5 — Cooperation 'cascade'.

The original message from an application entity is, metaphorically, the smallest figure in a nest of Russian dolls. As the message descends through the stack of layer entities the doll is encapsulated at each stage by the next bigger doll in the series. Finally, the fully assembled message (Matryoshkas) is transmitted between the end-systems. On its ascent through the stack of layer entities on the target end-system, the doll sheds a figure at each level. Eventually, the nugget of the message is presented to the end-system application entity.

The lowest (physical) layer is a special case, being the only layer to interface directly to a real communications medium. In a similar way the highest (application) layer is also special in that, unlike any other layer of the ISORM, the 'user' of this layer is not an entity of the layer above. The application layer 'user' is some practical application that can take many forms:

— a point of sale system in a store,
— a bank cash dispensing system,
— a library service, searching or reserving etc.,
— an automatic quotation service for insurance broking,
— an office mail system,
— a factory process control system.

A fundamental rule of the ISORM is that a potential 'user' of an OSI application can access OSI only by requests to an application entity. No other layer can be accessed directly by a 'user'. The 'stack' of entities that we see in Figure 1.5 on both of the cooperating end-systems can be regarded as a 'black box' with access only at the top.

The general rule of operation is that two peer entities of a particular layer (one on each end-system) cooperate to provide *services* to the next higher layer, and do so by the use of the services offered by the next lower layer.

The basic principles of the ISORM, outlined here, are examined in detail in Chapter 2.

2

Principles of the ISO reference model

In this chapter, we examine the mechanisms by which two peer layer entities achieve the functionality defined for that layer. In an expansion of the architectural principles outlined in the last chapter, we shall build upon the following terms introduced there: *end-system*, *layer*, *layer entity*, *peer*, *service*.

To reiterate, an *end-system* is a computer system with an attachment to some physical communications medium provided for the purpose of participating in OSI application activity; in this context it is often referred to as an *open system*. Any OSI application activity performed by this end-system will involve a cooperating end-system. A *layer entity* is an implementation of a layer on an end-system. The functionality of a layer can be achieved by the exchange of messages with a cooperating entity of the same layer on another end-system (a *peer* entity). A layer entity offers *services* to its 'user'; that user is, in all but the case of an application layer entity, an entity of the layer above. This was illustrated in Figure 1.5.

The aim of this chapter is to demonstrate how cooperation is achieved between peer layer entities and to introduce some concepts and definitions that are used throughout the book (and within the standards themselves). When examining the nature of this cooperation, we are not concerned with the specific functionality of the layers. Rather we shall focus on relationships between layers, layer entities and layer 'users'.

2.1 COOPERATION

One ground rule of the ISORM is that all seven layers of the model must be involved in any OSI application activity. Entities of each layer must be present in the cooperating end-systems to play their role in the mechanism of cooperation. When considering an OSI application activity, we must imagine a 'stack' of seven layer entities on each end-system. A 'user', via an application agent, uses the services of an application entity at the top of the stack, while the physical layer entity interfaces to the physical medium at the bottom.

Referring to Figure 1.5 as a schematic for two end-systems, we shall begin by looking at some layer, say layer n. We need not specify which, since here we are examining architectural, not functional, issues.

Consider Figure 2.1. A layer n user on end-system A requests of a layer n entity an n-specific service. Only if the layer happened to be the application layer would the

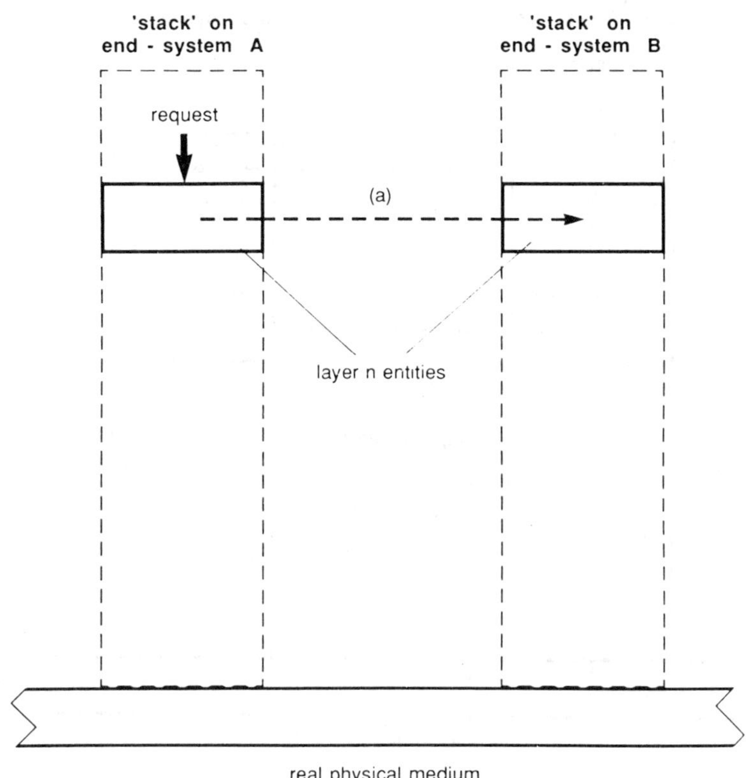

Fig. 2.1 — A general schematic.

user be related in some way to a 'real' user. In other instances the user will be a layer $n+1$ entity. The realization of this service over OSI requires the cooperation of two peer n entities, one on each of the cooperating end-systems, and involves the exchange of a control message between these peer n entities. This message indicates the nature of the required cooperation and carries any parameters associated with the particular service, encoded in a precisely defined format. This is represented by (a). Direct message exchange is only notional, since the only physical route between the end-systems is provided by the physical medium, and access to this medium is available only via the lower layers. The n entity can only achieve (a) by calling on the next lower layer, $n-1$, to act on its behalf. In general an n entity operates by utilizing services of an $n-1$ entity.

The process described above is now repeated for the $n-1$ entity. Having been invoked by the n entity, the $n-1$ entity satisfies the service request by cooperating with its peer on the remote end-system. To do this it constructs an $n-1$ control message. The n control message, (a), is passed to the $n-1$ entity as part of the service request and packaged into the $n-1$ control message.

Consider now Figure 2.2. We have:

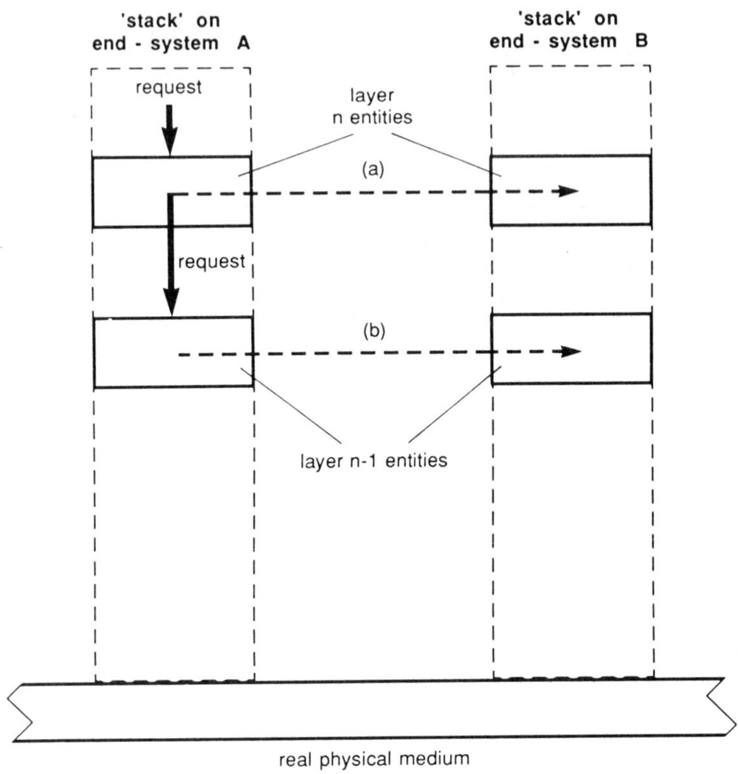

Fig. 2.2 — Use of subordinate layer entity.

(a) is the required transfer of an n control message. It may contain information provided by the user (an $n+1$ entity or application agent).
(b) is the transfer of an $n-1$ control message between peer $n-1$ entities resulting from the request by the user, the n entity. This message contains the whole of (a).

If $n-1$ is not the layer at which physical data exchange between the end-systems can occur, then the procedure is repeated with a service request by the $n-1$ entity acting as a user of an $n-2$ entity. This is continued until the physical layer is reached, at which level the data exchange consists of a series of *encapsulated* control messages.

The following sequence, shown in Figure 2.3, will then occur on end-system B in each layer entity, in ascending order:

The control message associated with the layer is examined and the activity implicit in that message is performed. The control message may just instruct the entity to pass on the residual part of the message, which contains encapsulated control messages for the higher layers, without any other action; this case is known a *normal data transfer*. Other types of control message instruct an entity to perform

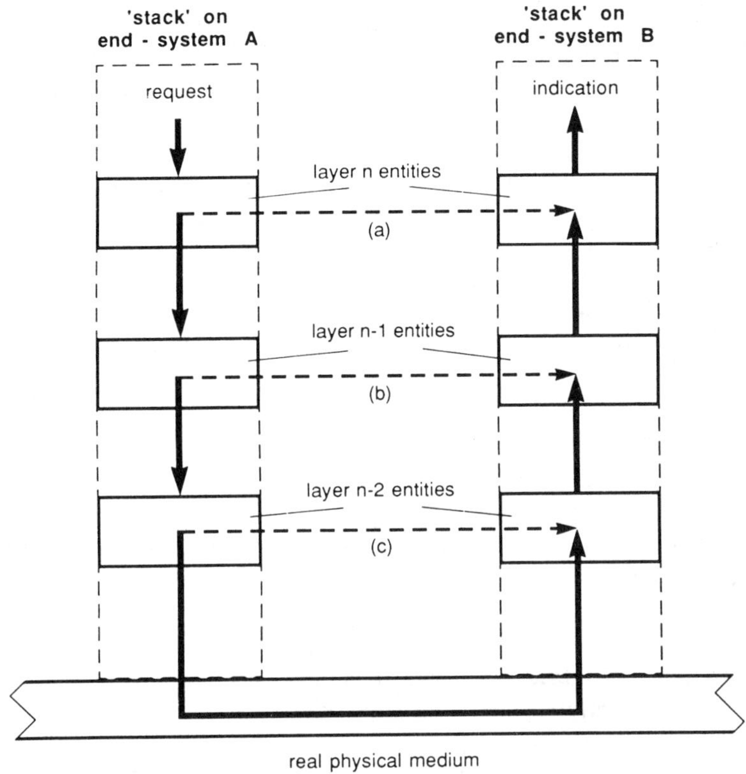

Fig. 2.3 — The 'cascade' reaches the real physical medium.

some layer specific activity, the nature of which will become clear as the book progresses.

The entity issues a report to its user (layer entity above), which corresponds to the request originally issued by the peer user. This report, known as an *indication* implies that the requested layer service has been performed by the cooperating peer entities. Together with the indication will be passed the residual part of the control message. This will result in the layer *n* entity (the peer of the *n* entity on end-system A from which a service was requested) receiving an indication that a service has been performed by the $n-1$ entity. The control message (a) that was constructed by the *n* entity on end-system A, will be presented along with this indication. The required *n* activity will then be performed as directed by the message and the *n* user on B given an indication that it has taken place.

2.2 SOME DEFINITIONS AND TERMINOLOGY

We can now relate some of these ideas to the terminology used in ISO/OSI.

A layer comprises a set of functions which, when activated by user requests, provides the realization of the services. Every function has an associated control message which conveys 'instructions' between peer layer entities in order that the function can be performed by the cooperating entities, without ambiguity. (As we shall see later, some functions have two control messages.) Every layer is defined by a precise set of functions and associated control messages. These functions, the formats and parameters of the control messages, and the actions to be taken on receipt of a control message or service request from a user, are all defined in a layer *protocol specification*. In effect it is a 'language' and set of procedures *private* to that layer. A control message is known as a *protocol data unit* (PDU).

The functionality of a layer is made available to a layer user as a set of *services*. That part of a protocol concerned with the realization of a particular service is a *service element*. A user may make use of a service element only when certain conditions are met or, perhaps, only after certain predicate service elements have been successfully invoked. (An analogy for this is the ordering of the driving instructions 'depress clutch' and 'engage gear'. Only one ordering of these is practical.) The specification of available services and of the rules of access to them constitute a layer *service definition*.

To summarize:

> **Every layer in the ISORM is defined by a STANDARD which comprises a SERVICE DEFINITION and a PROTOCOL SPECIFICATION.**

Every layer entity is therefore concerned with three areas:

— Service. The set of services it offers to its (superior layer) user.
— Protocol. The functions it performs, in conjunction with a corresponding layer entity in a remote end-system.
— Use of services. The services provided by its subordinate layer and used to carry out the (higher layer) services which it provides.

A layer user communicates a request for a service to a layer entity, or receives an indication of a service invoked by a remote peer user, in a *service primitive*. Every service element has a set of service primitives which are specified in the service definition.

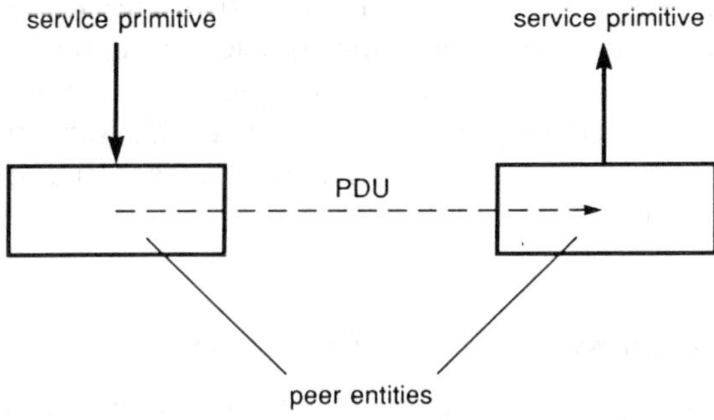

Fig. 2.4 — Peer cooperation.

The user of a layer entity is either a 'real user' (via an application agent) if the layer is the application layer, or is an entity of the next higher layer. This user, known as a *service user* (S user), requests a service by use of a service primitive. Together with this request the S user may include the control message (or protocol data unit—PDU) that it wishes to convey to its peer. We have then an *n* entity which, as an $n-1$ S user, issues an $n-1$ service primitive to request a service of an $n-1$ entity. The $n-1$ S user may include, as 'user data', any *n* PDU that it wishes conveyed to its peer. This 'user data', passed between the *n* entity and the $n-1$ entity as part of a service primitive call, is known as a *service data unit* (SDU). In this case, the *n* PDU is an $n-1$ SDU.

That part of an entity which generates or decodes PDUs, interprets events in relation to completed or outstanding layer activity, and polices the rules defined in the protocol specification, is known as a *protocol machine* (PM).

We can now summarize in standard terminology the *n* entity example described earlier in this chapter (Figure 2.5).

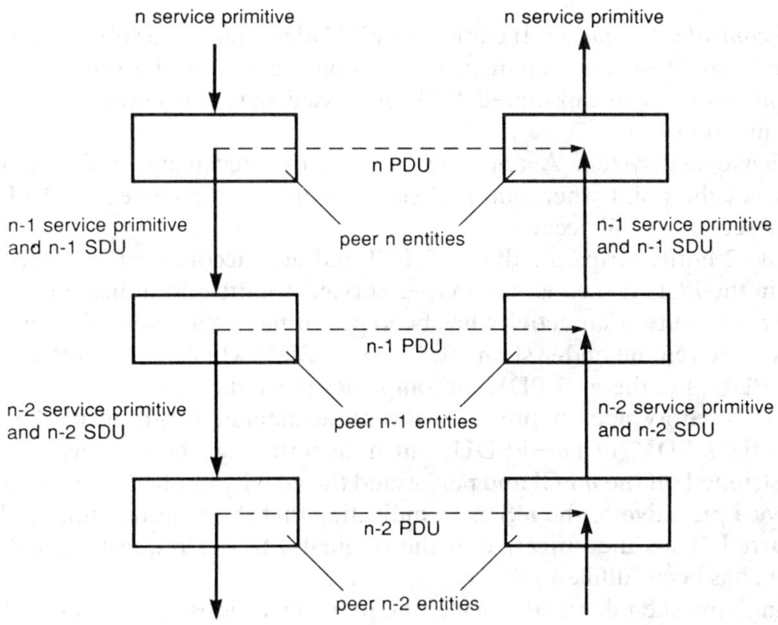

Fig. 2.5 — Peer cooperation by use of subordinate layer entities.

An *n* S user on end-system A uses an *n* service primitive to invoke a particular service element in the *n* entity. As a result the *n* entity generates an *n* PDU and issues an $n-1$ service primitive request to the $n-1$ entity, the *n* PDU becoming an $n-1$ SDU. In undertaking the requested service, the $n-1$ entity generates an $n-1$ PDU, which includes the whole of the $n-1$ SDU, and issues an $n-2$ service primitive to request a service of an $n-2$ entity. The $n-2$ entity similarly generates an $n-2$ PDU, and so on.

We can see that the $n-2$ PDU will look something like Figure 2.6. (PCI is

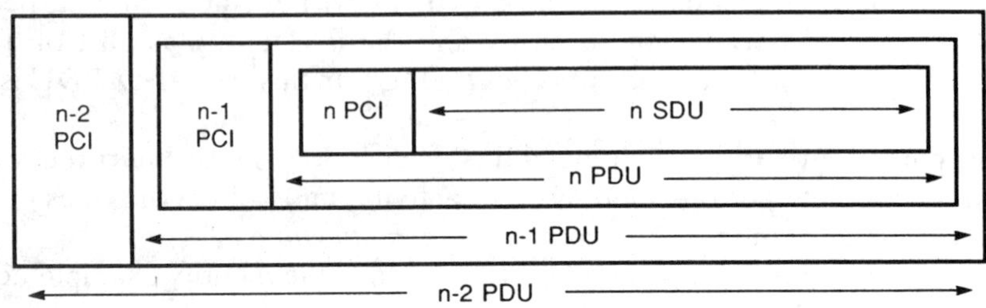

Fig. 2.6 — Encapsulation of PDUs.

protocol control information. It contains a PDU identifier and a series of parameters associated with the service element in question, defined in the protocol specification.) This form of encapsulated PDU is passed between end-systems over the physical medium.

We leave end-system A and now look at the 'receiving' end-system, B, in particular at the point where an $n-2$ entity interprets a received $n-2$ PDU. The following sequence will occur:

The $n-2$ entity strips off the $n-2$ PCI and acts according to the instructions implicit in the PCI. It then issues an $n-2$ service primitive to indicate to the $n-2$ S user, an $n-1$ entity, that activity has been performed as a result of an $n-2$ S user request on the remote end-system, A. The $n-2$ SDU which contains the residue of the $n-2$ PDU, i.e. the $n-1$ PDU, accompanies this indication.

The $n-1$ entity acts in precisely the same manner resulting in the n entity receiving the n PDU, in a $n-1$ SDU, which the initiating n entity sought to convey. Having stripped off the n PCI and performed the activity implied, the n entity issues an n service primitive to the n S user, indicating that the remotely initiated activity has occurred. Thus the objective of the original n S user request, issued on end-system A, has been fulfilled.

Having now been described twice, the basic operations of the model should be becoming clear. In reality, things are not as simple as this, but the complexities should become apparent as we examine the individual layers in detail.

Now we can further consider the interface between a layer and its service users. We have already seen that this communication is achieved by the use of service primitives.

Consider the boundaries indicated by lines (a) and (a') in Figure 2.7. Here there exists bindings between n S user and an n entity. OSI application activity is not feasible in an end-system unless there exists a complete 'stack' of bound entities. Such a binding is established through a *service access point* (SAP), in this case an n

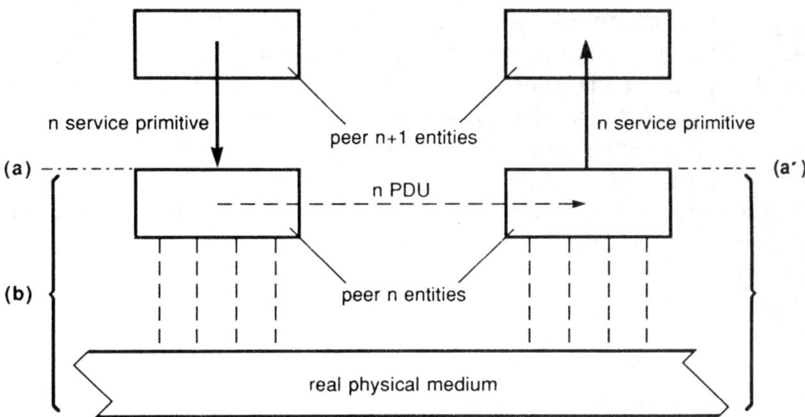

Fig. 2.7 — Boundary points.

SAP. An n entity offers services to an entity of the superior layer, an $n+1$ entity, through an n SAP.

In Figure 2.7 we see that everything below the notional line (a)–(a′) is represented by (b), down to and including the physical medium. In many instances, we can simplify the diagrams by fully representing end-systems only as far down as an appropriate SAP. In these cases we use a diagrammatical form as in Figure 2.8.

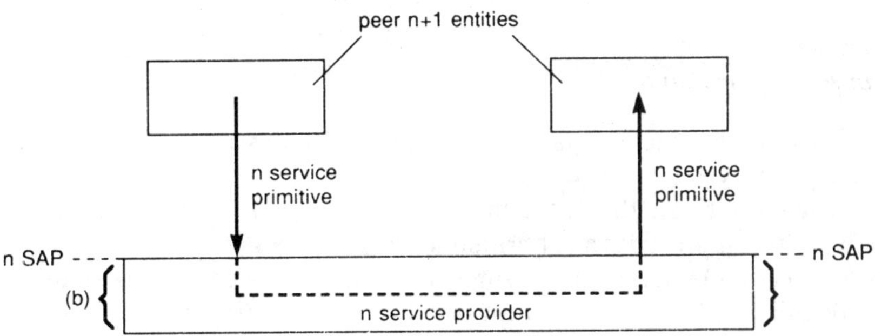

Fig. 2.8 — SAPs.

Here, everything below the corresponding SAPs is seen as a solid box which represents the layer directly below those SAPs and all layers beneath. The set of pairs of cooperating entities that reside below a particular pair of corresponding SAPs is known collectively as a *service provider* (S provider), in this case an n S provider.

When we are examining service primitives associated with a particular service element of a layer, we use a simpler version of this form of diagram. In this, the n S provider box is represented by two horizontal lines, one for each end-system. Everything below these lines is regarded as the *n* S provider, (b) (see Figure 2.9).

When this form of diagram is used, 'time sequence numbers' are added to indicate the order of the service primitives as a result of *n* S user activity or *n* S provider event, advancing time indicated by increasing numbers. As we use these two forms of diagram, their structure will become clear.

In expressing the example in standard terminology we saw that service primitives are used to request services or to indicate the occurrence of services. A service element has associated with it a set of service primitives. We can now see that these include:

— *request* service primitive,
— *indication* service primitive.

The consequence of issuing a request service primitive on an end-system is the activation of a service element, resulting in the exchange of a PDU with a peer layer entity. This brings about a cooperative activity and results in an indication service primitive on the remote end-system.

When an indication service primitive is issued to an S user, the activity involved in the realization of the particular service would appear to be complete. However the initiating S user has had no explicit confirmation that the service has been performed. A service of this nature is therefore classed as an *unconfirmed* service. There are many instances of services where a confirmation is desirable or indeed necessary to convey some information resulting from the activity. A service of this form is known as a *confirmed* service, and associated with confirmation are two further service primitives:

— *response* service primitive,
— *confirm* service primitive.

The service primitive sequence diagram in Figure 2.10 illustrates the use of the full set of service primitives by peer *n* S users.

A service element can therefore have a maximum of four service primitives associated with it. If it provides a confirmed service there will be four, if unconfirmed two. Certain service elements have a single associated service primitive, an *indication*. Consider Figure 2.11. Some event occurs in a lower layer, that is in the *n* S provider. This event could be a failure in intermediate communications equipment. In any event it is not brought about as a result of an *n* S user issuing an *n* request service primitive. The *n* S provider 'detects' the event and issues an *n* indication service primitive to both *n* S users.

Referring back to Figure 2.9, we see an unconfirmed service requested of the *n* entity. What if it had been a confirmed service? Clearly, the *n* S user on end-system B receiving the *n* indication service primitive would, if prepared to accept the service and its implications, issue a *n* response service primitive to the *n* entity. The entity would construct an appropriate *n* PDU and this would be transmitted to the *n* entity on end-system A in a mirror image of the mechanism already described. On receipt of this PDU, the *n* entity would issue an *n* confirm service primitive to the initiating *n* S user. The confirmed service would then be completed. Only in a confirmed service

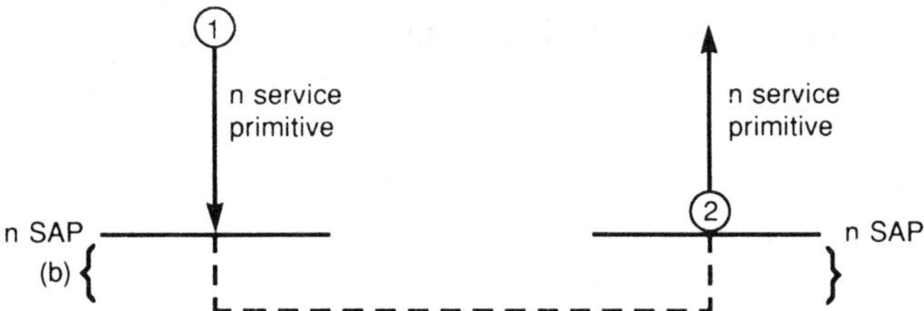

Fig. 2.9 — Service primitive time sequence diagram.

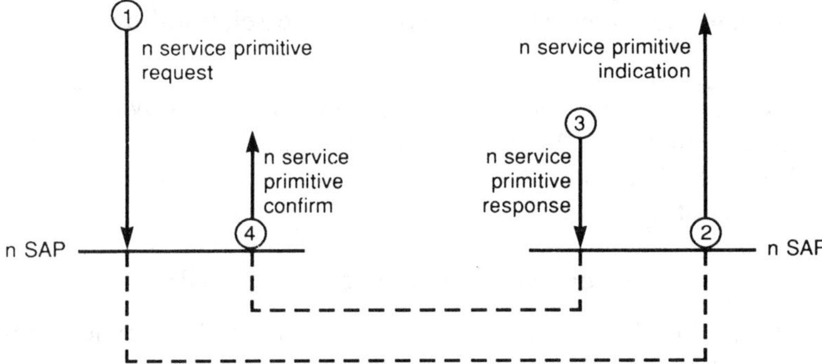

Fig. 2.10 — Example of a confirmed service time sequence diagram.

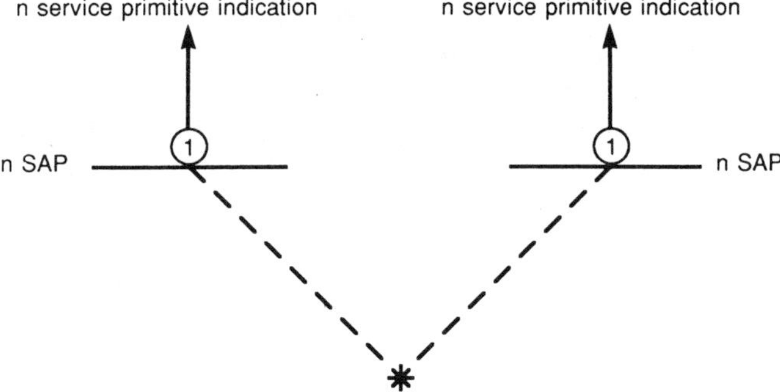

Fig. 2.11 — Special case brought about by lower layer event.

has the S user in receipt of an indication of a service any scope to 'negotiate'. How this is performed and the use to which it is put we shall see later.

2.3 SUMMARY

Rabbit turned round and nudged Piglet.
"The next time," he said, "Tell Pooh."
"The next time," said Piglet to Pooh.
"The next what?" said Pooh to Piglet.

A. A. Milne, *The House at Pooh Corner*

In this chapter we have defined the basic mechanism by which layer entities cooperate and bring about OSI activity between two end-systems. The reader has been introduced to the following terms and their interrelationships:

— End-system.
— Service; service element; service user (S user); service provider (S provider); service access point (SAP); service primitive (request, indication, response & confirm); service data unit (SDU).
— Layer; layer entity.
— Peer.
— Protocol; protocol data unit (PDU); protocol machine (PM).

In the latter part of the chapter we took to assigning '*n*' to a defined name, e.g. *n* PDU as a PDU of layer *n*. When we deal with specific layers, the *n* is replaced by a specific letter representing that layer. For session it is 'S' and so we talk of SS user, SS provider, SSAP, SSDU, SPDU, SPM, etc.

3

Connections and addressing

The higher layer standards that have reached Draft International Standard (DIS) or International Standard (IS) status are all *connection-oriented* standards. There is work under way to produce *connectionless* standards for these layers, but it will be some time before these appear as OSI 'products'. This chapter discusses connection-oriented and connectionless operation, concentrating on the former which is the mode of operation assumed in the remainder of the book.

3.1 CONNECTION-ORIENTED OPERATION

To understand connection-oriented operation we must understand what a connection is and how one is established. A connection is a concept primarily of interest in the layers involved in the realization of end-to-end data communication. In Chapter 1, we saw that the highest layer relating to data communication provision is effectively the session layer; application and presentation layer functionality being dependent on the data communications services offered by session. For this reason, for the remainder of this chapter we shall view an application entity together with its associated presentation entity as a single 'object', a session service user (SS user).

In connection-oriented operation the first task of the SS user, triggered by some application user initialization request, is to establish a data communications path between itself and the peer SS user on the remote end-system. This is known as a session connection. It is a relationship between two SS users which, once established and until released, is a 'channel' through which SSDUs can flow. The session connection can be released as the result of an SS user request, or because of a (possibly catastrophic) event in some lower layer. The SS user must wait until the session connection is established before it can send or receive SSDUs, i.e. before any application activity can begin.

In connection-oriented operation there is no mechanism to enable SSDUs to be exchanged between SS users other than over an established session connection. (Many readers will have used remote computer terminals to 'log on' to a multi-user computer system, and will be familiar with having to 'call' the host and provide a username and password before being granted access (a 'session') on that host. One could say that at this stage a 'connection' has been established and any data displayed on that terminal or entered on its keyboard will be understood to be 'travelling' over that connection. This connection will last until the user 'logs off', the host terminates the 'session', or a break occurs in the underlying network.)

Now let us follow the steps of a session connection establishment. As a result of a session connect request (a service primitive) from the SS user, a session entity will begin to establish a connection between this SS user and its nominated peer; we shall look at this 'nomination' later. At this time, all entities of the session and of the lower layers in this initiating end-system can be regarded as idle. Equally all entities on the nominated or responding end-system are idle. By 'idle', we mean that an entity is not bound into any regime of cooperation with a peer on another end-system; that is, it is not connected.

In the terminology and basic mechanism of the last chapter, a session connection is established as follows. On receipt of the session connect request from the SS user, the session service element concerned with establishing the connection constructs a 'connect' SPDU. It must then utilize a transport layer service to bring about the transfer of this SPDU to its peer.

At this point, the transport entity on the initiating end-system is 'idle'; that is, there is no transport connection established between peer TS users. As we have seen, in a connection-oriented environment *n* SDUs cannot flow between *n* S users until an *n* connection has been established, and so the session entity cannot use the transport service to transfer the connect SPDU (as a TSDU) until a transport connection is established. The session entity must hold on to the connect SPDU meantime, and issue a transport connect request (a service primitive) to the transport entity. The session entity then leaves the idle state and goes into an 'intermediate' state, viz. connecting. In this state it still cannot accept any SSDUs for transfer.

This process is repeated at the transport layer, with the transport entity holding onto its connect TPDU and entering a connecting state until such time as there is a network connection established between it and its peer. It issues a network connect request (a service primitive) to the network entity to bring about this connection. The session and transport entities on the initiating end-system hold back their respective connect PDUs until a connection is established on their behalf by their subordinate layers.

Upon receipt of the network connection request, the network entity will attempt to establish a network connection. To do this it must utilize the data transmission capability of the underlying sub-network(s) to exchange a connect NPDU with a peer network entity on the responding end-system. As we saw in Chapter 1, this may involve any number of sub-networks, traversed by the use of relaying computer systems. The network layer is responsible for establishing a route between end-systems and hence the involvement of intermediate relaying computer systems. The two lowest layers are concerned with the organization (transmission, receipt, error detection/correction) of data bits over a physical medium, that is, across a sub-network. If a sub-network is connection-oriented, then there is a concept of a connection in the data link layer, but this is simply the establishment of a state of readiness to receive and transmit data bits between two specific points on a particular physical medium. We refer the reader to Deasington (1986) for an in-depth explanation of link layer connection in an X.25 sub-network. Just as the upper two layers are not concerned with data communications issues, but in their exploitation, the lower two layers have no interest in high-level communications issues, but only in driving data over communications media (much as ship's boiler stokers are not involved in the navigation of a ship, only in ensuring its progress in passage).

We shall now complete the sequence of connection establishment events. The responding network entity receives the NPDU, (1) in Figure 3.1, and issues a network connect indication (service primitive) to the 'nominated' transport entity, (2). At this point, the transport entity must decide whether to reject or accept the

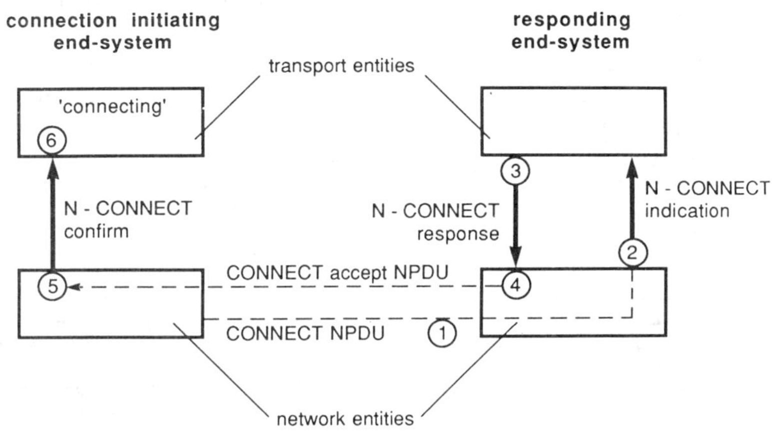

Fig. 3.1 — A part of the connection establishment process.

proposed connection between itself and the initiating transport entity; security or resource shortage may dictate rejection. Here we shall assume acceptance. The responding transport entity issues a network connect response (a service primitive), (3), and on receipt of this the responding network entity builds a 'connection accept' NPDU which it transmits to the initiating peer using the underlying data service, (4). On receipt of this NPDU the initiating network entity regards the network connection as established, (5), and informs the transport entity of this in an network connect confirm (a service primitive), (6). On receiving this the initiating transport entity 'releases' the held 'connect' TPDU which it now conveys to its peer (as a NSDU using a network data service).

A similar sequence, but this time at a layer higher, results in the initiating session entity receiving a transport connect confirm. Again this is followed by the 'release' of the 'held' SPDU which finally causes the session connection to be established and the initiating SS user informed by a session connect confirm.

At this point the SS user knows that a data communications channel has been established between it and its peer, and that SSDU exchange and associated session services are now available. The activity to be undertaken by the application can therefore begin.

3.2 ADDRESSING AND THE HIGHER LAYERS

In Chapter 1 we saw how the network layer is responsible for providing an end-to-end data transmission capability between two end-systems. It is also responsible for relaying and routing, i.e. the use of intermediate computer systems to cross between one sub-network and another. All these issues are transparent to the transport layer, which is offered an end-to-end data transmission capability (service) by the network layer.

We can consider addressing in two parts: the first concerned with network and the second concerned with transport and above.

A 'network address' is a form of address, provided to a network entity, which specifies the location within the OSI environment of the end-system which is the 'target' of the intended OSI application activity. It is the responsibility of the network entity to establish a route to the end-system specified, perhaps by consulting an OSI addressing and routing database. If necessary, it will use intermediate computer systems as relays between the various sub-networks that must be traversed on the chosen route (see Figure 3.2). The method by which this is achieved is specified by

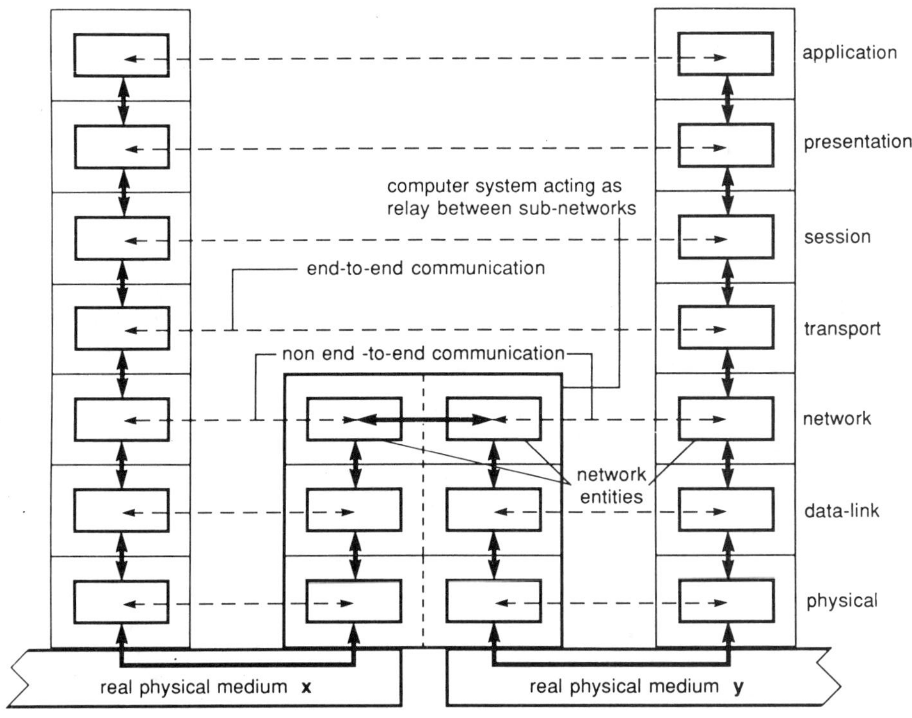

Fig. 3.2 — End-to end and non end-to-end communications.

network layer standards associated with the differing types of sub-network. In this book we are interested in end-to-end OSI issues, and so will not discuss network issues further (a full description of this topic can be had in the books referenced in Chapter 1).

The examination of higher layer addressing starts with the assumption that the network layer provides an end-to-end addressing capability. For the remainder of this section we examine addressing within the higher layers, using the general form of Figure 3.3 as the basis. We are retaining the concept, presented in the first section of this chapter, of a notionally unified application and presentation entity, the SS user.

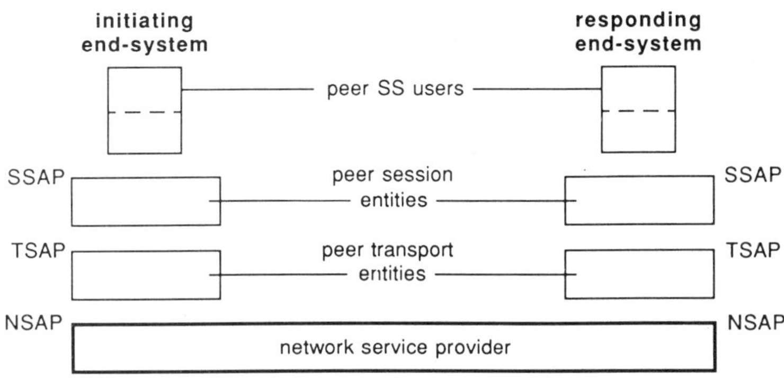

Fig. 3.3 — General form of diagram.

The basis of addressing in the higher layers is service user selection through SAPs. At first glance it is difficult to see how, within a stack-like structure of entities representing the layers within an end-system, addressing can be required. End-to-end addressing and intermediate routing are straightforward concepts, but addressing within an end-system appears neither necessary nor possible.

In our discussion of the realization of the ISORM on an end-system we have, up to this point, looked at a simple form of implementation architecture in which it appears that each layer can be represented only by a single entity, and that this entity is the only one separating the layer entity below from that above. If this were the case, then addressing, or any form of unique identification of entities within an end-system, would be redundant. This would mean that, on receipt of any 'connect' n PDU, an n entity would automatically pass a n connect primitive indication up to the only $n+1$ entity.

It is at the level of SSAP where it is most obvious that this would be a poor policy. The basis of a mechanism for invoking, as responder, an SS user of the same application type as the initiating entity, is the association of a unique identity with each possible SS user on an end-system. We have already seen that there are many possible standards within the application layer and that cooperation can be achieved only if initiating and responding application entities are of the same type. Consider Figure 3.4. As a result of some 'user' activity, an electronic mail standard entity (which, together with an associated presentation entity constitutes an SS user) issues a session connect request to the session entity (1). By mechanisms we have already explored, this results in a session connect indication being issued by the peer session entity to the peer SS user, (3). If the responding end-system includes entities of both

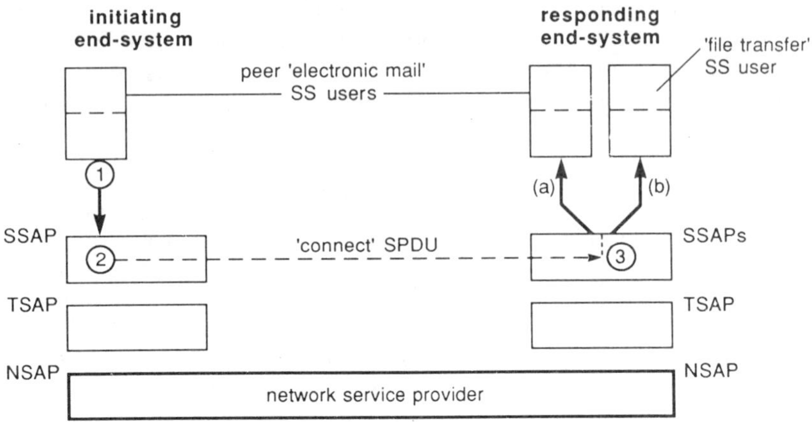

Fig. 3.4 — Example of SS user selection.

electronic mail and file transfer standards, then the problem is to select the correct SS user to invoke and subsequently issue with the indication service primitive. The choice is between (a) and (b). Clearly, each of these represents a different binding between the session entity and SS user; each is a distinct SSAP. Choice of SSAP is therefore the mechanism for selection. Each possible SSAP on an end-system (i.e. each possible binding between a session entity and SS user) is assigned a unique 'address', an *SSAP address*. Each distinct application entity on an end-system will be associated with one (or, as we shall see, more) SSAP address. This address is provided by the initiating SS user as a parameter of the session connect request service primitive, the 'nomination' mentioned in the last section.

SAP addresses are also defined at the level of TSAPs and NSAPs. Their purpose is the same as outlined above — to identify the TS users and NS users that are to be 'invoked' to receive a connect indication service primitive. Again, each of these addresses is provided as a parameter to the connect request by the initiating peer service user. It is at first sight less clear why these SAP addresses are required, since there is only one (connection-oriented) standard for the session and transport layers, and so it could be argued that a single entity would represent those layers on an end-system. However, there are reasons for having more than a single entity of each of these layers available for use on an end-system. For instance, some application standard may require minimal services of the session layer. If the end-system on which this application is mounted is resource-constrained and if efficiency is improved by providing a session entity 'tailored' to these minimal needs, then such an entity might be implemented. If on that same end-system another application that requires a 'complete' set of session services is made available, then a second session entity must also be provided to support this new application service. This results in two session entities being available on an end-system, each of which is identified by a unique TSAP address. It is by use of this TSAP address that the initiating end-system TS user ensures that the session entity with appropriate facilities is invoked for the application in question. This is represented in Figure 3.5.

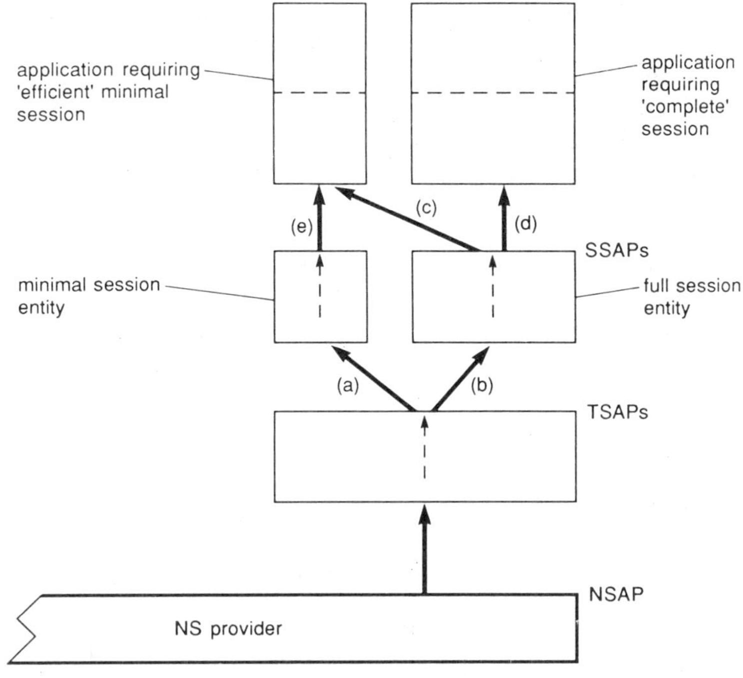

Fig. 3.5 — Internal 'stack' addressing.

We note that the 'full facility' session entity is capable of supporting the application that 'demands efficiency' but it may not 'perform' as required. The efficient route is TSAP address (a) and SSAP address (e), the usable alternative being TSAP address (b) and SSAP address (c). In addressing terms, (e) and (c) identify the same session entity and so (e) is equivalent to (c). Connection between SS users that require the 'full facility' session is only possible by addressing TSAP address (b) and SSAP address (d), since the TSAP address (a) will invoke a session entity which lacks the capability to provide the services required. We shall see in the next section of this chapter that this 'subsetting' of layer functionality is a part of standardization.)

In conclusion, we see that connection establishment not only establishes a data communications path between end-systems, but also identifies an 'internal' route through an end-system when a choice of layer entities must be made, finally identifying the target SS user. Once a connection is established it can be used to exchange SSDUs between the peer SS users, until released, without any further reference to addressing issues; that is, SSDUs can 'flow' between SS users over a session connection without having to carry destination addressing information explicitly.

3.3 CONNECTIONLESS OPERATION

Briefly, a 'connectionless' mode of operation is one in which a (SDU transfer) service can be requested of an entity at any time — there is no requirement for a connection between SS users, for example, to be established before session services can be utilized. In this way connectionless entities can never be regarded strictly as 'idle' but more accurately as 'ready'. Since no connection exists between SS users, the route, defined by the network address together with the SAP addresses identifying the 'internal' route through the receiving end-system, must be included explicitly with every SSDU transfer request.

Clearly, a connection-oriented *n* entity cannot cooperate with a connectionless *n* entity. On the other hand a connection-oriented transport service can be offered over a connectionless network service, leading to the possibility outlined in Figure 3.6.

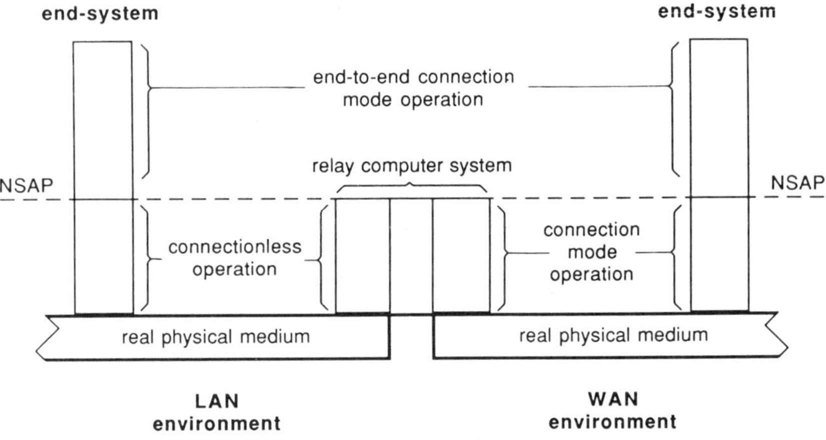

Fig. 3.6 — Use of relay computer system.

3.4 SERVICES REVISITED

A layer offers services, provided by the activity of service elements. Utilization of a service is via service primitives. Here we look a little closer at service primitives.

In the standards a service element is normally 'named' after the service it provides. As examples we use the following two session services.

(1) The session connection establishment service is used to bring about a session connection between two peer SS users. The service element supporting this service is the S-CONNECT service element of session. It is a confirmed service

and so has four associated service primitives: S-CONNECT request; S-CONNECT indication; S-CONNECT response; S-CONNECT confirm.

(2) The session normal data service is used to exchange application information between peer SS users. The service element providing this capability is S-DATA. It is an unconfirmed service and so there are only two associated service primitives: S-DATA request; S-DATA indication.

All standards follow this simple naming convention for service elements and associated service primitives.

The service definition defines the services, service primitives and the parameters associated with each primitive. The protocol specification specifies the mechanics of each service element.

In the following chapters we are going to look in detail at each layer, application down to transport. However, some more concepts must first be introduced.

3.4.1 Service types

In the data communication related layers, viz. session and below, there are two types of services, *control* services and *data* services.

A control service is one which has the objective of performing some layer specific function, for instance inserting a synchronization checkpoint in the flow of information. In many instances of this type of service it is possible to include in the request service primitive some 'user data' to be conveyed transparently between S users, but this exchange is a by-product of the service. (The response service primitive can also be used to convey user data to the initiating S user in the instance of a confirmed service). The primary purpose of a control service is, however, to perform a layer-specific service; it is not the exchange of user data.

A data service is a service which has the sole function of passing user data (an SDU) transparently (unaltered and complete) between S users. No other activity is undertaken. The data services of each layer provide the backbone of the mechanisms described in Chapter 2. They are the fundamental mechanisms by which a layer entity can exchange PDUs with a peer over an established connection. Consider Figure 3.7. Here we see that, as a result of a request for a control service by the S-'ACTIVITY' request service primitive, a PDU is to be exchanged between peer entities. This is achieved by the use of a data service of the next lower layer.

3.4.2 Functional units

In the section dealing with the need for addressing in the higher layers, we used an example in the session layer that suggested that an entity can be an implementation of a 'subset' of a layer standard, and noted that this subsetting is defined by the standards. Here we introduce the building blocks of the standards that make subsetting possible, namely *functional units* (FUs).

As we saw in Chapter 1, each layer has a specific area of functionality. More precisely, each layer can be seen as having a basic level of functionality providing the essential core of services, which can be augmented by the addition of further units of functionality. The layer standard defines the complete functionality of a layer but does so in a structured way. Services are grouped together by virtue of being associated with a specific type of activity, these groups being known as functional

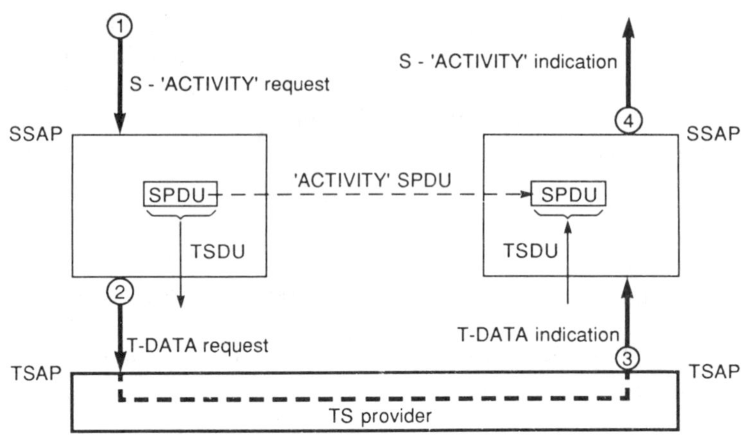

Fig. 3.7 — SPDU as a TSDU.

units. The group of essential 'basic' services are grouped together in a *kernel* FU; other FUs are named after the type of activity on which they are based.

The requirements for lower layer services are expressed in the application standards in terms of FUs. A specific application requiring services from the session layer over and above some defined basic level has its requirements stipulated in terms of FUs of that layer. If only one application, requiring basic services, is to be made available on an end-system A (perhaps a simple form of remote work station) then it is unnecessary to implement a 'complete' session entity (i.e. all the session FUs) on A. Now consider another end-system, B, which is to interwork with this 'simple' single application end-system. Suppose that B is a more comprehensive system, with many applications available. If these applications all use the same session implementation on B then that implementation will have a wide range of session FUs available. If B is the initiator of an application activity with A, we see that there is a mismatch in the capability of the session entities which are to cooperate. It is essential that the cooperating SS users are aware of the 'common denominator' level of the session service provider (FU availability), because many application standards offer optional services, the availability of which may be dependent on the availability of particular session services. An FU can be made available in a session connection only if it is available in both cooperating peer session entities. For this reason the peer entities must determine which FUs will be available over an established connection. This 'negotiation' of FU availability is done as part of the connection establishment process; that is, it is part of the connection establishment service element. (The connection establishment service element itself lies in the kernel FU and so this FU is clearly regarded as mandatory.) The negotiated level of service is conveyed to the initiating SS user in the confirm service primitive. It will then be in a position to determine which optional features can be made available.

The level of implementation of a standard in an entity is defined by the set of FUs of the standard which it supports. The kernel FU is always mandatory. The protocol specification of any layer is a very tightly defined document: every service element is unambiguously specified. The protocol specification (or at least some subset of it, defined in terms of FUs) will be mounted in a layer entity on an end-system. It will be expected to interwork with any other implementation (entity) on any other end-system with which it can agree (negotiate) an environment (common set of FUs) during connection establishment. (The prospect of failure to interwork because of a failure to agree such an environment, and the impact on OSI of such a situation, is discussed in Chapter 12, 'Functional standards'.) PDUs are exchanged between end-systems and so their encoding must be precisely defined and globally understood. The service definition does not embody this kind of rigour in specification. It defines the services offered and the access to these services in terms of service primitives. The information conveyed by these primitives is described in the form of service-specific parameters. The nature of this information is defined in the service definition, but the encoding is not, because this is an issue confined to the individual end-system implementation. The values carried by these parameters which are eventually placed in PDUs, to be exchanged between end-systems, have a precisely defined encoding in that context. The form of encoding used when they are passed between entities and S users is a local issue and is thus left to the implementor.

4

The application layer

The application layer differs fundamentally from the other layers of ISORM. Because it is the top layer of the model, its 'users' are not entities of the next higher layer; rather they are 'processes', e.g. programs or packages which provide services, often for the human clients of the end-system. The application layer provides system-independent application services to real users or user programs. It utilizes the services of the presentation layer, which offers controlled, error-free, exchange of information between co-operating peer application entities independent of local rules for representation. We shall examine how this is achieved in the following chapters. In order to help explain the relationship between the application layer (represented by application entities) and the end-system on which an entity is mounted, we introduce the concept of the *application process*.

The application process is that part of an end-system which carries out information processing for a particular application task over the OSI environment. It is invoked either by a local user/program request, or by the initiating activity (over a session connection) of some remote application process requiring its cooperation. It uses the services of the presentation service provider to cooperate with an application process of the same type on a remote end-system.

We can regard the application process as consisting of two parts: an *application agent* and an *application entity*. The application agent interfaces to the 'user' and to the operating system of the end-system on which it is mounted, in order to provide access to local, system-specific, resources such as the jobmill, filestore, or output devices. The operation of the application agent lies outwith the ISORM, which defines only system-independent activity. Clearly an agent which provides the interface between OSI application services and the local system environment is system-dependent.

The application entity performs the system-independent (standard) application activities, which are made available as application services to the application agent. By definition, the application entity lies within the application layer of the ISORM (see Figure 4.1).. (There is an implication here that entities of the layers below application have no interface with the system on which they operate, and for which they provide OSI functionality. Clearly this is not the case, since each layer entity must interface to its 'local' system in order to function, needing buffers and management services from the system. However such interfacing is purely part of achieving the specified functionality of the layer and not, as in the case of the application agent, the objective of that functionality.)

Layer entities bring about the services they offer by the exchange of PDUs with

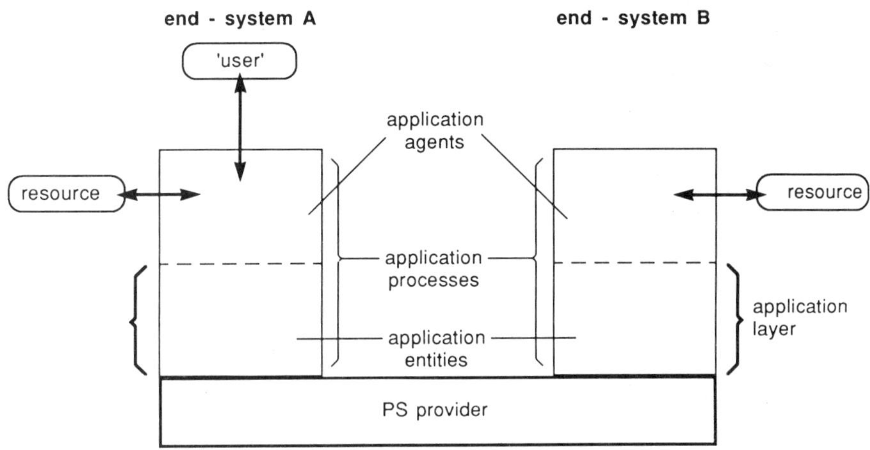

Fig. 4.1 — Application agents as a part of application processes.

peer entities. In this case application PDUs are exchanged by the use of presentation services.

As with all layers, an application standard is expressed in two parts. The services offered are defined in a service definition and the realization of these services and the associated PDUs in a protocol specification. A standard of this layer often includes extra descriptive documents.

In this layer one standard is not sufficient. Although many applications environments will require similar services and hence use the same application standard, others may require dissimilar services, and so quite a different standard. The application layer therefore comprises all possible application standards. As discussed in Chapter 1, some of these are well recognized and so are internationally standardized applications:

— *File transfer, access and management* (FTAM)
— Electronic messaging: MHS/X.400
— *Job transfer and manipulation* (JTM)
— *Virtual terminal* (VT)

As an example to demonstrate the relationship between an end-system and an application process, consider a point-of-sale (POS) system in a DIY store as end-system A. A requirement of this end-system is that it update stock records held on a stock control computer at the DIY HQ after every sale. Here, an application agent running on this POS system will have a 'user' interface in the form of a bar code reader; as each item sold is scanned, a stock control activity is initiated in the POS system. The application agent is simply a routine that will read the data off the bar code device, extracting from this a stock control identity key for the item.

Suppose the application layer services required by such an application agent are: 'select appropriate stock control file'; 'locate end of file'; 'write a transaction record'; 'release the file'. This is a very naive example and certainly not the best way a stock control system could work, but it will help to illustrate our points. The stock control application agent on the POS system will be interfaced to an application entity whose service definition provides for the activities defined. Together they form the POS application process. Let us call the application standard in question 'X'. The service elements to be utilized are then:

X-OPEN X-LOCATE X-WRITE X-CLOSE

The X entity on the POS system and peer X entity on the HQ end-system will perform the activities by the exchange of XPDUs, resulting in a stock file update on the HQ computer system.

Now consider a second, unrelated, end-system: B, a personal computer (PC). Here there is a requirement for the PC user to use dial-up facilities to obtain a copy of a book list stored as a file on some computer system. The application agent on that PC has the following characteristics:

— A user interface allowing the PC user to specify the book list required. In its simplest form, the book list is the name of a file on a remote computer system. The interface will inform the user when the copy has been obtained.
— A system interface ensuring that the book list received is stored on the backing store of the PC.

The services that an application agent of this sort require are : 'select the appropriate file'; 'read the contents'; 'release the file'.

The ISO application standard *file transfer access and management* (FTAM) is concerned with precisely this sort of activity. It has service elements F-OPEN, F-READ and F-CLOSE that provide these services. An FTAM entity would clearly be an appropriate application process 'partner' for this application agent.

FTAM has other service elements, including F-WRITE and F-LOCATE (at beginning, or end, or by 'index key') and so we see that FTAM also satisfies the needs of end-system A; it is equivalent to the 'X' standard. And so we have two differing application agents which achieve their respective OSI objectives by the use of the same application standard. Indeed if the book list were of DIY-related books, and maintained as a customer service by the DIY firm on its HQ computer, then that computer need only have an implementation of the application standard FTAM for these two apparently dissimilar applications to be supported over OSI (Figure 4.2).

4.1 THE ARCHITECTURE OF THE APPLICATION LAYER

In each of the layers below application there is a very specific but, as we shall see, complex functionality. The application layer, however, covers a very broad and general field of system-independent cooperation, e.g. electronic mail, remote access to database systems, the exchange of files or documents, etc. Each of thee application activities requires services that are specific to the activity; however, they may also require application services which could be made use of by a number of widely differing types of application. It would therefore be poor policy to approach the standarization of a particular application without a view to maximizing the use of common services already defined in existing application standards. Equally, in producing a new application standard, an eye to the future must be maintained to

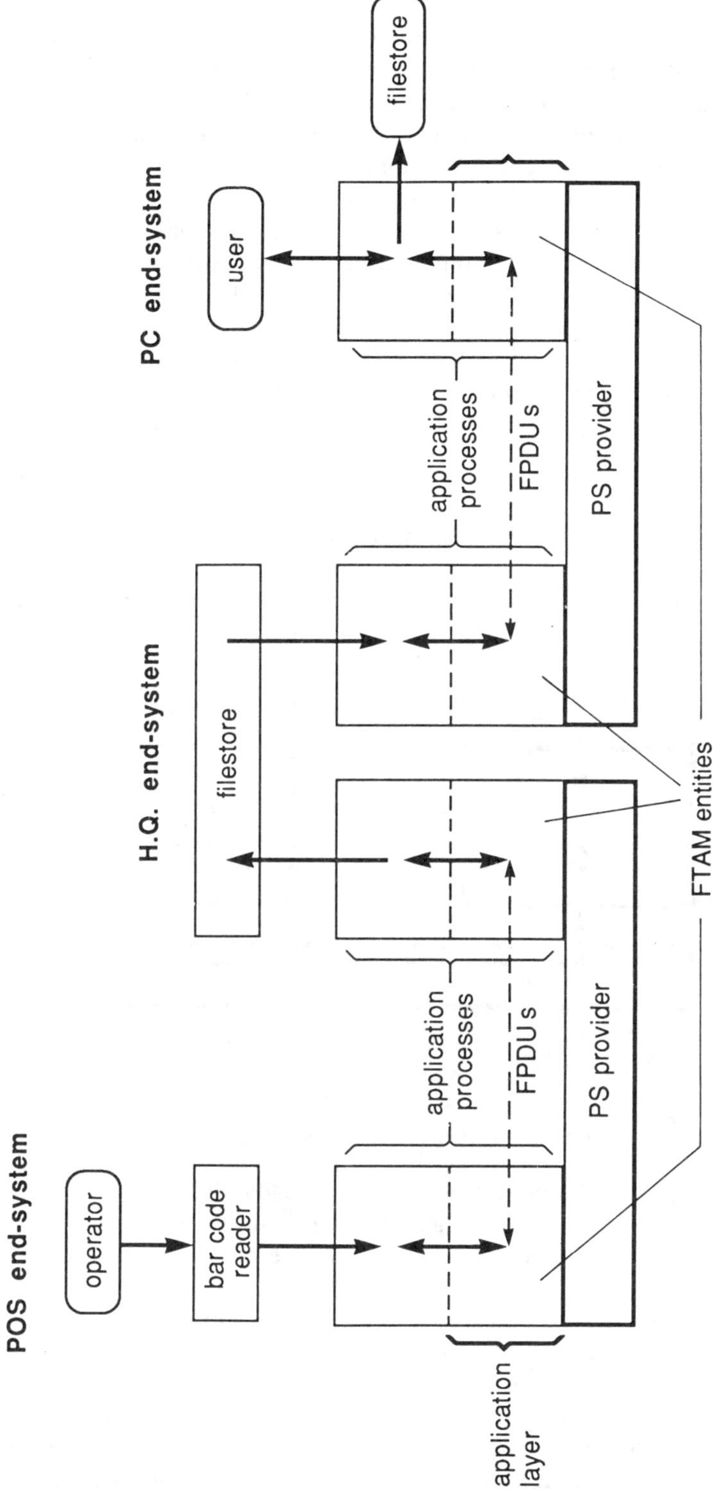

Fig. 4.2 — DIY HQ computer needs only an FTAM implementation.

ensure that introduced services that have a potential for common use are defined in general, rather than application-specific, manner.

In order to facilitate such a modular approach to standardization, a building block architecture for application standard definition has been adopted. It should be noted that this architecture was formulated in parallel with early application standardization activity, and so some application standards display a greater use of modular definition than others. Equally, some applications have such individual character as to warrant only a minimum level of modularization.

We shall use the standard FTAM that was briefly introduced earlier, as an example to introduce the basic architecture of the application layer. For the reasons noted above, FTAM is a standard defined with minimum modularity. From this example we shall progress to the more general architecture.

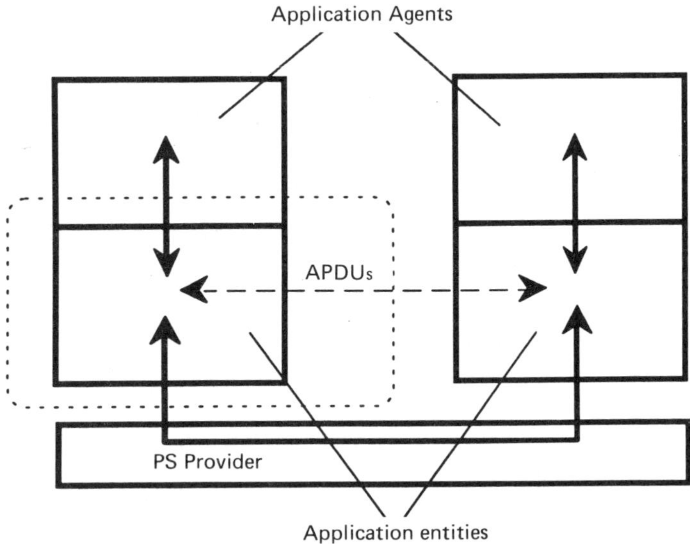

Fig. 4.3 — Cooperating application processes.

Consider Figure 4.3. here we see our already defined application process structure with one of the entities highlighted. It is in the 'exploded' version of this entity as an FTAM entity, Figure 4.4, that we begin to see the internal modular architecture.

In all applications, the first action that must be undertaken by the initiating application process is the establishment of a cooperative relationship between its own and a peer application entity. This relationship is known as an *association*. Companion functions to association establishment are association release, and user- or provider-initiated abort. The management of these functions, being common to all applications, is clearly a candidate for adoption as a single standard (module),

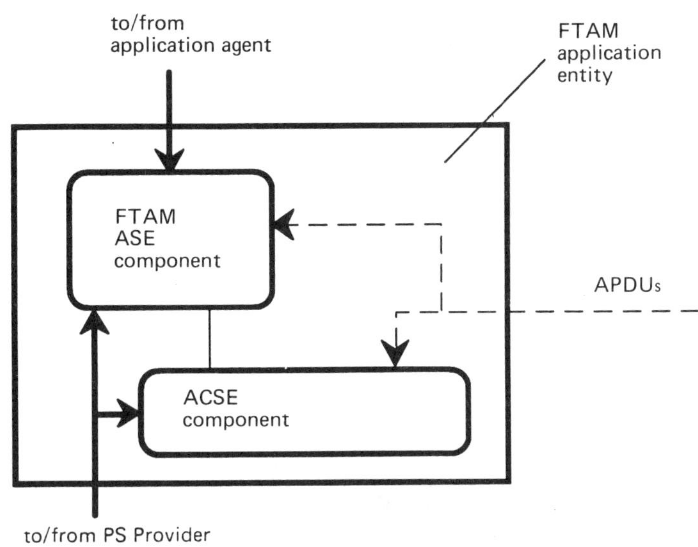

Fig. 4.4 — An FTAM application entity.

rather than being the subject of redefinition within each new application standard. *Association control* is therefore a fundamental module within the architecture of the application layer.

The association control standard comprises a service definition (ISO 8649) and a protocol specification (ISO 8650); it defines a set of services, together with a supportive set of service elements that facilitate all aspects of association control. It is known as the *association control service element* (*ACSE*) and, as such, is a generic grouping of all services and service elements concerned with association control. We shall examine this standard later.

Referring again to Figure 4.4, we see that the application entity under examination is made up of an ACSE component and an FTAM ASE component. **An ASE or *application service element* is a general term for a component of the application layer that is a generic grouping of services and service elements related to a specific application purpose**; in this case FTAM — file transfer, access and management.

In the case of FTAM, the degree of modularization is limited to the inclusion of two components, the mandatory ACSE and FTAM ASE. It is important to note that we are not talking of 'sub-layers' within the application layer, but of flexible modular architecture. In our example the FTAM ASE component, on being driven by the application agent, will only utilize the ACSE component if association control-related services are required, i.e. establish, abort, or close. In other instances of use of an association the ACSE component will remain dormant within the application entity.

Now consider Figure 4.5. here we have an example of a hypothetical application entity comprising an ACSE component and two ASE components. One of the ASE components is concerned with providing specific application management services, whilst the other is limited to providing simple document exchange services. Clearly the former is likely only to have impact on the specific application area it is designed to service, whereas the latter could be useful in many application environments.

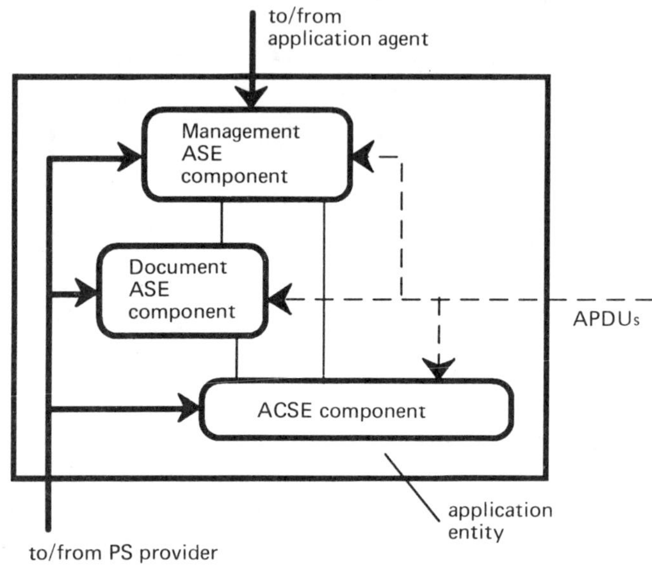

Fig. 4.5 — A complex application entity.

Application standards are therefore defined as being a union of a set of ASEs together with ACSE, which, when implemented on an end-system, form an application entity capable of furnishing the application services required. An application standard will, therefore, define the application-specific ASE(s) in detail, whilst having only to make simple reference to ACSE and other general ASEs that it requires to be bound into an application entity. It is possible that certain ASEs are optional to the operation of an application — perhaps only adding service enhancements to a basic level of functionality. Indeed, certain negotiable services of a particular ASE may also be optional to the application in question. It is therefore important that the coorperating application entities understand the architectural and operational all make-up of their peers. Achieving this understanding, known as an *application context*, is a part of the process of association establishment.

We shall see a real example of a complex modular application standard in the chapter on message handling systems.

We can further generalize our view of an application entity. Figure 4.6 shows an application entity composed of two arbitrary ASEs and an ACSE component. These components will be bound into an application context by the establishment of an association with a peer grouping of components. This component grouping within an application entity is therefore known as a *single association object* (SAO). To

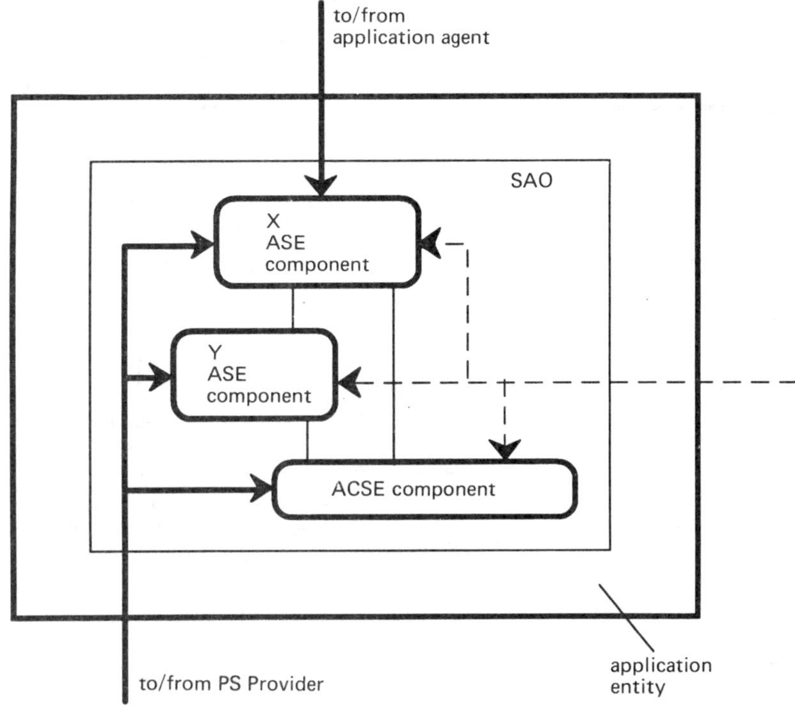

Fig. 4.6 — A single association object.

understand why we need such a sub-division of an application entity, consider the following example.

A company has a nationwide network of warehouses that are re-stocked by the action of an HQ central controlling 'hub' computer system as it detects item stocks running low. Stock changes — either sales or receipt of fresh stock — at any warehouse are indicated to the hub system utilizing OSI technology. If this particular company has a reputation built upon swift and efficient service it will require more of its computer support. In particular the following scenario is not an unreasonable requirement.

A customer arrives at warehouse 'D' to find that the item he wishes to purchase has been the subject of unexpectedly high turnover and that, even though the automatic re-stocking system ordered fresh supplies from the manufacturer for this warehouse when the threshold level was reached, no replacement supply has arrived. In this circumstance, the local computer system at 'D' could instigate the following 'fall back' procedure (thus ensuring the continued reputation of the company). An application process is instigated on this system — by the action of a warehouseman — and it automatically establishes communication with an appropriate peer application process on the hub computer system. It enquires whether an 'emergency' delivery of the item in question can be made by a transfer from the stock of any of the other warehouses (see Figure 4.7). The hub system checks the stock records to determine

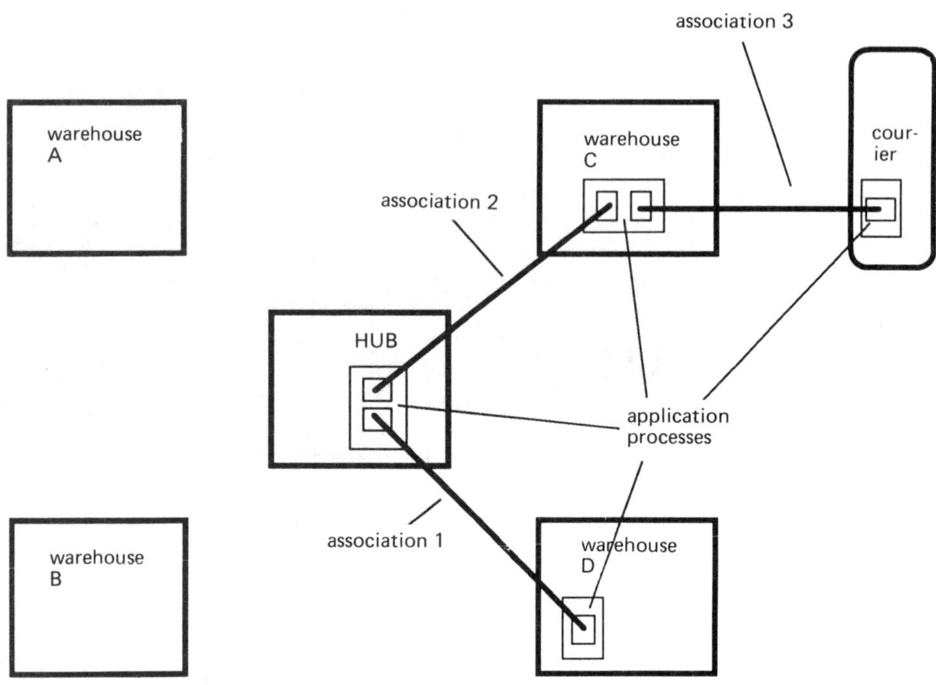

Fig. 4.7 — Stock control example.

which warehouses have stocks of the item, and establishes communication with an application process on the most efficient (in a transportation sense) warehouse computer system. On receiving the request from the hub system, the application process on the warehouse 'E' computer system places a 'holding' status on one item of the particular type in question. It establishes communication with an application process on an appropriate courier delivery company computer requesting a statement of when the item could be scheduled to be picked up and subsequently delivered by their service. On reply, the 'E' sytem provides the hub with the delivery information, which it then passes back to 'D', and so to the warehouseman and customer. If this is satisfactory to the customer then the whole thing is 'approved', resulting in an instruction being issued to warehousemen at 'E' to prepare the item for shipping, and in the hiring of the courier service under the conditions offered. All communications concerned with this activity can now be 'released'.

Although hypothetical, this example gives some idea of the potential power that coordinated use of OSI can provide to business; especially when one considers that it is very unlikely that the courier service computer will be of the same origin as that at warehouse 'E' which has been the normal barrier to this type of communication until now. Indeed, had the courier service been fully booked or offered unacceptable terms, then a poll around a number of courier companies would have been possible.

To demonstrate the power of OSI was not however the primary objective of introducing this example. What it is intended to do is to illustrate how the functionality required of an application process may require a number of instances of a 'communication with a peer application process', i.e. an association, to be in existence with that application process at any one time.

In order that such 'distributed' applications can be accommodated, an application entity may, at any time, be made up of a number of SAOs (single association objects). These SAOs are not constrained to the same application context — each may have a differing make-up to suit the application purpose they are to fulfil, and will be called into play as needed by the application agent.

In fact application layer architecture is modelled in a very general way in order to facilitate standards for complex distributed processing environments. The model for distribution builds upon the structures already examined, i.e. ASE, SAO, application entity, and application process; namely,

an application process may 'contain' one or more application entities at any one time;
an application entity may contain one or more SAO at any time;
an SAO must contain ACSE together with one or more ASE.

4.2 ACSE — ASSOCIATION CONTROL SERVICE ELEMENT

We have already seen in the last chapter how an SS user establishes a session connection between itself and a peer; now we consider ACSE in relation to this. In doing so, we must treat the SS user in a true layered manner, i.e. as a distinct presentation entity and an application process.

An initiating application process will first establish an association — a cooperative relationship with another application process. This is established over an OSI data communication 'channel' (essentially a session connection). Without such an association, application-specific activity cannot take place.

(**Note:** the concept of connection does exist in the presentation layer, but there it is a mechanism for establishing an 'initial working environment' for presentation activity over a session connection, and for providing the application process with a means to set, or be informed of, the parameters associated with the establishment of a session connection. This will become clear in the next chapter on presentation.)

ACSE, as we have already seen, is a generic grouping of services and service elements of the application layer concerned with association control. The services provided by ACSE are as follows:

— application association establishment;
— application association release (orderly release);
— application association abort (disorderly release).

and these are realized by the four service elements:

— A-ASSOCIATE (confirmed service);
— A-RELEASE (confirmed service);
— A-ABORT (unconfirmed service);
— A-P-ABORT (unconfirmed, initiated by the service provider).

The primitives associated with these service elements are shown in Table 4.1.

Table 4.1 — Service elements of association control

Service element	Primitives
A-ASSOCIATE	Request; Indication; Response; Confirm.
A-RELEASE	Request; Indication; Response; Confirm.
A-ABORT	Request; Indication.
A-P-ABORT	Indication.

The A-ASSOCIATE service element provides the mechanism by which an association can be established between two application processes. One function of association establishment is to determine the *application context* that is to be in force during the period of association.

This service element provides a confirmed service. The service primitives have associated parameters; these fall into two groups:

Group one:

recipient entity title,
initiator entity title,
application context name,
user information,
result.

Group two:

calling presentation address,
called presentation address,
responding presentation address,
presentation context definition list,
default presentation context name,
quality of service,
presentation requirements,
session requirements,
initial sync. point serial number,
initial assignment of tokens,
session connection identifier.

Group two parameters have no bearing on the nature of the association nor on the activity of any application layer service element. Rather, they are used in establishing the underlying presentation connection (initial environment) and session connection, which must be created before the association can be achieved. By means of these parameters, the application process has control over the nature of the underlying session connection. We shall not discuss these further here but leave them for the following chapters on the lower layers.

The first group of parameters have a direct bearing on the nature of the association established by the use of the A-ASSOCIATE service element. The service primitive sequence is shown in Figure 4.8. Notice here that the line we wouldhave expected to be labelled as a ASAP is instead labelled 'ASE/ACSE boundary'. This is because these interactions occur within an application entity —

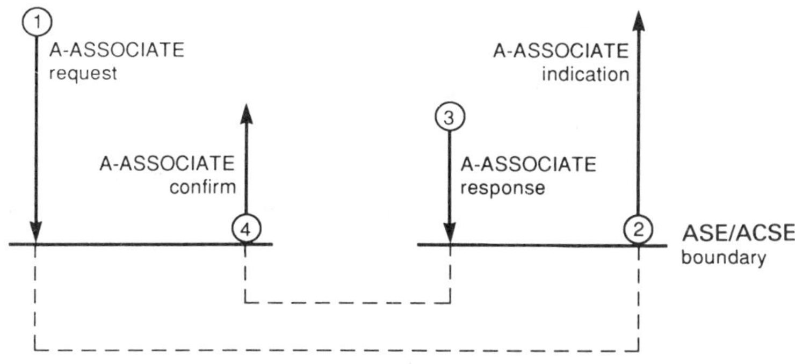

Fig. 4.8 — A-ASSOCIATE service primitive sequence.

between ASE and ACSE components — rather than between superior and subordinate entities where a SAP is defined as the binding between entities.

The **recipient application entity title** parameter identifies the specific application entity with which the association is to be established. It appears on the A-ASSOCIATE request and indication service primitives and, since it can be accepted with modification by the responding end-system, can also appear on the response and confirm. This modification may be the addition of useful information which can be passed back to the initiating application agent. It is an optional parameter and if it is not used on the request then the **PSAP address** parameter is regarded as sufficient identification. The **initiating application entity title** parameter is included, optionally, to identify the component application entity of the initiating application process, and appears on the request and indication only.

Here we have used a form of notation which we shall continue to use throughout the remainder of the book. If we are looking at a particular service element and if the context is clear, then all instances of words 'request', 'indication', 'response' and 'confirm' refer to those particular service primitives of that service element. For instance, above we were looking at the A-ASSOCIATE service element; a subsequent reference to response was therefore referring to the A-ASSOCIATE response service primitive. Should the context be unclear then the full form of the primitive will be used.

The **application context name** parameter is the context name discussed above. It is optional and if not provided by the initiating application agent it is assumed that a 'default' context is to be used. It appears on the request and indication, and the responder must return this name or perhaps some other choice of context on the response. This choice by the responder offers a limited scope for negotiation. The **user information** parameter can be used optionally by either or both application agents to carry meaningful information to their other. **Result** is a mandatory parameter on the response (and hence on the confirm), and indicates either the acceptance of the association by the responder, or a rejection, citing one of the following reasons:

Unacceptable application context

Unrecognized recipient AE title
Unrecognized initiator AE title
Temporarily unavailable
Permanently unavailable
User data not readable

If the **result** of the association on the confirm is positive, but the responder has modified the **application context name** to some unacceptable value, then the sequence of events shown in Figure 4.9 may occur; in which case no association remains.

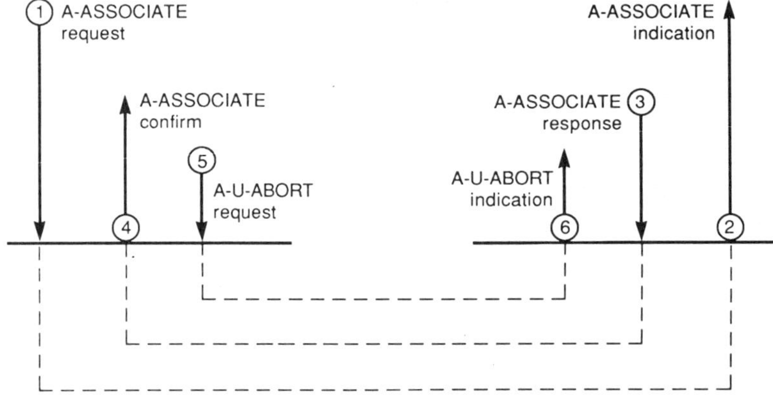

Fig. 4.9 — Rejection of unacceptable association.

The A-RELEASE service element provides for either of the application agents to release the association without any loss of information in transit. It is an orderly release and a confirmed service. It is possible for the application agent in receipt of an indication to refuse the release: this would normally occur because of the 'conversational' nature of the application in question whereby the need for further activity is seen only by one application agent. The facility to refuse to release an association is available to the application agents only if the session connection over which the association is provided has the 'session negotiated release' FU selected. More discussion of this will appear in later chapters.

The A-RELEASE service primitives have the following associated parameters :

Reason
User information
Result

We have already seen one use of the A-ABORT service element. Generally it is a *destructive* service, in that any information in transit over the association at the time of its use may be lost. The result of this unconfirmed service is the release of the association, and it can be initiated in either application process. It has a single parameter, **user information**.

The A-P-ABORT service element is used whenever problems are encountered in the service provider that are catastrophic to the association. The result is the release of the association. It is also a destructive service, potentially causing the loss of information in transit. (See Figure 4.10).

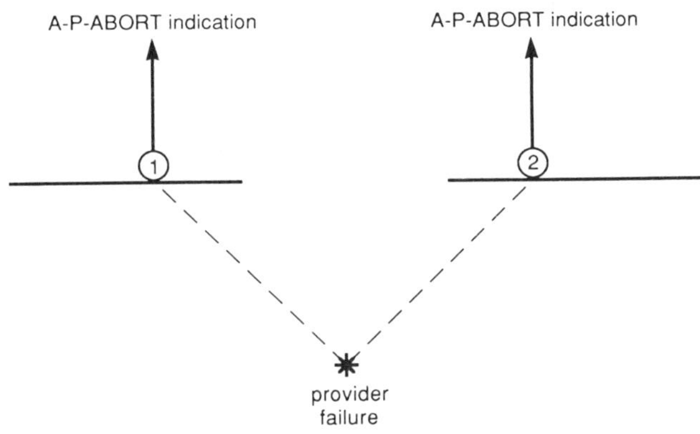

Fig. 4.10 — A provider failure.

4.3 ACSE PROTOCOL AND THE USE OF THE PRESENTATION SERVICE

Association establishment is the primary service offered by ACSE. There is a one-to-one correspondence between an application association and a presentation connection. The establishment of an association and a presentation connection (the nature of which we shall investigate in the next chapter) are not bound by the rules of establishment discussed in the last chapter. This procedure of establishment is examined below (in note 1). ACSE activity is, like all other instances of activity within a layer, achieved by the exchange of PDUs (APDUs) between layer entities (application entities in this case). Table 4.2 demonstrates the relationships between ACSE, service primitives, APDUs and presentation services.

Each of the entries in the table should be read left to right. They comprise five units as follows:

A. The ACSE primitive issued within an application process (i.e. by an ASE component) either to initiate a service or to respond to a confirmed service.
B. The APDU that is generated by the service element of the application entity as a result of A.
C. The presentation service primitive issued by the application entity as a result of A/B.

D. The presentation service primitive issued to the peer application entity on the cooperating end-system as a result of C.
E. The ACSE primitive issued to the peer ASE component as a result of A.

This tabular form will be used in the following chapters in a similar way.
Notes:
(1) Because of the one-to-one relationship between an association and a presentation connection, there is little point in using the mechanism described in the last chapter for lower layer connection establishment (where an *n* entity awaits an $n-1$ connect confirm service primitive before using an $n-1$ data service to convey the connect *n* PDU). The association is bound to a presentation connection in such a way that the two can be established in a single 'exchange' between end-systems. The P-CONNECT request carries, in the user data parameter, the AARQ (A-ASSOCIATE ReQuest) APDU. The AARQ APDU is carried 'up', in the responding end-system, within the user data parameter of the P-CONNECT indication (Figure 4.11). The responding application entity will use the user data parameter in the response to convey the AARE (A-ASSOCIATE REply) APDU to the initiator. Association establishment is described in a worked example in Chapter 9.
(2) The P-CONNECT request parameters provided by the initiating application entity are the group two parameters provided on the A-ASSOCIATE request. They are mapped onto the presentation service primitive without change by the application entity. In this way the application agent has indirect access to the presentation service.
(3) Having decoded the AARQ APDU presented in user data of the P-CONNECT indication, the responding application entity may be unable to service the proposed association, perhaps because of inadequate resources. If this is the case, then the application entity will not issue an A-ASSOCIATE indication but will build an AARE APDU, including a negative result, and send it by use of the user data parameter of the P-CONNECT response which it will subsequently issue.
(4) If the responding application process (either agent or entity) rejects the association for any reason, then the result parameter of the P-CONNECT response will be negative and a presentation connection will not be established.
(5) A provider abort occurs as a result of some event that causes the loss of the presentation connection. Loss of the presentation connection clearly implies loss of the association.

4.4 ROSE — REMOTE OPERATIONS SERVICE ELEMENT

Very many application areas, especially those which will operate within a distributed open systems environment (e.g. electronic mail, financial house and banking, transport signalling) often operate either partially or wholly in an *interactive* manner. That is, many activities take the form of an operation being *requested* by an application entity which a peer entity will attempt to perform; the outcome being the subject of a *reply* to the initiator.

To facilitate this type of operaiton a further building block ASE has been defined

Table 4.2 — ACSE and use of presentation services

A: ACSE Primitive →	B: PDU →	C: P Service Primitive →	D: P Service Primitive →	E: ACSE Primitive
A-ASSOCIATE request	AARQ APDU	P-CONNECT request (1)(2)	P-CONNECT indication (3)	A-ASSOCIATE indication
A-ASSOCIATE response	AARE APDU	P-CONNECT response (4)	P-CONNECT confirm	A-ASSOCIATE confirm
A-RELEASE request	RLRQ APDU	P-RELEASE request	P-RELEASE indication	A-RELEASE indication
A-RELEASE response	RLRE APDU	P-RELEASE response	P-RELEASE confirm	A-RELEASE confirm
A-ABORT request	ABRT APDU	P-U-ABORT request	P-U-ABORT indication	A-ABORT indication
—	—	—	P-P-ABORT indication (5)	A-P-ABORT indication

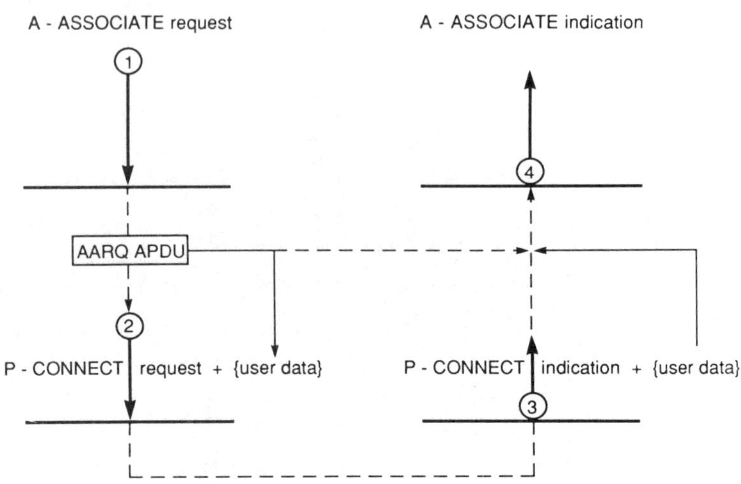

Fig. 4.11 — AARQ APDU conveyed in P-CONNECT user data.

— *remote operations service element* (ROSE). It provides a general framework of request/reply facilities over which any application operation can be invoked by one application ASE, to be performed by a peer.

ROSE provides five types of *classes* of operation:

Operation class 1: Synchronous, reporting success or failure (result or error).
Operation class 2: Asynchronous, reporting success or failure (result or error).
Operation class 3: Asynchronous, reporting failure (error) only, if any.
Operation class 4: Asynchronous, reporting success (result) only.
Operation class 5: Asynchronous, outcome not reported.

ROSE is defined in a two-part, service and protocol, standard — ISO 9072.

4.5 CCR — COMMITMENT, CONCURRENCY AND RECOVERY

One of the most sensitive areas of computer application is in computerized financial transaction processing. Here we have an example of an application area that frequently involves a number of distinct remote computer systems in a single coordinated transaction — a transaction of which no part should go ahead, i.e. be committed, unless the whole is guaranteed to succeed. If, for example, a financial transaction involving a number of banks and their respective computer systems is in progress when one of the systems 'crashes', then a total recovery to a pre-transaction commencement state must be assured.

Since many instances of distributed processing applications would find services facilitating this sort of reliable environment useful, they are standardized as a building block ASE. This ASE is known as *Commitment, Concurrency and Recovery* (CCR).

4.6 INTRODUCING THE ISO STANDARD APPLICATIONS

These are the five major applications which were well enough understood to be amongst the first to be standardized by ISO within the application layer.

4.6.1 File transfer, electronic mail and directory services

In the early days of OSI based services these areas will have the most impact on user activity. For this reason we devote a chapter to each of FTAM, MHS/X.400 and Directory Services towards the end of the book.

4.6.2 Virtual terminal, VT

In examining the architecture of the ISORM, we have regarded the end-systems involved as being autonomous computer systems. This, of course, need not be so. Indeed, in many applications of OSI, one party to the activity will be some highly specialized slave system (a robotic device perhaps), control of which will be actioned over OSI; this is a basis for the automation of a manufacturing plant. Another example is provided by the use of remote terminals to access a multi-user computer system over OSI. Such a system could have many applications accessible by remote terminal access and, ideally, any terminal 'attached' to OSI could be used for such access.

There are a vast range of computer terminals available, and amongst them there are many differing methods used for screen control. If, however, a 'virtual terminal' standard were available over OSI, then the problem of remote terminal access to packages or processes on computer systems would be vastly simplified. This is in fact what VT is; it presents to an end-system a single terminal type and, at the terminal end of an OSI exchange, maps the characteristics of this 'virtual' terminal to the 'real' terminal involved.

A package implementor need only write terminal handling routines to the services specified in the service definition of the standard, in order to provide access to the package from any terminal with ISO VT capability. There is no need for the package to have knowledge of individual terminal characteristics.

The terminal manufacturer will provide, within the terminal, an implementation of ISO virtual terminal standard. The only application entity in this terminal will be a VT entity. The level of implementation of the lower layers will be based upon the requirements of VT. The individual characteristics of the terminal will be interfaced to the appropriate services of VT. Such a terminal then will be in a position to access any application package on any computer system available over OSI (see Figure 4.12).

4.6.3 Job transfer and manipulation, JTM

This application layer standard is concerned with the control of tasks and associated documents between computer systems without loss or duplication. Traditionally, this is associated with job submission to remote computer systems and the control of the distribution of 'output' from such jobs. It includes the following services:

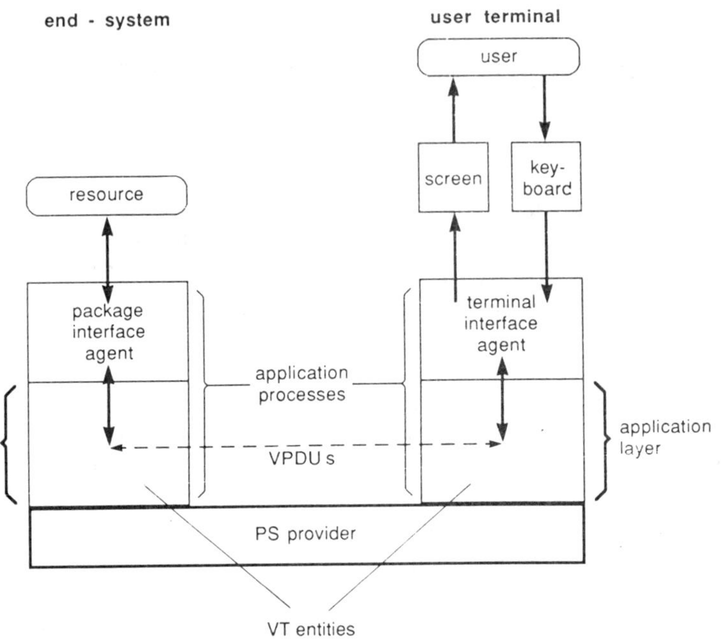

Fig. 4.12 — Use of VT.

— The transfer of a 'job control' document between the submitting 'user' and the jobmill (background job facility) on the 'target' end-system.
— The control of dependency; that is, the 'user' can make statements about the data documents to be assembled at the target end-system before the job can be executed. These documents may reside on any end-system in the OSI environment. The standard provides for the satisfaction of such dependencies before execution.
— The disposal of 'output' after job execution. The submitting 'user' can make statements about such disposal. The output documents may be returned to the submitting end-system, or to any other end-system. Indeed, an output document may be defined such that it itself becomes a new 'job control' document. This document could then be automatically submitted to any end-system as a job, together with any dependencies and disposal information. This process is know as *spawning*.
— Enquiry over OSI as to the progress of any JTM activity. The information returned would be a trace of the original submission and any disposal or spawned activity. Such an enquiry could involve many end-systems.
— Modification of any submission, dependency or disposal instruction at any stage before that instruction is carried out. For instance, if the disposal instruction on a JTM job is for all output to be sent to a graphics device at site X, then up to the

point where this is carried out this instruction can be modified (perhaps to direct some of the output to another site).

— JTM provides security control for every JTM job environment initiated by a 'user', such that enquiry and modification can be performed over OSI only by specified authorized JTM service users.

5

The presentation layer

> "It's a Missage," he said to himself, "thats what it is. And that letter is a 'P', and so is that, and so is that, and 'P' means 'Pooh', so its a very important Missage to me, and I can't read it"
>
> A. A. Milne, *Winnie-the-Pooh*

The ISO connection-oriented presentation layer is defined in two documents:

— ISO 8822 : Service definition
— ISO 8823 : Protocol specification

This layer deals with information representation issues. It provides a common representation for application information while it is in transit between peer application processes over an OSI 'data communication channel', i.e. a session connection. Peer application processes exchange information by the use of presentation services, the unit of exchange being known as an *information unit*. The representation of the contents of an information unit is the responsibility of the presentation layer.

Consider the use of presentation services by an application which performs the transfer of files between end-systems. Presentation is not concerned with any aspect of file structure. The preservation of any relationship *between* information units, e.g. that between records in a file of hierarchical structure, is the responsibility of the cooperating application processes.

There are three forms of representation (encoding) of the contents of an information unit:

Source: That in the real storage on the transmitting end-system.
Destination: That which will be used by the receiving end-system to store the information in its own real storage.
Transit: That understood by both end-systems and used whilst the information is in transit over a session connection.

An information unit may be 'a sequence of *integers*'. The transmitting end-system may have a (source) encoding for integer of 16 bit binary. The receiving end-system may use 32 bit binary (destination) encoding. The need for a commonly agreed transit encoding is clear.

Another information unit may consist of a 'sequence of characters', a line of text perhaps. One end-system may have a source encoding of 'a sequence of ASCII encoded characters'; while a receiving end-system's encoding may be 'a sequence of EBCDIC encoded characters'. A choice of transit encoding could be either of these or some other form.

Given that OSI concerns the interconnection of heterogeneous computer systems, it has to be assumed that the source encoding will not necessarily be the same as that of the destination. It is possible that the transit encoding may be either the source or destination encodings (or both in the special case of similar systems communicating), but it is often the case that it is neither of these.

There are therefore two possible encoding transformations to be performed in the course of information transfer: source → transit and transit → destination. The presentation layer is responsible for the realization of these transformations. The source → transit transformation will be done by the presentation entity on the transmitting end-system, and the transit → destination by the peer entity on the receiving end-system. The transmitting application process is aware of the nature of the information it is to transmit and it must convey this knowledge to its peer in order that that (receiving) application process can make a suitable choice of destination encoding. In essence the transmitting application process must, when making an information transfer service request, inform the presentation entity of the *syntax* of the information unit presented for transfer. Given this, the appropriate transformations can be performed on the information unit by the peer presentation entities. This syntax, known as an *abstract syntax*, formally defines the contents of an information unit without reference to any encoding technique that may be used to 'store' such a unit.

We shall now look at how the exchange of an information unit is achieved, bearing in mind the relationship between the information unit, the system-dependent encodings and the abstract syntax. On behalf of application processes, peer presentation entities exchange information over a session connection, encoded in a precise representational form understood by the peer presentation entities: the *transit encoding*. This encoding must satisfy two criteria:

(a) It must contain precise encodings for all aspects of the abstract syntax in question.
(b) It must have all the additional encoding features requested by the application process (for instance, encryption of information, compression of recurrent information sequences, etc.)

This (commonly understood) transit encoding is known as a *transfer syntax*. In effect it is this that defines 'the order in which the bytes go down the wire'.

Each aspect of representation in (b) is relevant only to the period of information transfer over a session connection and has no meaning outside the presentation layer; certainly there are no permanent relationships between these 'add-on' features and the local information encodings.

The peer presentation entities perform the transformations between the transfer syntax and the local encoding of an information unit.

Consider the following analogy. The captain of a British merchant ship at sea decides to send a greetings message to his counterpart on a naval vessel. He writes his message on paper in *shorthand*, and passes it to the radio officer who in turn transmits the message to the naval radio officer in *morse code*. The naval officer listens to the morse and writes the message on paper. The normal operational routine on this ship dictates that any message, regardless of source, be encoded in a 'code of the day' such that it cannot be read by any rating entrusted with its delivery. The message that subsequently passes to the captain will be in this *naval code*.

Contrived this may be, but it does demonstrate a relationship between abstract and transfer syntaxes. The message has a local (source) encoding on the merchant ship of *shorthand*. The abstract syntax associated with the basic unit of information of the message is: 'a sequence of characters from the Latin character set' (i.e. a word). The naval officer uses a local (destination) encoding, *naval code*. The transfer syntax is *morse code*.

Each instance of an exchange between peer radio operators is an encoding, in the 'agreed' transfer syntax (morse), of an information unit defined by the abstract syntax. In the example, the transmitting radio operator preserves the boundary between units of information by 'inserting' a pause in the flow of the morse code which is equivalent to the separate presentation service requests made by a transmitting application process to transfer each information unit (PSDU).

Other examples of abstract syntaxes are:

— *integer*,
— *floating point number*,
— *sequence of characters from the ISO IA5 character set*,
— *integer* followed by *floating point number*,
— *integer* followed by *boolean* followed by *sequence of characters from the ISO IA5 character set*.

Clearly, local encodings of abstract syntaxes such as *integer* and *floating point number* can differ widely. Whatever the local encoding may be, the encoding defined by the transfer syntax will be understood by both end-systems, enabling a meaningful transfer of information to take place.

An abstract syntax is assigned an identifier, an *abstract syntax name*. The final example above could, for instance, be assigned the name 'special-record-format-99' and registered as such with an ISO/OSI registration authority for general use. Similarly a transfer syntax has an associated *transfer syntax name*.

Notice that, in this last example, the abstract syntax defines an information unit made up of three items, each of which is logically indivisible. Such items are referred to as *presentation data values*.

An abstract syntax defines a set of one or more presentation data values

In requesting an information transfer service of a presentation entity, an application process presents an information unit for transfer, a PSDU. Together with this PSDU, the application process will provide the identity of the associated abstract syntax. The PSDU can be considered to 'contain' information in the local encoding of this syntax.

In servicing this request the presentation entity performs an encoding on the contents of the PSDU, determined by the rules of the transfer syntax appropriate to this abstract syntax. The encoded information is then packaged into a PPDU which also carries the identity of the associated abstract and transfer syntax. The PPDU is transferred to the peer presentation entity by the use of the SS provider.

On receipt of the PPDU from the SS provider, the receiving presentation entity examines the transfer syntax identifier and performs a transformation of the information carried by the PPDU into the local encoding of the specified abstract syntax. The result is then passed to the receiving application process as a PSDU.

Notice that the encoded form of the PSDU carried in the PPDU is meaningful only to the presentation entities. It has no meaning in any of the lower layers, which must handle it transparently (unaltered) as *data*. It also has no meaning to the peer application processes unless the transfer syntax chosen happens to be the same as either (or both) local encodings ('both' can obtain when like end-systems are cooperating; this clearly has efficiency implications).

ISO has defined a suitable notation for abstract syntaxes and a set of encoding rules for the generation of a transfer syntax. This standard, known as ASN.1, is described in Appendix 1. (We recommend reading this appendix after reading Chapter 11.)

Returning to the analogy, we can see that the transmitting radio officer could have chosen to transmit the message in a *secret code*, say CODEX, understood by himself and his peer on the naval ship. CODEX then is also a transfer syntax, so we have an instance where the abstract syntax could be associated with more than one transfer syntax — although, of course, it will only be associated with one in any particular transmission.

In general, an abstract syntax can be associated with one transfer syntax chosen from a set of appropriate transfer syntaxes. Conversely, a single transfer syntax may be suitable for encoding information units from a number of different abstract syntaxes. A presentation entity may know of many abstract and transfer syntaxes, and must be aware of the possible 'legal' pairings.

During the course of an application activity many information units may be exchanged. These information units may all be of the same type, i.e. defined by the same abstract syntax. Otherwise a number of abstract syntaxes are required to define the different types of information unit that are to be transferred. The peer presentation entities may therefore be required to handle many different abstract syntaxes during the period of a particular application association.

It is an implementation choice that determines the scope of a presentation entity. A simple entity may be able to handle only a single transfer syntax, thus reducing the range of information unit types that can be transferred by its services. Another may have many transfer syntaxes available.

Clearly, peer presentation entities must agree on a specific transfer syntax to be used for representation of information defined by a particular abstract syntax. Equally, it cannot be assumed that all transfer syntaxes at the disposal of one presentation entity are also available to a peer.

A pairing of abstract and transfer syntax must be negotiated between peer presentation entities before an information unit transfer, defined by the particular abstract syntax, can be requested by an application process. This pairing is known as a *presentation context*, and the negotiation is achieved as follows:

— An application process informs the presentation entity of one or many abstract syntax(es) that it wishes bound into presentation context(s). It is (they are) to remain available until the application process revokes that presentation context.

— The presentation entity examines each abstract syntax and selects the set of transfer syntaxes that are capable of encoding information units of each syntactic form. The choice can be further constrained by any requirement of the application process for 'add-on' facilities.
— The presentation entity then uses session services to pass the complete list of abstract syntaxes and their respective sets of transfer syntaxes to its peer.
— The peer determines, for each abstract syntax, a single available transfer syntax from the set provided. This results in a list of presentation contexts, which is returned to the initiating presentation entity.
— The initiating presentation entity is now aware of the presentation contexts in force. It informs the application entity that it can go ahead and use information transfer services involving the requested abstract syntaxes. It is possible for negotiation to fail and an abstract syntax to be rejected at this point. More of this later.

The list of negotiated presentation contexts is known as the *defined context set* (DCS).

The DCS is created by negotiation which occurs when peer presentation entities first enter into a cooperation; that is, immediately after a session connection has been established between the presentation entities. This is a result of an application process requesting the presentation entity to establish a presentation connection (the nature of which will be explored in the following sections). A part of the presentation connection establishment procedure is the negotiation of a DCS, described above.

It is, however, possible that the abstract syntax(es) to be used by the application process is (are) not known at connection establishment time. An example is a package to interrogate a remote database, where the abstract syntaxes to be called into use depend upon subsequent activity of the enquirer 'driving' the interrogation application.

In a case where no abstract syntax list is available from the application process at connection establishment time, the peer presentation entities will assume the availability of a mutually understood *default* presentation context. There is, therefore, in the presentation layer a service element that provides for the modification at any time of the DCS associated with a connection. The service provides the negotiated addition or removal of presentation contexts to or from the DCS. This service element makes up the context management FU of presentation. It is an optional FU, the use of which is negotiated as part of the connection establishment procedure.

Information units, PSDUs, are exchanged between peer presentation entities in data PPDUs in an encoded form defined by the transfer syntax of the appropriate presentation context. The PPDU carries, as well as encoded information, the identity of this presentation context. The receiving presentation entity can then perform the appropriate transformation of the received information before passing the PSDU (together with the identity of the associated abstract syntax) to the receiving application process.

5.1 THE PRESENTATION SERVICES

Presentation services fall into two sets. The first set, which we shall expand upon in the remainder of this chapter, provides the representational functions described above. The second set of services is concerned with providing a mechanism to enable application processes to exploit the data communication control facilities offered by the session layer; in effect these presentation services 'mirror' those offered by session. The operation of presentation service elements associated with the mirroring services does not entail any exchange of PPDUs between peer presentation entities, but causes a mapping of the parameters of the associated presentation service primitives to or from the equivalent session service primitives (which bear the same name) (see Figure 5.1).

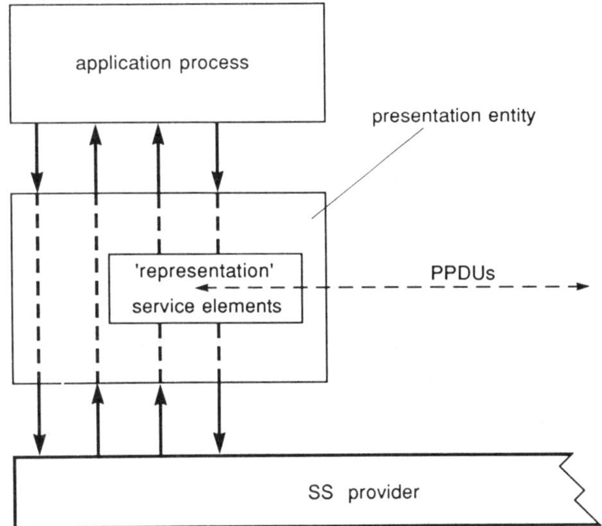

Fig. 5.1 — The two types of presentation service.

The mirroring services, examined in the next chapter on the session layer, are provided by the following service elements:

P-TOKEN-GIVE	P-TOKEN-PLEASE	P-CONTROL-GIVE
P-SYNC-MINOR	P-SYNC-MAJOR	P-SYNC-MINOR
P-RESYNCHRONIZE	P-U-EXCEPTION-REPORT	P-P-EXCEPTION-REPORT
P-ACTIVITY-START	P-ACTIVITY-RESUME	P-ACTIVITY-END
P-ACTIVITY-INTERRUPT	P-ACTIVITY-DISCARD	P-CAPABILITY-DATA
P-EXPEDITED-DATA		

In the remainder of this chapter we examine the information representation services in depth. The services are divided into three phases:

— connection establishment and release,
— application information transfer,
— context management.

The services in the first two phases form the *kernel* FU of the presentation layer, while that in the third forms the optional *context management* FU.

The service elements associated with these phases are as shown in Table 5.1.

Table 5.1 — Presentation service elements

Phase	Service element	Type
Connection establishment and release	P-CONNECT	confirmed
	P-RELEASE	confirmed
	P-U-ABORT	unconfirmed
	P-P-ABORT	(indication only)
Information transfer	P-DATA	unconfirmed
	P-TYPED-DATA	unconfirmed
Context management	P-ALTER-CONTEXT	confirmed

5.1.1 Connection establishment and release

Connection establishment is a confirmed service provided by the P-CONNECT service element. It provides the means by which an application process establishes a cooperative information exchange environment between itself and a peer. When established, this environment will have an agreed DCS which may, in its minimal form, be composed solely of a default presentation context.

This service element is really a mixture of the two types discussed above. Its use does result in a PPDU and has presentation-meaningful parameters but, in order that the presentation environment can be established, a session connection must be established. There are, therefore, parameters associated with this service element that have no meaning in this layer but are mapped directly onto equivalent parameters associated with the session connection establishment service element, S-CONNECT. (The relationship between the P-CONNECT service element and the S-CONNECT service element is discussed at the end of this chapter.)

The presentation environment is known as a presentation connection but this 'connection' is not, as we have seen, of the same kind of data communications concept as a session, transport or network connection. Real end-to-end *data communication* control is provided only in the session layer and below.

The parameters associated with P-CONNECT which have meaning only in relation to the session connection are as follows:

Quality of service
Initial synchronization point serial number
Initial assignment of tokens
Session connection identifier

These parameters are examined in the next chapter, on the session layer.

The remaining parameters have meaning within the presentation layer; they are:

Calling presentation address
Called presentation address
Responding presentation address
Multiple defined contexts
Presentation context definition list
Default context name
Presentation requirements
User data
Result

In the following description of the parameters it can be assumed that a parameter appears on the request, indication, response and confirm service primitives unless otherwise stated.

The **calling presentation address** appears only on the request and indication; it is the PSAP address of the application process initiating the connection. Likewise the **called presentation address** is the PSAP address of the intended responder application process. The **responding presentation address** is provided by the responder and so appears only on the response and confirm. It is provided only if the PSAP address to which the connection should be re-established in the event of failure, differs from the called presentation address. The **result** parameter appears only on the response and confirm and indicates the result of connection establishment. It has a range of symbolic values which include *acceptance* and *rejection*. The **multiple defined contexts** parameter appears only when the application process requires support for more than a single presentation context.

The **presentation context definition list** parameter is used to place one or many presentation contexts into the DCS. If the multiple defined context parameter is not included then this parameter is restricted to a single entry, otherwise it can be a list of entries. Each entry has two components:

— presentation context identifier,
— abstract syntax name.

By including this parameter on the request, the initiating application process provides the presentation entity with a list of abstract syntaxes (and corresponding identifiers), for each of which it must choose one, or a list of, appropriate transfer syntaxes. As a result of the connection establishment procedure, the presentation entity will negotiate, with its peer, a single transfer syntax for each abstract syntax (a presentation context); these pairings will be identified, during the connection, by the presentation context identifier. Since transfer syntax is transparent to the application processes, there is no reference to it in this parameter on any primitive. The presentation context definition list and the multiple defined context parameters on the indication are therefore identical to those on the request.

If an abstract syntax is unacceptable then the connection establishment fails with an appropriate **result** parameter value. If all abstract syntaxes are acceptable then the connection establishment can proceed. Since there is no 'middle ground' then there is no need for the presentation context definition list parameter to be included on a 'positive' response and confirm. The seven-stage procedure can be summarized as follows:

— The SS user issues a P-CONNECT request, which includes a presentation context definition list (PCDL) parameter. If the PCDL has more than a single entry then the multiple defined contexts parameter must also be set.
— The presentation entity chooses a list (one or many) of transfer syntaxes for each entry in the PCDL parameter. The PCDL is then expanded with transfer syntaxes and is encoded into the connect PPDU, which is sent to the peer (responding) entity.
— The responding entity chooses a single transfer syntax for each entry in the expanded PCDL. If a choice is impossible for any entry then connection establishment will fail at this point
— On successful completion of the step above, an indication is issued to the responding application process (identified by the called presentation address). The PCDL parameter will contain a copy of that provided with the request.
— The application process issues a response. If the connection is acceptable (because all abstract syntaxes are known) then the result parameter is positive. There is no PCDL parameter on the response since acceptance of the connection implies acceptance of all the presentation syntax requirements of the connection.
— The responding presentation entity transmits the refined PCDL (i.e. with only a single transfer syntax for each entry) to the initiating entity in an appropriately encoded connect accept PPDU.
— A confirm is issued to the initiating application process.

Once the DCS has been established in this way, it is possible to *tag* any information transmission by a presentation entity with the presentation context identifier; this is sufficient for the receiving entity to determine the abstract and transfer syntaxes of the encoded information received in a data PPDU.

Now consider the other parameters associated with the P-CONNECT service element. The **default context name** is included when the initiating application process requires the abstract syntax to be supported in the default context. If the parameter is not included then the implication is that there is some *prior arrangement* on the definition of the default context between the cooperating end-systems. The parameter value is an abstract syntax name and it occurs only on the request and indication. It is not negotiable by the application processes, and non-acceptance results in connection establishment failure.

The **presentation requirements** parameter is used by the initiating application process to select optional presentation FUs. In fact there is only one, context management. The inclusion of this FU is negotiated with the responder. Note that, should the responder accept a connection but negotiate out the initiators requirement of the optional FU, then the initiating application process, on receipt of the affirmative confirm, may issue a P-U-ABORT request to terminate the established but unacceptable connection if it cannot continue.

User data can contain application information to be conveyed to the peer application process. This information exchange is subject to representational manipulation since it originates above the presentation layer. It must be accompanied by a presentation context identifier from the list provided in the PCDL parameter, if present; otherwise use of the proposed or assumed default presentation context is implied. It can be used to convey application information from initiator to responder (request → indication) or from responder to initiator (response → confirm), or both.

Application processes can instigate the disorderly release of a presentation connection by invoking the P-U-ABORT service element. Disorderly release means that any information in transit between peer application processes may be lost as a result of use of this service. It can be issued at any time by the initiator of the connection and at any time, after issuing the P-CONNECT response, by the responder. It is an unconfirmed service with a single, optional, parameter, **user data.** This parameter carries application information between the peer application processes using the default presentation context. One use of this service which was indicated in the last section is illustrated in Figure 5.2.

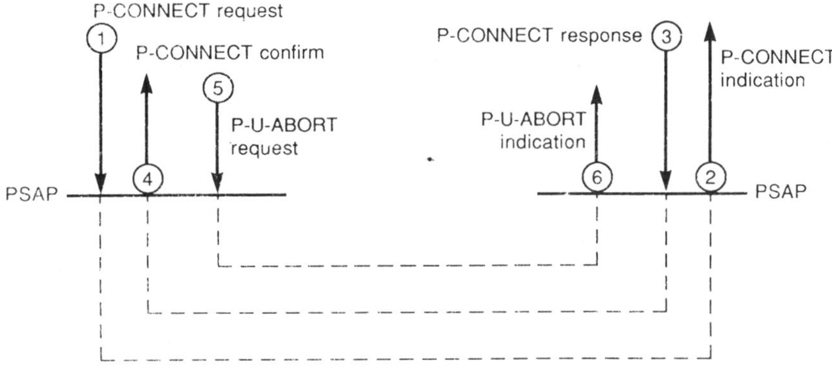

Fig. 5.2 — Rejection of unacceptable presentation connection.

Should any event occur in the underlying layers or in either of the peer presentation entities (which together form the PS provider) whereby the service is disrupted (i.e. a lower layer connection is lost) then the peer presentation entities issue a P-P-ABORT indication to their respective application processes. This is a disorderly release and information in transit can be lost. There are no associated parameters.

Orderly release of a presentation connection is achieved by invoking the P-RELEASE service element. As we shall see at the end of this chapter, this service is really one falling into the category of presentation 'transparency'. The presentation connection is released as a result of the release of the underlying session connection; this is instigated by the use of the session normal release service via the P-RELEASE service element. It is a confirmed service and will be expanded on in the next chapter, being included here only for completeness.

5.1.2 Context management

We now consider the service element that constitutes the optional context management FU.

The P-ALTER-CONTEXT service element adds new presentation context(s) to, or removes existing presentation contexts from, the DCS. It provides a confirmed service (since negotiation is involved) and has a number of associated parameters.

The **presentation context addition list** parameter is associated with the addition of new presentation contexts to the DCS. It is governed by the same rules and negotiation mechanisms defined for the presentation context definition list parameter in the P-CONNECT section above.

The **presentation context deletion list** parameter is associated with removal of presentation contexts from the DCS. It comprises a list of identities of the presentation contexts to be removed from the DCS.

A **result list** parameter is used, optionally, by either instance of the service, on the response and confirm. If it does not appear then the assumption is that all the DCS manipulations have been accepted and performed. If it is present, it comprises a list of entries, exactly the same in number and order as the list of presentation contexts in the corresponding parameter on the request. Each entry is a **result**, taking the value of *acceptance*, *rejection by user* or *rejection by provider* (addition only).

User data is an optional parameter to both services. It can contain application information in any abstract syntax appearing in the DCS.

5.1.3 Information transfer

There are two presentation service elements offering the information unit transfer described in the opening section of this chapter. These are P-DATA and P-TYPED-DATA.

P-DATA offers the normal information unit transfer service, giving a representation-independent information exchange capability between peer application processes.

P-TYPED-DATA is a specialized service element offering the same service as P-DATA but only used by application processes to exchange information *against* the current setting of the *data token*. This is examined in detail in the next chapter.

A transmitting application process initiates an information unit exchange by use of a P-DATA (or P-TYPED-DATA) request. The information unit to be exchanged (the PSDU) and a tag (presentation context identifier) indicating the abstract syntax of that information unit, are provided by the application process. The peer presentation entities perform any transformations indicated by the presentation context defined for the abstract syntax; and subsequently an indication (of the appropriate service) will be issued to the peer (receiving) application process, together with the PSDU containing the application information unit and the presentation context identifier indicating its abstract syntax.

"Oh, are those 'P's Piglets? I thought they were Poohs."

A.A.Milne, *Winnie-The-Pooh*

5.2 PRESENTATION PROTOCOL AND THE USE OF SESSION SERVICE

As we saw earlier in the chapter, there are two distinct sets of parameters associated with the P-CONNECT service element. One set is unrelated to the functionality of the presentation layer, but gives the application process control over the parameters of the session connection establishment service. Now, in addressing terms, there is a one-to-one relationship between PSAP and SSAP addresses. Further, there is no aspect of the session service which can be negotiated out of use during session connection establishment that affects the provision of representational services by the presentation layer. For these reasons there is no need to perform the presentation connection establishment in the same way as the lower layers (as described in Chapter 3). The presentation entity need not wait for a session connection to be established before transmitting the connection (CP) PPDU to its peer. Instead the CP PPDU is generated by the initiating presentation entity from the parameters associated with presentation functionality, and then, instead of being 'held' until a session connection is established, it is placed in the user data parameter of the S-CONNECT request. The other parameters of this service primitive are derived directly from those parameters of the P-CONNECT request that are related only to session connection establishment. The CP PPDU will be presented unaltered to the peer (responding) presentation entity, in the user data parameter of the S-CONNECT indication, whereupon that entity will subsequently issue a P-CONNECT indication to the responding application process. (Association establishment, including presentation connection establishment, is illustrated in a worked example in Chapter 9.) Subsequently, the responding application process will issue a P-CONNECT response; the resultant connect accept (CPA) PPDU will pass this back to the initiating presentation entity via the user data parameter of the S-CONNECT response and confirm.

It is not our intention in this book to present the standards right through to the actual encoding of PDUs etc. Any reader who feels a need to progress to this level of understanding should be ready to take on the standards documents themselves (preferably with a stiff drink). Here we use the table form (introduced in the last chapter) to look at the relationships between presentation services, presentation protocol and session services. In Table 5.2 each entry is read from left to right and comprises five units, as follows:

A. The presentation service primitive issued by an application process to initiate a service or to respond to a confirmed service.
B. The PPDU that is (or may be) generated by the service element of the presentation entity as a result of A.
C. The session service primitive issued by the presentation entity as a result of A/B.
D. The session service primitive issued to the peer presentation entity on the cooperating end-system as a result of C.
E. The presentation service primitive issued to the peer application process as a result of A.

Notes:
(1) As discussed at the start of this section, the PPDU is conveyed by use of the user data parameter of the S-CONNECT service primitive.
(2) There is no PPDU. The peer presentation entity detects that the connection is

Table 5.2 — Presentation and the use of session layer services

A: PS Primitive →	B: PPDU →	C: SS Primitive →	D: SS Primitive →	E: PS Primitive
P-CONNECT request	CP PPDU	S-CONNECT request (1)	S-CONNECT indication	P-CONNECT indication
P-CONNECT response +ve	CPA PPDU	S-CONNECT response (1)	S-CONNECT confirm	P-CONNECT confirm
P-CONNECT response −ve	CPR PPDU	S-CONNECT response (1)	S-CONNECT confirm	P-CONNECT confirm
P-RELEASE request — (2)		S-RELEASE request	S-RELEASE indication	P-RELEASE indication
P-RELEASE response — (2)		S-RELEASE response	S-RELEASE confirm	P-RELEASE confirm
P-U-ABORT request	ARU PPDU	S-U-ABORT request	S-U-ABORT indication	P-U-ABORT indication
— (3)	ARP PPDU	S-U-ABORT request	S-U-ABORT indication	P-P-ABORT indication
P-DATA request	TD PPDU	S-DATA request	S-DATA indication	P-DATA indication
P-TYPED-DATA request	TTD PPDU	S-TYPED-DATA request	S-TYPED-DATA indication	P-TYPED-DATA indication
P-ALTER-CONTEXT request	AC PPDU	S-TYPED-DATA request	S-TYPED-DATA indication	P-ALTER-CONTEXT indication
P-ALTER-CONTEXT response	ACA PPDU	S-TYPED-DATA request	S-TYPED-DATA indication	P-ALTER-CONTEXT confirm

being released through receipt of an S-RELEASE indication. There is no PPDU because no specific presentation action is required of the entity other than the issuing of a P-RELEASE indication to the application process, and so there is no presentation-specific information to be encoded in a PPDU.

(3) There is no service primitive request since this event originates within the PS provider.

6

The session layer

The ISO connection-oriented session layer is defined in two documents:

— ISO 8326 : Service definition
— ISO 8327 : Protocol specification

Chapter 5 explains how presentation layer functionality ensures that a common representational form is understood and used for application information exchanged between cooperating application processes. The layer below the presentation layer, therefore has no concern with the syntax or semantics of such information, or with its encoding for transfer. Session handles *data*, that is, instances of a sequence of octets passed 'down' by an SS user to the session layer for transfer, subsequently being presented 'up' to an SS user after transfer. The syntax of the data is of no concern to the session, or any lower, layer. We say that the data is handled *transparently* by these layers.

The SSAP is a boundary point between information handling and data handling. Above the SSAP the object of exchange over OSI is information. The SS users handle information which is presented up or down through the SSAP in SSDUs, and SSDUs are regarded by the session layer as data objects to be handled transparently.

The session layer provides data transfer, control and management services over a session connection. These facilities enhance the reliable end-to-end data transfer service provided by the layer below, transport. By the nature of the presentation layer, discussed in the last chapter, we can see that the 'intelligence' behind the control of session services lies with the peer application processes. They access the session service by use of the second set of presentation services (the mirroring services).

6.1 THE SESSION SERVICE

6.1.1 Grouping the services

The session layer services fall into four distinct groups.

6.1.1.1 Group one

The first group consists of services associated with: session connection establishment between peer SS users; the exchange of data between peer SS users; and the orderly release of a session connection. These services should now be becoming familiar to the reader and we shall leave them for the moment without further comment.

6.1.1.2 Group two

Group two consists of *synchronization* and *resynchronization* services.

Synchronization of an information transaction between peer SS users is achieved by the insertion of synchronization points (in between SSDUs) into the information flow. The insertion of these points is a service provided by the session layer. Their positioning is the responsibility of the transmitting SS user but the issuing of the *identity* of a synchronization point is the responsibility of the session layer. The session entity, on instruction from the SS user, inserts a synchronization point and informs the initiating SS user of the identity of that point. This identity is known as a *synchronization point serial number* (SPSN).

There are two types of synchronization point, *major* and *minor*. Major synchronization points are used by the SS user to structure the information exchange into a series of distinct *dialogue units*. A major synchronization point indicates the end of one dialogue unit and the start of the next. The information within a dialogue unit can be regarded by the receiving SS user as completely separated from any in a previous or subsequent dialogue unit. That is, the information within the dialogue unit can be regarded as a complete piece of application information which may have followed, or be followed by, a separate, complete piece of application information. Other than storing the received information, an application process may take other specific action only on notification of a complete exchange, signalled by the end of a dialogue unit.

Minor synchronization points are used to establish commonly understood points in the information exchange *within* a dialogue unit. The peer SS users relate these points to positions in *secured* application information (e.g. written out after transfer to a 'non-volatile' storage medium), but, unlike major synchronization points, they have no other significance.

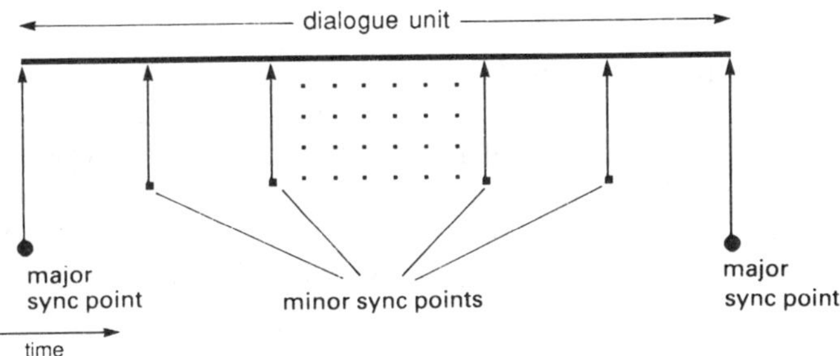

Fig. 6.1 — A dialogue unit.

Resynchronization is the session service supporting the restarting of an information exchange at some negotiated point (synchronization point) where information up to that point is known to be secured by the receiving SS user. As we look more closely at synchronization and resynchronization services, later in the chapter, it will become clear that the resynchronization service is a tool provided by the session layer to the peer SS users. The responsibility for the realization of a negotiated restart of information exchange lies with the peer SS users. It includes the use of this service to reset the session connection to a defined state with respect to the SPSN and the available tokens (which are introduced later).

6.1.1.3 Group three

Services in this group are associated with activity management, permitting SS users to order work into *activities*. An activity is assigned a unique name and consists of one or a series of dialogue units. During the *lifetime* (between establishment and orderly — or disorderly — release) of a connection any number of activities can take place but only one at any one time. There are service elements supporting the following:

Start an activity
End an activity
Interrupt an activity
Resume an activity
Abandon an activity

In the *interrupt* and *resume* we can see how the activity concept can be utilized. Let us assume that an application process is being driven in some sense in *real time* by a user (a real user sitting at a terminal perhaps). The user demands services of the application process; these services are structured by the application process into activities over a session connection established between itself and a cooperating peer application process. Let us assume that the current activity is demanding a considerable resource (for example, as a result of a large amount of information being exchanged). This results in a delay visible to the user. If the user has reason to demand a separate (higher priority) service of the application process then, with sufficient intelligence in the implementation of the peer application processes, the current activity can be interrupted (to be resumed later) and the new activity started. The original activity can be resumed over the same session connection or it may be resumed over a new session connection, perhaps hours later. The activity will be resumed at some point within the *last* dialogue unit, specified by reference to a synchronization point. A simpler instance of the use of an activity interruption and resumption in a new session connection is where a computer system service is about to close whilst an application operation is in progress. Activity management can be used to prevent the waste of resource inherent in restarting the complete application transaction from the beginning when the system which has been closed down returns to service.

6.1.1.4 Group four

These services are concerned with providing the mechanisms to support the orderly control of the use of a session connection by the SS users. Control is maintained by means of *tokens*. Tokens exist to control four aspects of the session service, each of which is negotiated into use during session connection establishment. If a particular service is not in use over a connection then the associated token is regarded as *unavailable* in that connection. Only the current *owner* of the token associated with a particular service may perform certain actions with respect to that service. The tokens are as follows:

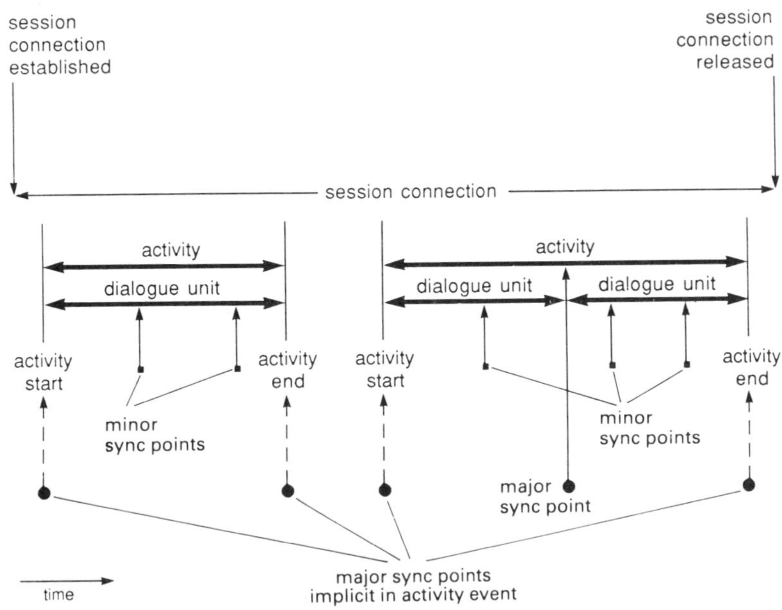

Fig. 6.2 — Relationship between session connection and activities, and between activities and dialogue units.

Data — controls access to data transfer initiation in a half-duplex environment.

Release — only the SS user owning this token may initiate an orderly release of the session connection.

Sync-minor — only the owning SS user may initiate minor synchronization or resynchronization services.

Major/activity — determines the right to initiate a major synchronization or to initiate activities.

A token is defined as being either available or unavailable in a connection. If it is unavailable then neither SS user has exclusive use of the associated service(s), which are then either inherently available to both SS users (in the case of data token and release token), or unavailable to both (in the case of sync-minor token and major/activity token).

Tokens can be exchanged between SS users during a session connection by the use of *token management* services.

6.1.2 Functional units of the session service

The session service has twelve FUs. Only the *kernel* FU is mandatory, that is in force or *selected* over every session connection, the remainder being negotiable by the SS users at session connection establishment time. The FUs are as follows:

The *kernel* FU supports the basic session services of connection establishment, normal data transfer and connection release.

The *negotiated release* FU is associated with the release token, meaning that if this FU is selected then the release token becomes available over the session connection. Either of the cooperating SS users can request an orderly release of the session connection between them and this is supported by the kernel FU. If the negotiated release FU is not selected over the connection then, once requested, the release must be accepted by the SS user in receipt of the release indication. If, however, the negotiated release FU is selected then only the owner of the release token can initiate a release. Further, when this FU is selected, the SS user responding to a release may choose not to accept the release and continue to use the session connection. This is clearly of use in a 'conversational' application environment where an SS user may initiate a release and mean 'I have done all the work I had to do', but the responder may choose to reject the release on the basis of its having more work to do which is unknown to the initiating SS user.

Duplex and *half-duplex* FUs. Only one of these can be selected over any session connection. If the half-duplex FU is selected then the data token is available over the connection; otherwise it is unavailable. In half-duplex working, normal data transfer can only be initiated by the token owner.

The *expedited data* FU supports the session expedited data service. Expedited data is a special form of data transfer in that data carried by this service is guaranteed to arrive at the receiving SS user at a time not later than the next data transmitted by a further call on any session data service. Indeed it is intended that data transferred by the use of expedited data will, if possible, arrive before data already submitted for transmission by the SS user, by use of the session normal data service. Expedited data will be examined in greater detail in the next chapter.

The *typed data* FU supports the typed data service. This FU is only meaningful when the data token is available but not owned by an SS user needing to transmit data. Typed data is a service that carries SS user data against the control of the data token.

The *minor synchronize* FU supports the minor synchronize service already introduced. The sync-minor token is available when this FU is selected over a connection.

The *major synchronize* FU supports the major synchronize service. The major/activity token is available when this FU is selected over a connection.

The *resynchronize* FU supports the resynchronize service.

The *exceptions* FU supports the *user* exception and *provider* exception reporting services, the latter for handling potentially catastrophic errors. Use of these services leaves the connection in a usable state for possible error recovery activity, unlike the alternative to these services, a disorderly release. This FU can only be selected together with the half-duplex FU.

The *activity management* FU supports the activity management service. The major/activity token is available when this FU is selected over a connection.

The *capability data* FU supports the capability data exchange service. When the activity management FU is selected it is illegal for an SS user to use major or minor synchronization services *outside* an extant activity. The capability data exchange service is used to provide a confirmed data exchange service between SS users when no activity is in progress. This FU can only be selected if the activity management FU is also selected.

A digression in the form of an example here will help to bring together a number of the concepts introduced in the last sections, particularly synchronization, resynchronization, activity management and capability data. Consider an automated manufacturing environment, controlled from a central computer system. In particular consider a sophisticated robotic paint spray unit whose function is to spray assembled items. The application controlling this unit could make use of session services as follows:

— Activity start: move on to the next item in line
— Normal data: spray facet according to the instructions inherent in the information conveyed in this data transfer
— Minor synchronize: (inserted between instances of normal data) establish, on acknowledgement, the 'successfully painted' areas of the facet.
— Major synchronize: confirm, by acknowledgement, that facet painting is completed (end of dialogue unit) and rotate to next facet, the rotation being defined by information carried in the user data parameter of this control service; normal data will now follow.
— Activity end: confirm, by acknowledgement, that item painting is completed. Move on the completed item as specified by information carried in the user data parameter of this control service, and then become 'dormant' until activity start is received.

If an error event were to occur in this activity, say a 'jammed' paint spray nozzle, then the activity could be restarted after repair at a point defined by the current dialogue unit (facet) and the acknowledged minor synchronization points, thus preventing the waste of respraying already painted areas of the facet. Should there be a requirement for the paint colour to be changed *between* items — that is, outside of an activity — then the capability data service can be used to convey the specific instruction. Confirmation, which is offered by capability data, is clearly necessary since a new activity cannot start until the change is completed.

It was the need for standards for automated process control of the sort demonstrated in this example that brought about *Manufacturing Automation Protocol* (MAP), which has developed in conformance to the ISORM. MAP specifies use of the ISO standards for the end-to-end upper layers, the sub-network basis of MAP being a 10 megabit token bus.

6.1.3 Phases of the session service

From the point of view of the SS user, the session service can be in one of three phases at any time:

— session connection establishment,
— data transfer,
— session connection release.

We now examine each of these phases in detail.

6.1.3.1 Session connection establishment phase

In this phase the service is concerned with the establishment of a session connection between peer SS users. Several items must be negotiated as a part of connection establishment.

First there are twelve FUs in the session service, of which only kernel is mandatory. Other FUs are selected for use over the connection by negotiation between the SS users. The subset of FUs selected will contain the kernel with a number of other FUs and be subject to rules of interdependency. It is also subject to the availability of the services associated with the FUs in the peer session entities (a dependency on the level of implementation of session entities).

The second negotiation issue concerns the initial settings of tokens. In proposing a connection which includes an FU that requires a particular token to be available, the initiating SS user must propose an initial setting (ownership) for that token. This initial setting of ownership can be one of:

Calling SS user side
Called SS user side
Called SS user choice

Only in the last instance does the *called* SS user (i.e. the SS user that responds to connection establishment) have a choice in the matter which it will indicate in its response.

If a token is not required over a connection then it is taken to be unavailable.

The final item for negotiation during session connection establishment is the initial synchronization point serial number (SPSN). If the subset of FUs chosen by the peer SS users includes any that imply the use of synchronization points then the initial SPSN must also be negotiated. If the activity management FU is included then the initial SPSN need not be negotiated because the SPSN is set to '1' at the start of any activity. The calling SS user is of course aware of proposing a subset that implies a need for an initial value of SPSN, but it cannot assume that proposing the activity management FU removes the need to negotiate the initial SPSN, since the called SS user may accept a reduced subset by negotiating out the activity management FU. The calling SS user must then always include a proposed value for the initial SPSN if synchronization points are implied by its proposed subset. The called SS user will not respond with a value for the initial SPSN if activity management is included in the final subset or if use of synchronization points is excluded in the final negotiated subset.

There is only a single session service element in this phase, S-CONNECT, and it provides a confirmed service. The parameters associated with S-CONNECT are as follows:

Session connection identifier
Calling SSAP address
Called SSAP address
Session requirements
Initial synchronization point serial number
Initial assignment of tokens
Quality of service

Result
SS user data

Unless otherwise stated, a parameter is assumed to appear on all four service primitives associated with this service element.

The **session connection identifier** is provided in part by both SS users and assigns an unambiguous name for the particular session connection. The session entities have no interest in the value assigned to this parameter. The parameter is mandatory and composed of four parts which are built up by the peer SS users during the negotiation of the session connection. These parts are:

Calling SS user reference	(max 64 octets in length)
Called SS user reference	(max 64 octets)
Common reference	(dictated by the calling SS user but modifiable by the Called SS user, max 64 octets)
Additional reference	(max 4 octets)

The **calling SSAP address** and **called SSAP address** are mandatory parameters and are, in respect of addressing (discussed in Chapter 3), self explanatory. The calling SSAP address parameter only appears on the request and indication. In the mandatory **session requirements** parameter the calling SS user proposes the subset of FUs of session that it would like to see selected for this connection. The called SS user will either accept these by explicit confirmation on the response, or include on the response the modified subset it will support. In the **initial synchronization point serial number** parameter the negotiation discussed earlier is achieved. Its presence in the primitives is clearly conditional on the FUs proposed and accepted by the calling and called SS users. A similar comment applies to the **initial assignment of tokens** parameter.

Quality of service (QOS) is a mandatory parameter and is, on the request, a statement by the calling SS user of the level of service it expects to see over the established connection. The SS provider may then modify this level of service to suit the (network) environment over which the session connection is to be established. This — perhaps modified — QOS will appear on the indication. The called SS user may also modify the parameter to take account of its view of a desired or achievable service level. The final level of QOS will appear to the initiating SS user in the subsequent confirm. The parameter is itself a list of parameters, the final values of which represent an agreement on the level of service expected (in a series of categories) of the established session connection by the SS users. Should the level of service subsequently achieved fall below this expectation, the SS provider is expected to inform the SS users who will take whatever action the application demands. A drop in service level could, for instance, be a fall in data throughput below the agreed threshold. If the network over which this connection is established includes a charging element related to elapsed usage time and not to data volume, then this drop in service level has financial implications and the application may chose to *back off* until the operating conditions are more suited to achieving the service level. As QOS is large topic, we shall leave it until the next chapter before exploring it further.

The **result** parameter is included on the response and subsequent confirm. It

indicates the success or otherwise of the connection establishment. Table 6.1 gives a possible range of symbolic values for this parameter.
(The standards do not constrain an implementation of a session entity in assigning values to the symbolic results; these values will be specified by implementors in product documentation.)

Reasons marked in the table by an asterisk may be regarded by the calling SS user as persistent, that is, it may assume that the application user behind the connection establishment initiation may be informed of a permanent failure. In other cases the application process may choose not to inform the user of the failure but to take remedial action (such as waiting for a short time before retrying). At first glance the asterisked reasons seem to be the same. Local tables in the called end-system will contain valid SSAP addresses and if the called SSAP address does not appear in these tables then the first of these reasons will result. However, should the address appear in the tables but the relevant application service be withdrawn for any reason, then the latter reason will result.

The **SS user data** parameter can contain, on the request, useful information provided by the calling SS user, to be conveyed transparently to the called SS user on the indication. The called SS user may use this parameter for the same purpose on the response.

Note: We saw in the section on 'use of session' in the last chapter that the presentation entity, on making a S-CONNECT request to a session entity, includes its CP PPDU as the SS user data parameter of this primitive. If the session connection is accepted by the called SS user, then the presentation accept or reject PPDU will be conveyed in the SS user data parameter of the S-CONNECT response (and subsequent confirm). If result is 'success' then SS user data on S-CONNECT response (and confirm) is the CPA PPDU or CPR PPDU. If result is 'rejected by SS user' (that is, no session connection can be established and so presentation connection is not attempted) then SS user data may contain additional information.

6.1.3.2 The data transfer phase

The services that make up this phase of session can be examined under the following headings:

Data transfer
Token management
Synchronization
Exception reporting
Activity management

6.1.3.2.1 Data transfer services

The data transfer services provide the transparent exchange of SSDUs between SS users over an established session connection. These services are summarized in Table 6.2.

These services have a single associated parameter, **SS user data**. The earlier section on FUs indicated when the different data services would be used. It is

Table 6.1 — Result parameter values

Category	Reason
Success	
Rejected by SS user	No reason specified Temporary congestion at SS user More information in SS user data
Rejected by SS provider	No reason specified SS provider congestion Called SSAP address unknown * Called SS user not attached to SSAP *

Table 6.2 — Data services

Service	Service element	Type
Normal data transfer	S-DATA	unconfirmed
Expedited data transfer	S-EXPEDITED-DATA	unconfirmed
Typed data transfer	S-TYPED-DATA	unconfirmed
Capability data transfer	S-CAPABILITY-DATA	confirmed

important to note that the fundamental mechanism for providing transparent data transfer between SS users is normal data transfer, provided by S-DATA.

There is no restriction on the amount of SS user data that can be transferred in a single call on this service: that is, on the length of an SSDU (known as an NSSDU to indicate 'normal'). However, the SSDUs of other data services are restricted by the standard (Table 6.3).

Table 6.3 — Restrictions on data SSDUs

Service element	SSDU	Restriction
S-EXPEDITED-DATA	XSSDU	max 14 octets
S-TYPED-DATA	TSSDU	no restriction
S-CAPABILITY-DATA	—	max 512 octets

Notice that the SS user data parameter is unnamed for S-CAPABILITY-DATA. This is because capability data is not regarded as a 'true' data service (as defined in Chapter 3), but as a control service whose function is to bring about a confirmed exchange of a limited amount of SS user-provided data when the activity management FU is selected, and only when there is no extant activity.

6.1.3.2.2 Token management services

Certain services can only be initiated by an SS user if it is the owner of an associated token, or if that token is unavailable and the rules are such that that service is understood to be inherently available to both peer SS users. We have already seen the association of tokens with FUs. The ownership of these tokens is initially defined as part of the connection establishment phase, but thereafter ownership is controlled by the use of token management services. These services are summarized in Table 6.4.

Table 6.4 — Token services

Service	Service element	Type
Give tokens	S-TOKEN-GIVE	unconfirmed
Please tokens	S-TOKEN-PLEASE	unconfirmed
Give control	S-CONTROL-GIVE	unconfirmed

The 'give tokens' service allows the SS user who is currently the owner of one or more token(s) to surrender one or more of them to the peer SS user. Which tokens are involved is the subject of the sole parameter, **tokens**. The parameter is a list of tokens whose ownership is to be transferred. The possible tokens are:

— data token
— synchronize minor token
— major/activity token
— release token.

The 'please tokens' service allows an SS user to request one or more token(s) that it does not currently own to be released to it by the owner. On receiving the S-PLEASE-TOKENS indication the owner will, if satisfied that the token(s) can be relinquished, issue an S-TOKEN-GIVE request to transfer ownership. There are two parameters: **tokens** is mandatory and is a list of the tokens in question; **SS user data** is optional and is used to convey any qualifying information between SS users. The S-CONTROL-GIVE service element is only available for use when the activity management FU is selected and can be used when no activity is in progress. In using this service the initiating SS user relinquishes *all* available tokens to its peer. There are no associated parameters.

Of course the token management services can only be used with reference to *available* tokens.

6.1.3.2.3 Synchronization services

Synchronization consists of the three services shown in Table 6.5. These are all confirmed services but, as we shall see, the nature of the 'confirmation' of the minor synchronization service is unlike that of any other confirmed service.

The transmitting SS user determines the frequency of insertion of minor synchronization (minor sync) points in the flow of information between peer SS users. On instruction from the SS user — an S-SYNC-MINOR request — the session entity will 'insert' a minor sync point in the data flow, that is, between the last SSDU presented by the SS user for transmission and the next, as yet unpresented, SSDU. Only normal and typed data can be synchronized in this way. The SS user can only use this service if it owns the sync-minor token and the data token (if available). The value of the synchronization point serial number (SPSN) is provided to the receiving SS user in the **synchronization point serial number** parameter of the indication.

If the activity management FU is selected over the connection then minor, and major, synchronization can only be used *within* an activity.

It is the responsibility of the transmitting session entity to maintain the SPSN; this is achieved simply by incrementing the current value by one after a minor sync SPDU has been transmitted. The SPSN initially has a value that was determined during connection establishment, and it is only reset when either an activity is started, in which case it is reset to 1, or when the session connection is resynchronized, the setting of the new value being part of the resynchronization procedure. The initiating SS user can specify that it requires *explicit* confirmation of a minor sync service request; in this case the service operates like any other confirmed service and requires a response from the receiving SS user, resulting in a confirm. The sequence, as seen by the transmitting SS user, might be:

S-DATA request →
S-SYNC-MINOR request →
S-SYNC-MINOR confirm ←
S-DATA request →
S-SYNC-MINOR request →
etc.

Here, the use of the explicit confirmation variant of the sync minor service is equivalent to the effect that would be achieved by a confirmed normal data service, but has the added benefit of identifying known points in the information flow for use if restarting that flow becomes necessary.

When the activity management FU is selected, synchronization services are not available outside an activity, so this form of confirmed data transfer is not available. It is, however, available to some extent in the guise of another service provided by S-CAPABILITY-DATA.

The initiating SS user selects the explicit version of the minor sync service by setting the **type** parameter of the S-SYNC-MINOR request to 'explicit', which then appears on the indication. This parameter is unused on the response/confirm. If the initiator sets this parameter to 'optional' then we have a variant of the concept of confirmed service: it is a statement by the SS user that he does not require confirmation of all minor sync points and that confirmation is at the discretion of the receiving SS user, who will either confirm all minor sync points or only occasional

Table 6.5 — Synchronization services

Service	Service element	Type
Minor synchronization point	S-SYNC-MINOR	confirmed
Major synchronization point	S-SYNC-MAJOR	confirmed
Resynchronization	S-RESYNCHRONIZE	confirmed

ones. In the latter instance the transmitting SS user, on receipt of a confirm, will regard the confirmation as being for the sync point in question (identified by the SPSN parameter), and also for all preceding sync points since the last confirmation. The following sequence is an example of what the peer SS users may see:

Transmitting SS user		Receiving SS user
S-DATA request	→	S-DATA indication
S-MINOR-SYNC request 1	→	S-MINOR-SYNC indication 1
S-DATA request	→	S-DATA indication
S-MINOR-SYNC request 2	→	S-MINOR-SYNC indication 2
S-DATA request	→	
S-MINOR-SYNC confirm 2	←	S-MINOR-SYNC response 2

.

.

etc.

The transmitting SS user decides how many data service requests to issue between minor sync points. In our example above, the transmitting SS user has continued to transmit information, using normal data service, after a S-SYNC-MINOR request. Indeed we see that there is data in transit to the receiving SS user at the time it issues a response (in this instance confirming both outstanding sync points). Neither the explicit nor optional versions of the service prevent the transmitting SS user from making further data service requests when sync point confirmation is outstanding. This is consistent with the definition of the optional form but it may surprise the reader that it also applies to the explicit form. It does not necessarily break any rule to request a further service before one previously invoked has been completed. Indeed, in this case, continuous information flow is only possible by doing just this, for otherwise an uneven flow would result.

> Underneath the knocker there was a notice which said:
> PLES RING IF AN RNSER IS REQIRD
> Underneath the bell-pull there was a notice which said:
> PLEZ CNOKE IF AN RNSR IS NOT REQID
>
> A. A. Milne, *Winnie-The-Pooh*

One can envisage a situation where an SS user transmits information (as NSSDUs or TSSDUs), punctuated by minor sync points and where no minor sync points are confirmed over a long period. This could result from a failure or congestion somewhere in the network, or perhaps on the receiving end-system. To continue to transmit beyond a certain point might be wasteful and might be damaging, squandering the resources of the transmitting end-system. The management of this problem rests with the transmitting application process. A *window* mechanism should be provided in an application process to ensure that there is a bound on the number of unconfirmed minor sync points allowed over a session connection at any time. When this window is reached, the application process will cease information transfer and await confirmation(s), terminating the application if none are forthcoming after a certain time has elapsed. This window must be negotiated between peer application processes as a part of their initialization procedure so that the information receiver is aware that it must confirm minor sync points within that defined window. The session layer has no knowledge or involvement in windowing.

There is a third, optional, parameter associated with S-SYNC-MINOR, namely **SS user data**.

The major synchronization service, provided by the S-SYNC-MAJOR service element, allows an SS user to set a major synchronization point in the information flow between itself and its peer. It denotes the end of a dialogue unit. Unlike the minor sync service, this service indicates that a complete dialogue unit has been exchanged and that the receiving application process may need to take some action defined by the nature of the application. By its nature this service is confirmed and no further data service may be invoked by the initiator until confirmation is received. The confirmation of a major sync point implicitly confirms all outstanding minor sync points in the dialogue unit in question. Unlike the minor sync service this service may be used with XSSDUs as well as NSSDUs and TSSDUs. The token restrictions on the initiating SS user are as follows:

— the data token must be unavailable or owned,
— the sync-minor token must be unavailable or owned,
— the major/activity token must be owned.

The parameters associated with this service element are **synchronization point serial number** (SPSN) and **SS user data**. The SPSN appears on the indication but is not required on the response/confirm since no further sync points (or data) can be issued until confirmation is received. Clearly, like the minor sync service, this service results in a common understanding of a point in information flow, identified by the SPSN, between the peer SS users and from which information flow could, potentially, be restarted.

Now we turn to resynchronization, provided by the S-RESYNCHRONIZE service element. In a *well behaved* information transfer it is likely that no further use will be made of the synchronization points established in the information transferred. They only come into play when one of the SS users (the transmitter or receiver) concludes that it is necessary to restart the information exchange; this, of course, can only commence at some commonly agreed point.

Part of the process of restarting an information flow is the resynchronization of the session connection to some known state. In particular, it involves selecting the SPSN that will be initially used in the restarted environment, the *resynchronized SPSN*. The understanding between the peer application processes defining the nature of the (restarted) environment can be re-established by the exchange of some application-specific 'restart' PDU. The precise restart point is defined in terms of a previously confirmed SPSN. In using the resynchronization service, the SS user ensures that:

— a value for the SPSN to be used initially over the resynchronized session connection is established,
— token ownership over the resynchronized session connection is well defined.

The following demonstrates a use of resynchronization to achieve the restart of information transfer in a coordinated manner:

(i) An application process detects the need to attempt a restart.
(ii) The application entity restart service element builds an appropriate restart PDU that will bring about a coordinated understanding of the nature of the 'restart' between the peer application processes.
(iii) The application entity, via the 'mirror' presentation services, issues an S-RESYNCHRONIZE request, providing values for parameters related to the resynchronized SPSN and to token ownership. The application restart PDU is passed in the user data parameter of this request.
(iv) The session resynchronize service will result in the resynchronization of the session connection as described, and at the same time will have conveyed the application restart PDUs between application entities.
(v) On receipt of the confirm, the resynchronization initiating application process will have either 'recovered' the situation or learnt that there is no hope for such recovery. (If data exchange is really jammed up in the lower layers then no confirm will be received, and after a time out period has elapsed this would be assumed and the connection released).

It is not necessary for an application restart service element to have a PDU associated with it, since receipt of an S-RESYNCHRONIZE indication by an SS user can be assumed to convey the intention of information flow restart. In this case the value of the SPSN parameter of the indication will be used by the application restart service element in establishing the restart point in the information flow. (This form of application information flow restart is likely to be used only by the 'simpler' application environments.)

On issuing an S-RESYNCHRONIZE request an SS user must not invoke any further session service, other than initiating a *disorderly* termination of the session connection, until such time as the confirm is received. Similar restrictions constrain the activity of the SS user in receipt of an indication: it may only invoke a disorderly release (utilizing the S-U-ABORT service element which we examine later) before it issues a response. The transmitting SS user, on either issuing an S-RESYNCHRONIZE request or receiving an indication — remember the service can be initiated by transmitting or receiving SS user — assumes that all information transmitted from the point of the last S-SYNC-MINOR confirm has not been 'seen' by the receiving SS user. In effect, when the S-RESYNCHRONIZE request is issued, all data in transit between SS users is regarded as purged. In fact, provision is made in the standards for implementations to ensure that any data passed by an SS user for transfer in an S-DATA request (or other data service request) that has not yet resulted in an indication at the receiving peer, may under some conditions remain *undelivered* to that SS user, even though the 'data channel' between SS users is functioning at that time. This has clear efficiency implications, in that the receiving SS user need not handle information rendered meaningless by a subsequently issued resynchronization. How this is achieved in practice we shall discuss in the next section.

Four parameters are associated with the S-RESYNCHRONIZE service element. The first, **resynchronize type**, is mandatory, appearing only on the request/indication; it specifies the nature of the resynchronization to be undertaken by the peer session entities. There are three types, the first of which, *abandon*, can be seen as a complete purge of the session connection. The initiating SS user is effectively asking the SS provider to choose a new value for the resynchronized SPSN that is 'greater' than any previously used. This SPSN cannot therefore convey a 'known' point in the interrupted information flow and so the indication itself cannot imply a restart at a specific point in the information flow. The initiator is 'cancelling' the flow over this connection in favour, perhaps, of starting from scratch. The second type of resynchronization is *restart*. Here, the application processes agree to restart the information flow at some agreed point. As we have seen, this process may also involve the exchange of application restart PDUs qualifying the nature of the restart, but in either case the session connection will be resynchronized such that the resynchronized SPSN will be in line with the SPSN sequence in use at the time of resynchronization. It will have a value greater than that of the last major synchronization, but less than the SPSN that was next to be used at the time of resynchronization. The final resynchronization type is *set*. In using this type, the SS user is specifying that the session connection is to be resynchronized with the resynchronized SPSN being *any* (valid) value dictated by the SS user. In effect it is a little like the 'abandon' type; any further implication it may have on the information flow is a matter for the application processes to convey in PDUs which they may exchange at the time.

The second parameter, **synchronization point serial number**, needs no comment. The third parameter, **tokens**, is used to effect any changes in token ownership as a part of resynchronization. In this respect it is similar to the initial assignment of tokens parameter of S-CONNECT. Finally, the **SS user data** parameter allows user information to pass between peer SS users during the resynchronization process. We have already seen how this can be used for application-specific PDU exchange, qualifying the effect of resynchronization on the specific application activity.

6.1.3.2.4 Exception reporting services

The exception reporting services of the data transfer phase provide mechanisms to support notification of unanticipated error events to SS users when detected by the SS provider or an SS user. An attempt to recover from the event can then, perhaps, be undertaken. Without such mechanisms the only option, on detection of such errors, would be to initiate a disorderly termination of the connection. The FU supporting these mechanisms is only available if the half-duplex FU is selected. There are two types of event. When an event is detected by the SS provider, peer SS users must be informed of the event and this is effected by the S-P-EXCEPTION-REPORT service element. It has only a single associated primitive, the indication, since it is unconfirmed and its use is determined by the provider (on detection of such an event) and not by an SS user (see Figure 6.3). It has a single mandatory parameter,

reason, which takes one of two values: 'protocol error' (meaning that a standard protocol specification has been contravened by an entity) and 'unspecified error'.

When an event is detected by an SS user, the S-U-EXCEPTION-REPORT service element is invoked by the detector to inform its peer. It also is an unconfirmed service and has two parameters: **reason**, with a wider range of possible values than in the 'provider' case, and **SS user data**, which is optional.

After an S-P-EXCEPTION-REPORT indication has been received or an S-U-EXCEPTION-REPORT request has been issued, and until the error condition is cleared, the following SS user climate prevails:

- — NSSDUs, TSSDUs and XSSDUs will be discarded by the SS provider.
- — Sync point indication service primitives will not be issued to the SS user initiating the **U** service or, in the case of the **P** service, to either SS user.
- — In the **U** service case, the initiating SS user can only issue an S-U-ABORT request which will bring about an abnormal release.

The error situation can possibly be cleared by one of the following actions by an SS user:

Resynchronizing
Activity interruption or discard
Giving the data token
Aborting

If the activity management FU is selected then the exception services are only available *within* an activity.

6.1.3.2.5 Activity management services

The final group of services making up the data transfer phase are the five 'activity management' services. They are summarized in Table 6.6. Only one activity can be in progress over a session connection at any time, and only if the activity management FU is selected. An activity is initiated by the use of the activity start service; this can only be done by the SS user owning the major/activity token and, if they are available, the data and sync-minor tokens (ownership of the last two tokens is irrelevant if they are not available). Use of this service always results in the SPSN being set to '1'. The initiating SS user assigns an identity to the activity, and this is conveyed to the peer in the mandatory **activity identifier** parameter. The optional **user data** parameter may be used to convey other information.

If this FU is selected and there is no activity underway, then an SS user is restricted to use of the following services:

Activity start
Activity resume
Capability/normal/typed/expedited data
Give tokens
Please tokens
Give control
Orderly release
User abort

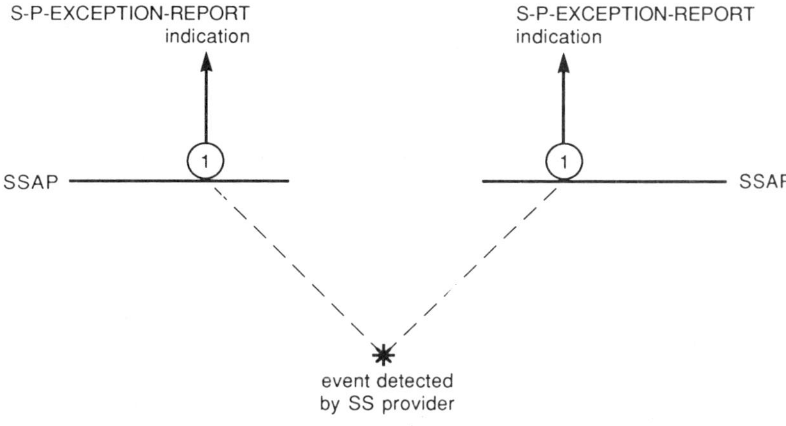

Fig. 6.3 — Provider-detected event.

Table 6.6 — Activity management services

Service	Service element	Type	Parameters
Start	S-ACTIVITY-START	unconfirmed	Activity identifier SS user data
Interrupt	S-ACTIVITY-INTERRUPT	confirmed	Reason
Resume	S-ACTIVITY-RESUME	unconfirmed	Activity identifier Old activity identifier SPSN Old session connection id. SS user data
Discard	S-ACTIVITY-DISCARD	confirmed	Reason
End	S-ACTIVITY-END	confirmed	SPSN SS user data

When an activity is completed, that is, an SS user has completed a *task*, it is terminated by the use of the 'activity end' service. This is a confirmed service because implicit in it is a major synchronization point which must, of course, be acknowledged. The SPSN associated with this sync point is conveyed in a mandatory parameter of the S-ACTIVITY-END indication. An **SS user data** parameter is also available. Initiation of this service is subject to the same token restrictions as the activity start service.

There are two services elements whose use brings about the termination of an activity. The first, S-ACTIVITY-DISCARD, cancels the activity and is destructive, in that all services that have completed *within* that activity are deemed not to have occurred, the SS users returning to their positions prior to activity start. Realization of such a cancellation is the responsibility of the SS users. Any data that is still in transit over the SS provider will be lost and any unacknowledged sync points will remain so. This service can only be initiated by the SS user owning the major/activity token. S-ACTIVITY-INTERRUPT enables the SS user owning the major/activity token to terminate the activity in progress but without cancelling the work already done within the activity. As in the discard case, any data in transit will be lost and unacknowledged sync points will remain so. Implicit in the use of this service is an intention to resume the activity at some later time and from some mutually acceptable point (sync point), perhaps in a new session connection. Both the discard and interrupt services have a single parameter, **reason**. Resumption is achieved by use of the S-ACTIVITY-RESUME service element; this allows an SS user to resume an interrupted activity, subject to it owning the major/activity token and, if they are available, the data and minor-sync tokens.

There are a number of parameters associated with this service. The **activity identifier** assigns a new identity to the activity to be resumed, the **old activity identifier** identifies the precise interrupted activity that is being resumed; any number of activities can be in the 'limbo' state of 'interrupted', only implementation details or resource constraints imposing any real limit. The **old session connection identifier** parameter is only used when the resumption is in a different session connection from that of the interrupted activity. It has the same construction as the equivalent parameter on the session connection establishment service.

The value of the **synchronization point serial number** is provided by the SS user initiating the resumption and dictates the next SPSN to be used by session in the resumed activity. Its effect on the session layer is the same as that of the resynchronize ('set') service and, as such, does not necessarily say anything about where the information flow between SS users in the activity will be restarted. This resumption point is a matter for the peer SS users to agree, and this they can do in one of two ways. First by use of the **SS user data** parameter of the S-ACTIVITY-RESUME request to convey — embedded in an appropriate application PDU — the precise point at which the interrupted activity is to be restarted. This will be at an SPSN which was acknowledged before the activity was interrupted. Notice that there is no reason here for the identity of this SPSN to bear any relationship to the value of the SPSN parameter of the activity resume service, the set value. The second method is, simply, to use the value of the set SPSN that will, as a matter of course, be conveyed between SS users to define the point at which the interrupted flow should restart. In this case use of the SS user data parameter is not necessary.

How long the 'environment' of an interrupted activity is preserved on an end-system (a resumption being possible at any time within the same session connection or a subsequent connection) is an implementation decision and not specified in the standard. Details such as this should be available in product specifications.

6.1.3.3 Session connection release phase

A session connection can either be released in an 'orderly' or 'disorderly' manner during the data transfer phase. An orderly release is invoked at the completion of a cooperation between peer application processes when the connection is no longer required. If the activity management FU is selected over such a connection then, clearly, orderly release will only be invoked outside of an activity. If synchronization services have been used over the connection then the initiator of the orderly release believes the connection to be 'quiet', that is, there are no outstanding synchronization point acknowledgements. Indeed, this service can be initiated by an SS user only if it owns all available tokens. If this were not the case then the initiating SS user could not know that the connection was 'quiet'.

If the negotiated release FU is not selected over the connection then the SS user in receipt of a release indication must accept the release. However, if that FU is selected, then that SS user may choose not to accept the release and the initiating SS user must be prepared to receive a refusal. The service element supporting orderly release is S-RELEASE which offers a confirmed service, since an ability to refuse exists. It has two associated parameters, **result**, taking one of two symbolic values (affirmative or negative), and **SS user data**.

The need for a disorderly release mechanism is clear when an SS user or the SS provider can no longer continue a communication within the bounds of the standard definitions or when some environmental event, such as resource allocation being exceeded, makes continuation of the communication impossible. In these cases a release is required that will immediately cause the session connection to be terminated and allow the SS provider and SS users to clear up resources associated with the connection. Any data in transit over the connection will be lost.

A need for such action can be detected by either an SS user or by the SS provider. There are therefore two service elements associated with disorderly release. The first, S-U-ABORT offers an unconfirmed service which can be initiated by either SS user. It cannot, of course, be refused. It has a single parameter, **SS user data**, which can be used to convey additional information. The second service element, S-P-ABORT, deals with SS provider-detected errors. It has, like the case of S-P-EXCEPTION-REPORT, only a single associated primitive, the indication. It has a single parameter, **reason**, which takes one of the symbolic values:

Transport disconnect
Protocol error
Undefined

Transport disconnect occurs when the transport connection over which the session connection is established is seen to go down by the peer session entities.

This, at last, completes the overview of session services.

6.2 SESSION PROTOCOL AND THE USE OF TRANSPORT SERVICES

As in the last chapter we shall complete the description of the layer by looking at some of the activities performed by the protocol machine which are not reflected in the services already described, finishing with an examination of the relationships between session services, SPDUs and transport services.

6.2.1 Additional activities performed by the protocol machine

There are two aspects of session activity that are unseen by the SS users but defined as being provided and used by the protocol machine: *segmentation* and *extended concatenation*.

6.2.1.1 Segmentation

This facility is negotiated in or out of use as part of session connection establishment. The negotiation is entirely between session entities and is unseen by SS users; there are no parameters of primitives associated with S-CONNECT that reference this facility. Segmentation is the facility by which an SSDU, as an object of a data request, can be transmitted between peer session entities not in a single SPDU but in 'segments', that is, in several consecutive SPDUs. Figure 6.4 illustrates this activity.

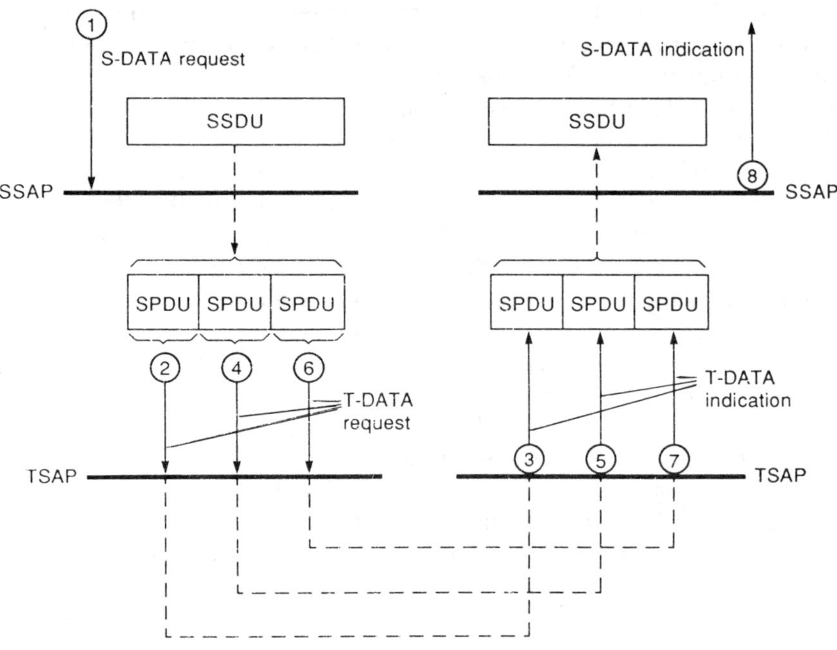

Fig. 6.4 — Segmentation.

Here the SSDU is transmitted in three SPDUs, each of which is — as we see later — transmitted by use of T-DATA request, the transport normal data service. When segmentation is in use over a connection the transmitting entity will determine whether a submitted SSDU should be segmented, and if so will construct and transmit SPDUs with appropriate sized data segments. In each SPDU it includes an indication as to whether it is an intermediate or final segment of an SSDU. When segmentation is in use the receiving session entity rebuilds the SSDU from the segments, which are received in the order transmitted; ensured, as we shall see, by the transport layer. Only when an SSDU has been completed (signalled by an SPDU with 'final segment indication' set) will the receiving entity issue a data service indication to the receiving SS user.

Why is segmentation required? Consider the higher layers of the ISORM, in particular an application process. At this level it is not desirable to constrain activity with arbitrary limits on the size of the units of information that are to be transferred, that is, on the size of SSDU that can be presented to a session entity for transfer. It is more appropriate that the size of such SDUs remain unconstrained such that they can be 'meaningful' to the application in question, for example a complete 'mail' message. However, within implementations of the lower layers of the ISORM there will be constraints on resources — for example, size and availability of buffers — that may impose restrictions on the size of SDUs acceptable to lower layer entities. The level of TSAP can be regarded as a boundary between the end-system unconstrained environment and the communication constrained environment, and consequently we can expect transport entities to impose restrictions on the size of TSDUs, within which SPDUs will be conveyed. Segmentation, then, is a method of accommodating any size of SSDU requested for transfer by SS users, regardless of the limitations there may be on TSDUs in the local or remote end-systems involved. The limitation on TSDUs is conveyed to the session entities as part of the transport connection establishment, a precursor to session connection establishment, and so when such limits are imposed session entities will attempt to include the segmentation option in the session connection. If, however, this option is unavailable in either or both session entities then a restriction will be imposed upon the communicating application processes.

6.2.1.2 Extended concatenation

The objects being concatenated are SPDUs. With this facility a number of SPDUs can be included in a single TSDU, subject to rigid rules imposed by the protocol specification. This facility, like segmentation, is negotiated as part of session connection establishment by the peer session entities. It is invisible to the SS users. The purpose of this facility is to improve efficiency: in certain instances it makes sense to send a sequence of SPDUs in a single transport data service request. Some valid concatenations are:

Activity Start SPDU + Data Transfer SPDU
Activity Resume SPDU + Data Transfer SPDU
Activity Resume SPDU + Minor Sync SPDU + Data Transfer SPDU

The efficiency is most noticeable in an end-system that has, perhaps, implemented the end-to-end data communications environment (up to the level of TSAP) in a 'front-end' processor which provides transport services, across an interface, to a multi-access mainframe on which a stack of the higher layer entities are implemented. The front-end system is well suited to handling the 'real-time' communications environment, whereas the responsiveness of the mainframe may be less predictable. Any reduction in the number of interactions between front-end and mainframe will decrease inherent delays in the OSI communications environment as seen by 'users'. The placement then of, say, three SPDUs in a single TSDU in effect reduces the interaction over the TSAP from three activities to one.

6.2.2 Use of the transport service

Finally, as in the last two chapters, we look at the relationship between session service primitives, SPDUs, and the transport service for each of the service elements we have introduced. We shall use the same format of table as before, five columns reading left to right with the following headings:

A. The session service primitive issued by a presentation entity to initiate a service or to respond to a confirmed service.
B. The SPDU that is (or may be) generated by the service element of the session entity as a result of A.
C. The transport service primitive issued by the session entity as a result of A/B.
D. The transport service primitive issued to the peer session entity on the cooperating end-system as a result of C.
E. The session service primitive issued to the peer presentation entity as a result of A.

Notes on Table 6.7:

(1) When a session connection is released there is provision within the standard for the transport connection over which it was established to be retained. This is beneficial in instances of end-systems that are in a semi-constant state of cooperation over OSI, where an ability to establish a new session connection over an existing transport connection between the peer end-systems removes considerable overheads. Such reuse of a transport connection is only available to the end-system that originally initiated the connection (this avoids possible contention). Either end-system may choose not to permit the connection to be retained for reuse. Once a transport connection is established or found available for reuse, the transport normal data service will be used to convey this SPDU. Transport connection reuse is not available if transport expedited data service is available over the connection in question.

(2) If the transport expedited data service is available then it will be used to convey this SPDU simply because there may be 'undelivered' data in transit between SS users which, now that this service has been initiated, have no meaning and can be discarded. Clearly, transport normal data service is used if expedited is not available.

(3) If the transport connection is not to be reused then the session entity issuing the S-U-ABORT indication also issues a T-DISCONNECT request to disconnect the transport connection. In the case of reuse, there is provision in the standard for this session entity to reply to its peer with an AA (Abort Accept) SPDU, using transport normal data service, to complete a 'handshake' that says to the initiator of the abort that the transport connection is indeed clear for reuse. An indication that the transport connection is to be retained is included in the AB SPDU and, indeed, in the FN SPDU, where the session connection release is orderly.

(4) Here there is no associated service primitive request because it is a *provider* abort. The session entity that detects an error transmits an AB SPDU to its peer and issues an S-P-ABORT indication to its SS user.

(5) The same SPDU is used to convey both a *user* and a *provider* abort event. The AB SPDU carries an indication of the 'detector' such that an appropriate service primitive indication can be issued. Note (3) also applies to S-P-ABORT.

Table 6.7 — Session and the use of transport layer services.

A: SS Primitive →	B: SPDU →	C: TS Primitive →	D: TS Primitive →	E: SS Primitive
S-CONNECT req	CN	T-DATA req (1)	T-DATA ind	S-CONNECT ind
S-CONNECT resp +ve	AC (ACcept)	T-DATA req	T-DATA ind	S-CONNECT conf +ve
S-CONNECT resp −ve	RF (ReFuse)	T-DATA req	T-DATA ind	S-CONNECT conf −ve
S-RELEASE req	FN (FiNish)	T-DATA req	T-DATA ind	S-RELEASE ind
S-RELEASE conf +ve	DN (DiscoNnect)	T-DATA req	T-DATA ind	S-RELEASE conf +ve
S-RELEASE conf −ve	NF (Not Finished)	T-DATA req	T-DATA ind	S-RELEASE conf −ve
S-U-ABORT req	AB	T-DATA req	T-DATA ind	S-U-ABORT ind (3)
		(2) [T-EXP-DATA req	T-EXP-DATA ind]	
S-P-ABORT ind ← (4)	AB	T-DATA req	T-DATA ind	S-U-ABORT ind (5)
		(2) [T-EXP-DATA req	T-EXP-DATA ind]	
S-DATA req	DT (DaTa)	T-DATA req	T-DATA ind	S-DATA ind
S-EXP-DATA req	EX (EXpeditied)	T-EXP-DATA req (6)	T-EXP-DATA ind	S-EXP-DATA ind
S-TYPED-DATA req	TD (Typed Data)	T-DATA req	T-DATA ind	S-TYPED-DATA ind
S-CAPABILITY-DATA req	CD	T-DATA req	T-DATA ind	S-CAPABILITY-DATA ind
S-CAPABILITY-DATA resp	CDA (CD Ack)	T-DATA req	T-DATA ind	S-CAPABILITY-DATA conf
S-TOKEN-GIVE req	GT (Give Token)	T-DATA req	T-DATA ind	S-TOKEN-GIVE ind
S-TOKEN-PLEASE req	PT	T-DATA req	T-DATA ind	S-TOKEN-PLEASE ind
S-CONTROL-GIVE req	GTC (GT Confirm)	T-DATA req	T-DATA ind	S-CONTROL-GIVE ind
— (7)	GTA (GT Ack)	T-DATA req	T-DATA ind	—
S-SYNC-MINOR req	MIP (MInor Point)	T-DATA req	T-DATA ind	S-MINOR-SYNC ind
S-SYNC-MINOR resp (8)	MIA (MInor Ack)	T-DATA req	T-DATA ind	S-SYNC-MINOR conf
S-SYNC-MAJOR req	MAP (MAjor Point)	T-DATA req	T-DATA ind	S-SYNC-MAJOR ind
S-SYNC-MAJOR resp	PR (PRepare) (9)	T-EXP-DATA req	T-EXP-DATA ind	(10) —
	MAA (MAjor Ack)	T-DATA req	T-DATA ind	S-SYNC-MAJOR conf

Table 6.7 — Cont.

A: SS Primitive →	B: SPDU →	C: TS Primitive →	D: TS Primitive →	E: SS Primitive
S-RESYNC req	PR	T-EXP-DATA req	T-EXP-DATA ind	(11) —
	RS (ReSynch)	T-DATA req	T-DATA ind	S-RESYNC ind
S-RESYNC resp	PR	T-EXP-DATA req	T-EXP-DATA ind	—
	RA (Resync Ack)	T-DATA req	T-DATA ind	S-RESYNC conf
S-P-EX-REPORT ind ← (12)	ER (Excep Report)	T-DATA req	T-DATA ind	S-P-EX-REPORT ind
S-U-EX-REPORT req	ED (Excep Data)	T-DATA req	T-DATA ind	S-U-EX-REPORT ind
S-ACT-START req	AS	T-DATA req	T-DATA ind	S-ACT-START ind
S-ACT-RESUME req	AR	T-DATA req	T-DATA ind	S-ACT-RESUME ind
S-ACT-INTERRUPT req	PR	T-EXP-DATA req	T-EXP-DATA ind	—
	AI	T-DATA req	T-DATA ind	S-ACT-INTERRUPT ind
S-ACT-INTERRUPT resp	PR	T-EXP-DATA req	T-EXP-DATA ind	—
	AIA	T-DATA req	T-DATA ind	S-ACT-INTERRUPT conf
S-ACT-DISCARD req	PR	T-EXP-DATA req	T-EXP-DATA ind	—
	AD	T-DATA req	T-DATA ind	S-ACT-DISCARD ind
S-ACT-DISCARD resp	PR	T-EXP-DATA req	T-EXP-DATA ind	—
	ADA	T-DATA req	T-DATA ind	S-ACT-DISCARD conf
S-ACT-END req	AE	T-DATA req	T-DATA ind	S-ACT-END ind
S-ACT-END resp	PR	T-EXP-DATA req	T-EXP-DATA ind	—
	AEA	T-DATA req	T-DATA ind	S-ACT-END conf

(6) If transport expedited data service is not available over the transport connection then session expedited data service is likewise not available.

(7) An S-CONTROL-GIVE request demands that all available tokens are to be given to the peer SS user. As far as the initiating SS user is concerned it cannot fail, and so, from its point of view, it is an unconfirmed service. However the session entities will not proceed without such confirmation: the responding session entity must acknowledge that it now has *control* by sending an acknowledge SPDU. This is an instance of an unconfirmed service having an *invisible* confirmation in a protocol-defined exchange within the service element; this is necessary to avoid conflicts developing between the protocol machines. The session entity on the initiating end-system will not be reset into an 'all's well' state until a GTA SPDU is received.

(8) As we saw in the discussion of minor syncs, a response is not always required.

(9) The PR (PRepare) SPDU is a special SPDU used to achieve a 'signalling' effect. If the transport expedited data service is available, this SPDU is sent on that service immediately before the service element-specific SPDU which it is to signal is sent on the transport normal data service. In this way it can arrive at the peer session entity ahead of the SPDU which it is signalling, possibly overtaking other session normal data SPDUs already transmitted on transport normal data. If this is the case and if the event signalled makes pointless the handling of further received session normal data, up to the signalled SPDU, then the data SPDUs can be discarded by the receiving session entity. 'Prepare' is only used if transport expedited data service is available. To use the transport normal data service to convey the PR SPDU would mean that it would arrive just before the SPDU which it was meant to signal — clearly of little use. It is used in conjunction with the following SPDUs:

RS (ReSynchronize)	RA (Resynchronize Ack)
MAA (MAjor sync Ack)	AI (Activity Interrupt)
AIA (Activity Int Ack)	AD (Activity Discard)
ADA (Activity Dis Ack)	AEA (Activity End Ack)

(10) On receipt of this prepare, the session protocol machine enters a state whereby it expects the signalled SPDU (the PR SPDU carries within it an indication of the type of SPDU it is signalling). In this case the session normal data flow is processed as if nothing had occurred, with data service indications issued as appropriate.

(11) Again a PR SPDU is received and in this instance signals an SPDU of a type that dictates that any session normal data received after this event, and up to the signalled SPDU, may be discarded. A discard of this nature is an implementation choice but, whatever the session entity does about discard, the information contained within such data will be of no use to the receiving application process. The signalled SPDU is of the destructive type. The sequence is demonstrated in Figure 6.5. Note that PR SPDUs associated with AI and AD SPDUs have the same effect.

(12) Identical in reasoning to note (4) above.

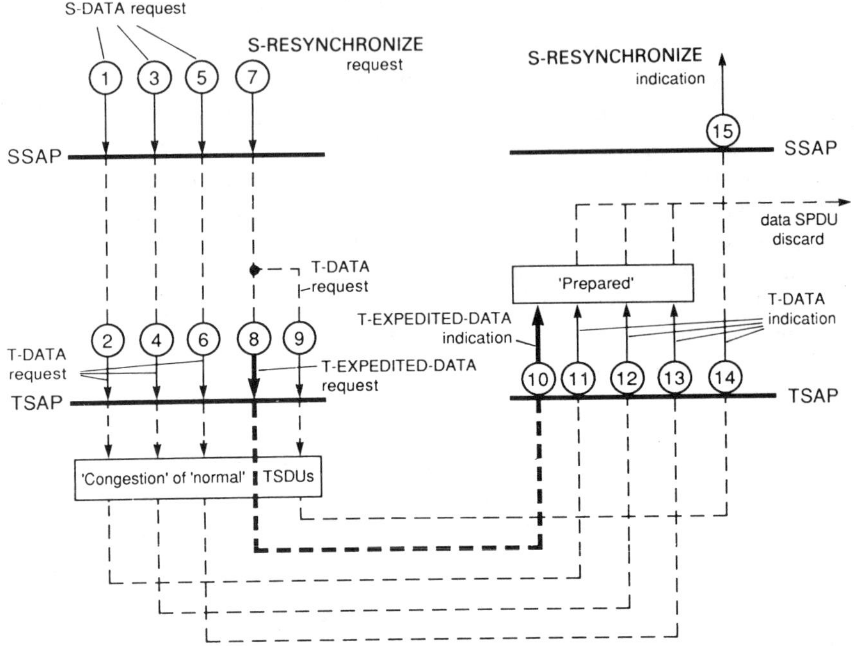

Fig. 6.5 — Use of 'prepare'.

During the course of the last three chapters we have identified the PDUs that are exchanged between peer layer entities as the principle instrument of cooperation. A PDU is generated by the protocol machine generally as a result of S user influence, a service primitive, and such generation is part of a procedure laid down by the protocol specification for the layer. This procedure may also involve the assignment of new values to layer variables associated with the particular activity (for example, incrementing the current SPSN by one before sending a MIP SPDU as a result of an S-SYNC-MINOR request), and will involve the changing of the *state* of the protocol machine. The state of a protocol machine reflects its understanding of the current position of activity between it and its peer. Based upon this, any further event (a service primitive from an S user or a PDU from its peer) will be judged for *legality*: that is, the event and the current state will be checked against *state tables* provided by the protocol specification to determine whether the particular event should occur in the current state. If the event is legal then the state table dictate the action(s) to be taken by the protocol machine and the new state to be entered. If the event should not occur then there is a protocol violation, and an appropriate action dictated by the protocol specification is undertaken. This is generally destructive of the connection. An example of (part of) a session protocol state table is given in Table 6.8.

Notes:

This is a cross-reference table. The column titles give the 'current state' of the protocol machine, the row titles give the event which triggers a state table look-up.

Table 6.8 — Example of part of a session state table

	STATE					
EVENT	STA01A await AA	STA01C idle TC con	STA02A await AC	STA03 await DN	STA04A await PR or AEA	STA04B await PR or AEA
DT	STA01A	TDISreq STA01		p05&p10 SDTind STA03	p05 SDTind STA04A	p05 SDTind STA04B
EX	STA01A	TDISreq STA01	[10] STA02A	p09 SEXind STA03	p08 SEXind STA04A	p08 SEXind STA04B
TD	STA01A	TDISreq STA01		p06&p10 STDind STA03	p06 STDind STA04A	p06 STDind STA04B

The action to be taken is specified in the state/event intersection. This is either blank or a list of one or more 'instructions'. A blank intersection is one that cannot occur during 'legal' operation; if it does then a protocol error is implied.

For example, the third column title breaks down as follows:

STA02A — The mnemonic for the current state.
await — A (two line) description of the
AC state: 'awaiting an AC SPDU'.

The event titles are, in this case, all instances of SPDU receipt from the peer: DT is Data Transfer SPDU received, EX is EXpedited data SPDU received and TD is Typed Data SPDU received. The events can also be service primitive receipt from the user or provider, for example, 'SDTreq' is S-DATA request received from user.

The intersections, when not blank, are formed by one or many 'instructions'. The last of these is *always* the next state to enter (and so has the same form of label as the column title: 'STAxx'). The other possible instances are as follows:

pnn This is a *predicate* statement and governs what follows in the intersection. If the predicate is *true* then the following instructions(s) are followed: if *false* then either alternative instructions are given or it is an error situation where the protocol machine must take appropriate action. Such predicate statements are often logically combined to for a complex predicate. For instance, 'p05&p10' refers to a check on the *data token* and upon previous protocol machine activity.

[nn] This is a reference to a particular action defined in the standard. For instance '[10]' is an instruction to 'store the event in a queue'.

text For instance 'TDISreq' and 'SEXind'. This form of text is an instruction to issue either a service primitive request ('TDISreq' is a T-DISCONNECT request) to the subordinate layer, or an indication ('SEXind' is an S-EXPEDITED-DATA indication) to the service user.

The state table is a fundamental element of all layer protocol specifications: it is from the state table that the implementation of a layer standard (entity) is achieved. Before leaving this brief foray into the depths of the protocol specifications themselves this is an appropriate point to look at PDUs. The general format of PDUs associated with a particular layer is specified in the layer protocol specification. There is no reason why the structure of PDUs of one layer should be the same as another, given that the layers are completely independent. To the layer providing a service by which a PDU of the layer above is transferred, the latter appears to be simply a string of octets. As an example of a PDU we consider the Minor sync SPDU, MIP. It is generated by a session entity as a result of an S-SYNC-MINOR request, and is encoded as follows:

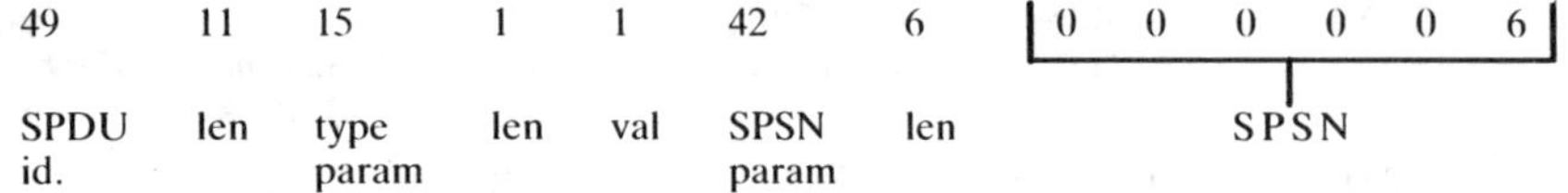

We see a string of octets that make up the SPDU, starting with an SPDU identifier (49 indicates an MIP) followed by the overall length (11) which is a count of the number of octets forming the parameters of the SPDU. This is followed by all the parameters, each composed of a code identifying the parameter, a length and a parameter value. In this case the type parameter (code 15) has a value, contained in 1 octet, of 1 (meaning that the minor sync is of the non-explicit confirmation type). The second parameter, SPSN, has a value contained in 6 octets, each of which represents a digit (0–9) of the SPSN (the SPSN is always with the range 000000–999999). The user data parameter is optional and in this case does not appear.

This example does not in fact show the full extent of SPDU encoding, being simplified for presentation. The point to note is that the SPDU is a precisely defined encoding of information that appears, to the transport service provider, as a string of octets. The reader who wishes to see the precise encoding techniques should refer to the standards.

7

The transport layer

In Chapter 1 the transport layer was described as a layer with a 'coercive responsibility'. It ensures that a reliable end-to-end data transmission capability of the quality demanded by the session layer is offered to that layer, regardless of the nature of the underlying network (potentially comprising many sub-networks) over which the data is transferred.

We shall examine transport in two sections: first looking at the services offered to transport service users (TS users), and then describing how transport provides the services at the level stipulated for the TS user — *quality of service* (QOS). Before commencing our look at transport services we reiterate the concept of end-to-end activity and its relationship to the transport and network layers.

Consider the instance of OSI activity between two end-systems which are 'attached' to the same sub-network. The realization of an OSI application activity

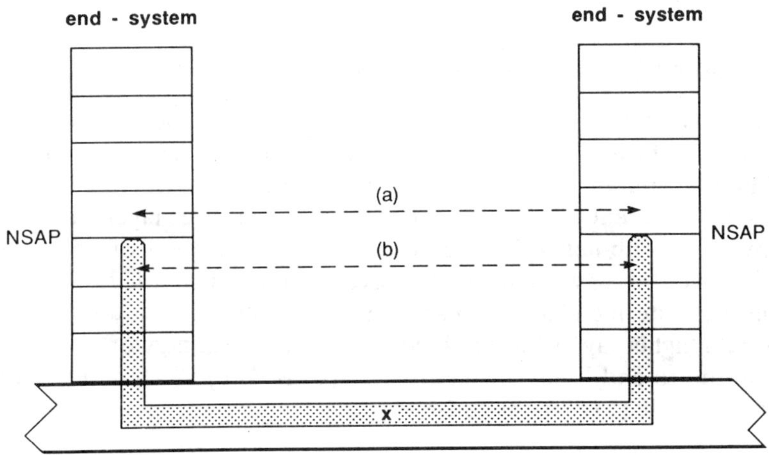

Fig. 7.1 — Cooperating end-systems on the same sub-network.

relies upon a reliable end-to-end data transmission capability. It is provided by the transport layer, (a) in Figure 7.1. This in turn is achieved by use of network data services, in this case by the cooperation of two, peer, network entities of a type appropriate to the nature of the particular sub-network. Any additional facilities over and above those provided by the network layer which are needed to achieve the required QOS will be provided by the transport layer. We have, then, a sub-network of type 'X' over which a data transmission capability, (b), is provided.

In the example it is clear that not only do the transport entities operate on an end-to-end basis but so also do the network entities. However, consider the case where the end-systems communicate over different sub-networks.

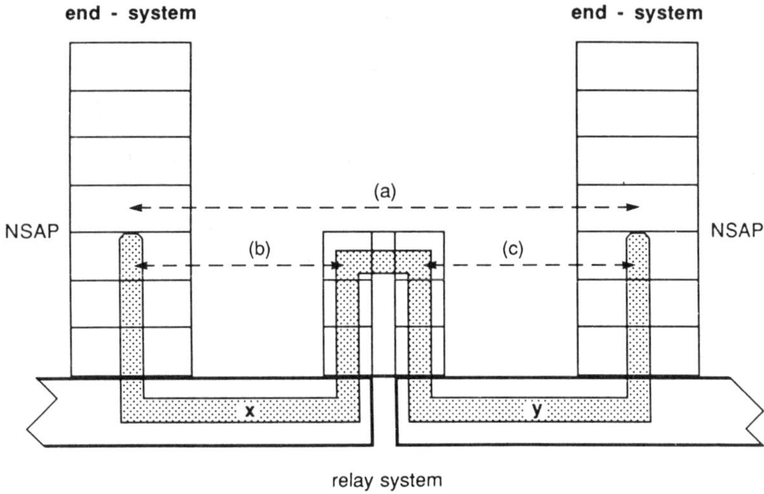

Fig. 7.2 — Cooperating end-systems on different sub-networks.

Now we see that the network no longer appears 'end-to-end' because, in order to facilitate the use of two differing sub-networks, an intermediate computer system is brought into play, but only up to and including the network layer. This intermediate system has two different 'stacks' of entities of the lower three layers, each reflecting the nature of the sub-network it represents. The realization of end-to-end data transmission over this environment is achieved by the network layer; any necessary routing through intermediate systems being the responsibility of the network layer. Transport and higher layers have independence from such network issues, working only on an end-to-end basis. In Figure 7.2, (b) and (c) are 'point-to-point' data transmissions, while (a) remains end-to-end.

7.1 THE TRANSPORT SERVICE

The connection-oriented transport service is defined in ISO service definition document 8072.

The transport service is in one of three phases at any time:

(i) transport connection (TC) establishment,
(ii) data transfer,
(iii) transport connection release.

In the TC establishment phase a connection is established between peer TS users (session entities). The session entity initiating the TC specifies the QOS required of the connection, in terms of reliability and other aspects of the service; we examine QOS in detail at the end of the chapter. Once a TC is established the session entities can exchange data (TSDUs) transparently over the connection. In the release phase the TC is unconditionally released by either TS user.

Each phase has associated services which are summarized in Table 7.1.

Table 7.1 — Transport services

Phase	Service	Service element	Type
TC establishment	TC establishment	T-CONNECT	Confirmed
Data transfer	Normal data transfer	T-DATA	Unconfirmed
	Expedited data transfer	T-EXPEDITED-DATA	Unconfirmed
TC release	TC release	T-RELEASE	Unconfirmed

The reliable end-to-end (normal) transmission of data is provided by the T-DATA service element; that of expedited data by T-EXPEDITED-DATA. The required level of service of the TC is dictated to the initiating transport entity in the **quality of service** parameter of the T-CONNECT request; this is used as a basis for negotiation, during TC establishment, of an acceptable and attainable QOS between the end-systems. This negotiated QOS must then be maintained by the TS provider throughout the lifetime of the connection.

The primitive sequences associated with the use of these service elements follow the basic rules, but there is one 'oddity' that must be mentioned, concerning the rejection of a TC by the responding TS user. In this case the connection is rejected by the issuing of a T-DISCONNECT request rather than, as we might expect, a T-CONNECT response with a negative 'result'. This is illustrated in Figure 7.3. In the

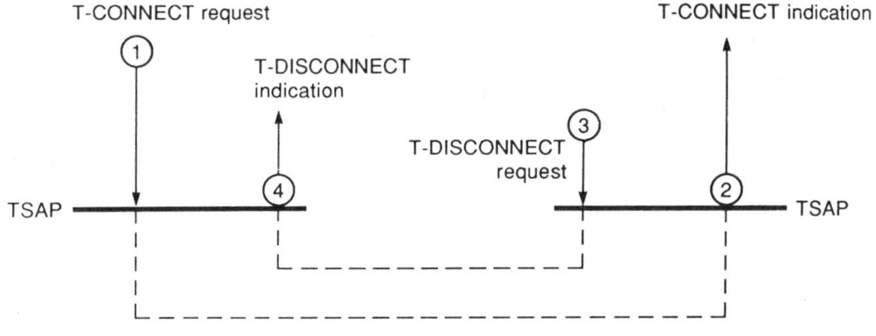

Fig. 7.3 — Transport connection rejection.

initiating TS user, the outstanding T-CONNECT confirm is overridden by the more dominant T-DISCONNECT indication. Indeed should the TC have been rejected by the TS provider rather than the responding TS user then the result would be exactly the same — a T-DISCONNECT indication to the initiating TS user.

Table 7.2 — Transport service primitive parameters

Primitive		Parameters
T-CONNECT	request indication	Called address Calling address Expedited data option Quality of service TS user data
T-CONNECT	response confirm	Responding address Expedited data option Quality of service TS user data
T-DATA	request indication	TS user data
T-EXPEDITED-DATA	request indication	TS user data
T-DISCONNECT	request	TS user data
T-DISCONNECT	indication	Disconnect reason TS user data

Table 7.2 shows the parameters associated with each TS primitive. The **called address** and **calling address** are TSAP addresses and identify the TS user initiating the TC and the intended responder. The **responding address** conveys the TSAP address of the responding TS user accepting the TC. Generally this will be the same as the called address, only differing from it when that address has been supplied by the initiating TS user in some 'generic' form. Such a form results in a selection, by the responding end-system, of a specific TSAP address which is based upon the provided generic; it is this selection that is returned in the parameter. The **expedited data option** parameter is used to negotiate the availability of transport expedited data service over the TC. Note that, if the calling TS user or TS provider does not offer this service, which is apparent in the T-CONNECT indication, then the called TS user may not insist upon it by including it on the response.

TS user data is a parameter that, in the case of T-DATA and T-EXPEDITED-DATA, is the mechanism for provision of transparent, reliable, TSDU exchange over a TC between peer TS users. In the case of the other services this parameter enables a limited amount of transparent user data to be passed between TS users which may qualify the service in question. TS user data is restricted in length by the standard as shown in Table 7.3.

The unconstrained size of normal data TSDUs will often not apply in practice. Constraints on implementation or on the operational environment of a transport entity, such as the size of available buffering, lead to a limit being imposed on TSDUs. Such a limit will have repercussions on the higher layers but, as we saw in the last chapter, these can be overcome by the use of segmentation by the peer session entities.

The quality of service parameter is itself a 'list' of parameters. It is, on the T-CONNECT request, a statement by the initiating TS user concerning the level of service it requires of the, as yet unestablished, TC. It is concerned with such things as acceptable error rates and minimum acceptable (data) throughput. Both the calling *and* called transport entities may amend the QOS to a level they regarded as feasible, given knowledge of aspects of the network not necessarily visible to the initiating TS user. In the course of establishing the connection the (possibly modified) QOS is passed to the responding TS user in the indication. Acceptance of the connection results in a T-CONNECT confirm which carries the final QOS. If this is modified to an unacceptable level then the initiating TS user has the option to terminate the established connection by issuing a T-DISCONNECT request with an appropriate **reason** parameter value and, perhaps, qualifying user data, such as 'QOS negotiated to unacceptable level'.

The reason parameter of the T-DISCONNECT indication gives the cause of the TC release. It shows whether the release was user or provider initiated. Possible values are:

Quality of service fallen below level agreed for this TC.
Congestion or failure of local or remote TS provider.
Unknown reason.
Called TSAP address not valid.
Called TSAP address not available.

7.2 REALIZATION OF THE TRANSPORT SERVICE

The connection-oriented transport protocol is defined in ISO protocol specification document 8073.

The QOS-defined level of reliable end-to-end data transmission is realized by the transport layer, by the use of a combination of standard defined procedures, each of which extends, modifies or manipulates the services offered by the network layer. The level of service offered by the network is dictated by the nature of the underlying sub-network(s) of which it is composed. Clearly the attainable data throughput depends upon two issues. The first is the physical limitation of a sub-network or of its components; for instance, if a 'packet switch' in a particular X.25 sub-network has a restricted switching capability of n packets per second then the sub-network data throughput has an absolute upper bound dictated by n. The second aspect is 'errors': the level of errors which a sub-network is prone to limits the level of reliable service that can be offered over it.

Table 7.3 — Restriction on TS user data

Service element	Restriction
T-CONNECT	Maximum of 32 octets
T-DISCONNECT	Maximum of 64 octets
T-EXPEDITED-DATA	Maximum of 16 octets
T-DATA	No restriction

7.2.1 Sub-network reliability

Errors originating in a sub-network and consequently observed by the transport layer are of two types, *signalled* and *residual*.

A signalled error is one detected by the network layer but where no steps are taken within that layer for recovery. The event is just signalled to the transport layer for action. Two examples are network disconnection (the network connection is lost) and network reset (the network connection is reset to a known state, possibly with loss of data in transit — but the connection remains available for use).

Residual errors are all those apart from signalled errors. In effect they have not been detected by the network layer. Examples are loss, corruption, duplication, and delivery out of sequence of TPDUs.

If sub-networks are analysed in terms of these two types of error they can be divided into three categories:

(i) where the rate of both types of errors are acceptable,
(ii) where the rate of residual errors is acceptable but not that of signalled errors,
(iii) where the rate of residual errors is unacceptable.

A network connection over a single sub-network of type (ii) say, is said to offer a (ii) category of service, but what of a network connection offered over a number of sub-networks (via relays) of different error categories? The answer is simply that the category of service to be expected from a network is the same as that of the 'poorest' level of service of the sub-networks over which it operates.

As part of transport connection establishment the peer transport entities must establish the level of network service 'enhancement' that must be undertaken in order to provide the agreed QOS for this connection. This involves the selection of the set of procedures that will be used during the connection. This selection is achieved as part of the connection establishment procedure in parallel with QOS negotiation.

If we have a network composed of two sub-networks, one of type (i) and the other of type (iii), then the level of service enhancement, in terms of error detection and correction, that will be carried out over the network by the transport entities is determined by the poorest service level of the two sub-networks. The transport entity on the initiating end-system will offer a level of enhancement based upon its knowledge of the underlying sub-network to which its end-system is attached. The responding entity will either accept this level of enhancement as suitable, given its own 'local knowledge', or propose an alternative enhancement level to the initiator.

In this way an appropriate set of enhancement procedures is chosen for use over the connection. This negotiation is done as part of the TC establishment procedure but, unlike QOS, it is transparent to the peer TS users. Choices of other enhancement procedures, not directly related to 'errors' and perhaps only indirectly related to the nature of the underlying sub-network(s), are solely based upon final value of the negotiated QOS.

7.2.2 Transport classes

There are a set of five basic levels or *classes* of network service enhancement available from the transport layer. Each class is in some way related to the three categories of sub-network identified above.

Transport entities, during TC establishment, perform the procedure negotiation described above by agreeing on a transport class to be used over the network for this particular TC. Inherent in a choice of class is a set of associated transport procedures.

Class 0, the *simple class*, provides the most basic transport connection and is designed to be used with type (i) quality of network service. Given that this type of network service provides reliable data transmission, only a basic level of transport activity is required.

Class 1, the *basic error recovery class*, provides, with minimal overhead, a basic transport connection designed to be used with type (ii) network service. It handles signalled errors such as network disconnect without, of course, involving the TS user.

Class 2, the *multiplexing class*, is as class 0 but with additional mechanisms to support the multiplexing of transport connections onto single network connections.

Class 3, the *error recovery and multiplexing class*, is as class 1 but with additional multiplexing mechanisms.

Class 4, the *error detection and recovery class*, provides all the capability of class 3 together with mechanisms required to detect and recover from errors not signalled by the NS provider. This class also provides for increased throughput and for additional resilience against NS provider failure. It is designed to be used over a type (iii) network.

Negotiation of a transport class between transport entities is achieved as follows. The initiating entity proposes a *preferred* class together with, optionally, an *alternative* class. The preferred class is either accepted or modified to another, numerically lower, class by the responder. Such modification is done by reference to a table, Table 7.4.

The responder can choose to accept any class indicated in the appropriate intersection in the table.

7.2.3 Transport procedures

The transport protocol is defined as a set of *procedures*, each of which relates to a particular activity. Implicit in the final negotiated transport class is the choice of a subset of those procedures that is necessary to provide the functionality of that class. As we examine the procedures it will become clear that many are fundamental to basic transport service provision. These form a set of procedures common to all transport classes.

The (simplified) relationship between each procedure and the five transport classes is summarized in Table 7.5.

Table 7.4 — Look-up table for transport class selection

Preferred class	Proposed alternative class					
	0	1	2	3	4	none
0	—	—	—	—	—	0
1	1 or 0	1 or 0	—	—	—	1 or 0
2	2 or 0	—	2	—	—	2
3	3,2,0	3,2,1,0	3 or 2	3 or 2	—	3 or 2
4	4,2,0	4,2,1,0	4 or 2	4,3,2	4 or 2	4 or 2

Table 7.5 — Relationship between transport procedures and classes

Mechanism	Procedure No.	Variant	0	1	2	3	4	Note
Assignment to network Conn.	1		★	★	★	★	★	
TPDU Transfer	2		★	★	★	★	★	
Segmenting/Reassembling	3		★	★	★	★	★	
Concatenation/Separation	4		–	★	★	★	★	
Connection Establishment	5		★	★	★	★	★	
Connection Refusal	6		★	★	★	★	★	
Normal Release	7	Implicit	★	–	–	–	–	
		Explicit	–	★	★	★	★	
Error Release	8		★	–	★	–	–	
TPDU association with TCs	9		★	★	★	★	★	
DT TPDU Numbering	10		–	★	m	m	m	
Expedited Data Transfer	11	Net. normal	–	m	★	★	★	(1)
		Net. Exped.	–	+	–	–	–	
Reassignment after failure	12		–	★	–	★	★	
Retention until Ack. of TPDU	13	Conf Receipt	–	+	–	–	–	(2)
		AK TPDU	–	m	–	★	★	
Resynchronization	14		–	★	–	★	★	
Multiplexing/Demultiplexing	15		–	–	★	★	★	
Explicit Flow Control	16			–	m	★	★	
Checksum	17		–	–	–	–	m	
Frozen References	18		–	★	–	★	★	
Retransmission on Timeout	19		–	–	–	–	★	
Resequencing	20		–	–	–	–	★	
Inactivity Control	21		–	–	–	–	★	
Treatment of protocol errors	22		★	★	★	★	★	
Splitting and Recombining	23		–	–	–	–	★	

★: Procedure always included in class; –: never available in this class; m: negotiable procedure whose implementation in a transport entity is mandatory; +: negotiable procedure whose implementation in a transport entity is optional and the use of which depends upon availability within the network service.

Notes

(1) Not applicable in class 2 if explicit flow control is not selected. 'Net. Normal/Expedited' refers to the use of the normal or expedited data services of network.

(2) 'Conf. Receipt' refers to use of the network confirmed receipt service, and 'AK' to the use of a transport facility for acknowledgement.

The procedures are introduced in some depth in the following pages and, from this description, the fundamental mechanisms of the transport layer can be seen. However the descriptions are not complete and many operational details are omitted for simplification. Like all other chapters of this book, this chapter should not in any way be used as a substitute for the standards themselves.

7.2.3.1 Assignment to a network connection

This procedure is common to all classes — indeed, until an initial assignment is made a transport connection (TC) cannot be established. Assignment is the association of a (potential) TC with a network connection (NC); 'potential' because, in the TC establishment stage, establishment cannot proceed until an assignment is made. However, once made and the TC established, then, in the event of the NC being lost, the TC can be retained and assigned to a different NC. In either case the transport entity may chose to establish a new NC (by use of the N-CONNECT service element) or use a suitable existing NC. We shall see later that a single TC can be assigned to more than one NC at any time (*splitting*) and that more than one TC can be assigned to a single NC (*multiplexing*).

7.2.3.2 Transport protocol data unit transfer

This procedure coordinates the conveyance of TPDUs between peer transport entities. It uses the network normal and expedited data service elements N-DATA and N-EXPEDITED-DATA (the latter used, if available, only to convey expedited data related TPDUs and only in class 1). This procedure is common to all classes of transport.

In the transport data PDUs, DaTa (DT) and Expedited Data (ED), the structure is such that the 'control' section of the PDU, the *protocol control information* (PCI), comprises an identifier together with a length parameter giving the length of the PCI within the PDU. However, there is no length indication for the data field (unbounded in the case of DT) of the PDU. The whole is passed to the NS provider as an NSDU and it is from the overall length of this NSDU that the receiving transport entity can determine the size of the data field: i.e. NSDU length minus PCI length.

7.2.3.3 Segmentation and reassembling

A TSDU requested for transfer by a TS user may exceed the limit placed upon the amount of data that can be conveyed between peer transport entities in a single data (DT) TPDU. Such a limit reflects constraints within the network service on NSDUs associated with the N-DATA service element. In this case segmentation is invoked to break the TSDU into a series of appropriately size DT TPDUs. In other cases a single DT TPDU will suffice (see Figure 7.4).

On receipt by the peer transport entity, the sequence of DT TPDUs representing a segmented TSDU will be reassembled into the single TSDU, and only when this complete TSDU has been received will a data service indication be issued to the receiving TS user. In order that a segmented TSDU can be recognized by a receiving transport entity, there is a parameter, **EOT**, in each DT TPDU which is only *set* when

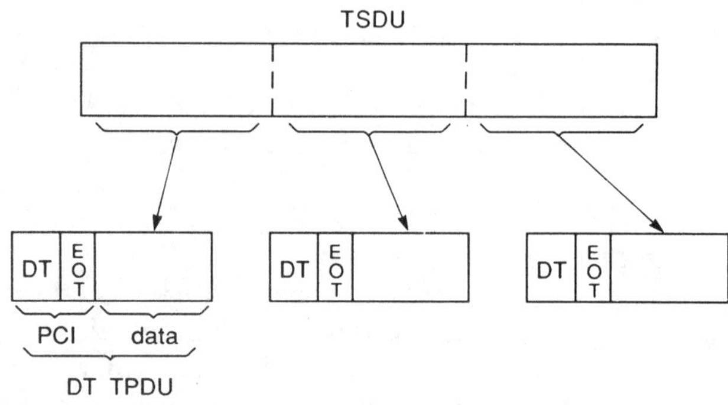

Fig. 7.4 — Segmentation.

a complete TSDU has been transferred. In the case of TSDUs contained entirely within DT TPDUs this will be set on every DT TPDU. This procedure is available in all classes.

7.2.3.4 Concatenation and separation

In this procedure, subject to certain rules, a number of TPDUs can be concatenated into a single NSDU for transmission, and separated by the receiving transport entity on receipt. It is available in all classes except 0.

Now, remembering what was said about the structure of data TPDUs, it is clear that, if a data TPDU is to be one of group of concatenated TPDUs then it must be the last TPDU of the concatenation and, therefore, the *only* data TPDU. This is simply because any further concatenated TPDU would be 'invisible' on receipt at the receiving transport entity, since it would appear to be part of the data field (data length = (length of remainder of NSDU)−(DT TPDU PCI length)).

The same argument applies to extended concatenation within the session layer.

7.2.3.5 Connection establishment

This procedure is available in all classes of transport to establish a TC after successful assignment to a network connection.

A transport connection is established by negotiation between peers, by the exchange of appropriate PDUs, which in this case are conveyed by the use of network normal data, N-DATA. As a result of negotiation the QOS to be maintained and the transport class to be used over the network are determined. There are procedures associated with particular classes that are in themselves optional within the class, and so negotiation of these optional features is also carried out at this time. The two TPDUs involved in the confirmed exchange are Connect Request (CR) TPDU and Connect Confirm (CC).

In the course of TC establishment, information is exchanged between transport entities in parameter form (on the CR and CC TPDUs). This information defines and constrains the resultant TC as follows:

— **References** are arbitrary references chosen by the transport entities to identify the TC.

— **Addresses** define the calling and called TSAPs.
— **Initial credit** is concerned with explicit flow control (discussed in the section on the initial credit procedure).
— **User data** is transparent data supplied by the TS users.
— **Acknowledgement time** and **checksum parameter** are concerned with class 4 only; they are discussed later.
— **Security parameter** is a general security parameter whose semantics are defined by the TS user, that is by the 'environment' of the OSI activity to which this TC is related.

The aspects negotiated between transport entities during TC establishment are:

— Protocol class.
— Maximum bound on TPDU size. The initiator may propose a bound; the responder may accept it or propose a lower bound.
— Use of checksums on TPDUs, only applicable to class 4 and optional in that class.
— Quality of service, being aspects of the transport service which are adjusted by negotiation to mutually acceptable levels. These include: throughput, transit delay, priority, residual error rate. This is discussed further at the end of the chapter.
— Use of explicit flow control. It is mandatory in classes 3 and 4 and optional in class 2. In class 2 then it can be excluded by negotiation. It is discussed in the section on the explicit flow control procedure.
— Use of network receipt confirmation and network expedited. Both are of concern only to class 1 and optional within that class. They are discussed later.
— Use of transport expedited data service, available in all but class 0.

7.2.3.6 Connection refusal

This procedure is initiated by the responding transport entity in response to either (i) a T-DISCONNECT request from the responding TS user, or (ii) an inability to conform to the requirements of the initiating transport entity conveyed in the CR TPDU. It is common to all classes and is achieved by sending a Disconnect Request (DR) TPDU to the initiator using network normal data.

7.2.3.7 Normal release

Common to all classes and used to terminate a TC.

In class 0 there is a one-to-one relationship between the 'lifetime' of a TC and that of the NC to which it is assigned. In this class normal release is achieved, by either transport entity, by disconnecting the NC (using N-DISCONNECT request). The receipt of an N-DISCONNECT indication is considered, in class 0, to imply the release of the associated TC. This is known as the *implicit* variant of normal release.

The other variant, *explicit*, is associated with all other classes and here the TC is released by a confirmed activity involving the exchange between peers of Disconnect Request (DR) and Disconnect Confirm (DC) TPDUs, using network normal data. The need for an explicit variant becomes clear when multiplexing is considered.

7.2.3.8 Error release

This is a mechanism used only in classes 0 and 2 to release the transport connection after a signalled error has been received from the NS provider. In these 'simple' classes (designed for networks of type (i)) this is the only possible course of action. The TS users are, of course, informed of the release by a T-DISCONNECT indication. In the other classes, procedures are available for recovery from signalled errors.

7.2.3.9 Association of TPDUs with transport connections

This is a procedure used in all classes while data is being received. Whenever a transport entity receives an NSDU from the NS provider it must take the following steps:

(1) Check that the NSDU can be decoded into one or more concatenation of TPDUs.
(2) If concatenation is detected then invoke the separation procedure.
(3) If the NC over which this NSDU is received has associated with it multiple TCs (i.e. multiplexing), then ensure that the TPDUs are associated with the appropriate TC.

Step (3) raises a general point which, until now, we have not explored. Implicit in this action is an understanding that the transport entity in question can 'manage' more than a single transport connection at any time. The general point is that an *n* entity can handle any number of *n* connections at any time. Any restriction on this will be placed by the operational environment or by the complexity of implementation of the entity, there being no constraint imposed or suggested by the standard. What is unique amongst the higher layers is that the TSAP is the only boundary at which a one-to-many or many-to-one relationship between connections (TCs and NCs) is permitted.

Obviously the action to be taken should any of the activities 1, 2 or 3 fail — and indeed whether each is invoked — depends upon the transport class. For instance if class 0 was extant over a network then:

— Step (1). In this class only a single TPDU can be present (concatenation not being allowed). If this NSDU does contain concatenated TPDUs then the procedure protocol error is invoked.
— Step (2) is never invoked in this class.
— Step (3) is never invoked — the TPDU is automatically assigned to the only TC.

7.2.3.10 TPDU numbering

In order that certain procedures can be successfully undertaken it is necessary for each DT TPDU to carry, as a parameter in the PCI, a sequence number. The procedures in question are those concerned with recovery, flow control and resequencing. TPDU numbering is used in classes 1, 3 and 4, and in 2 when non-use of explicit flow control was negotiated during TC establishment.

7.2.3.11 Expedited data transfer

How the expedited data effect is achieved is discussed later in this chapter. The procedure places the TS user data provided by a T-EXPEDITED-DATA request into the data field of a Expedited Data (ED) TPDU. Although the transport Expedited data *service* is unconfirmed, transport protocol demands that the peer entity procedure be confirmed, and so each ED TPDU must be acknowledged by the receiving peer transport entity by use of an Expedited data Acknowledge (EA) TPDU. Indeed no more than one unacknowledged ED TPDU can be outstanding (over the network) for each data flow direction of the TC at any time.

In classes 2, 3 and 4 the ED and EA TPDUs are conveyed between peers by use of network normal data, that is, by use of N-DATA request. In class 1, either network normal data can be used or, if negotiated during TC establishment, network expedited data.

This procedure is unavailable in class 0.

7.2.3.12 Reassignment after failure

Available in classes 1, 3 and 4. When a network signalled error is received, indicating the loss of the NC (N-DISCONNECT indication) to which a TC is assigned, this procedure is called into play. The result will be that the TC is assigned to a different NC, which either already existed and was 'owned' by this transport entity or is newly 'created' for the purpose. When this reassignment is achieved the procedure *resynchronization* is invoked. However should a reassignment not be achieved then the TC will be considered released and the transport reference frozen; this is considered later, in the section on procedure *frozen references*. If splitting is in use — the association of this TC with many NCs — and the quality of service required can be maintained by the remaining NC(s), then the reassignment may not be attempted, the TC remaining in use.

7.2.3.13 Retention until acknowledgement of TPDUs

Available to classes 1, 3 and 4, this provides mechanisms whereby the transmitting transport entity can retain 'copies' of TPDUs until an explicit acknowledgement of receipt is received from the peer. Should no acknowledgement be received after a certain period of time has elapsed (class 4 only), or should a signalled error occur (classes 1, 3 and 4), then the TPDUs can be retransmitted.

The reader can now see that in these classes, even though the transport data service is unconfirmed, the protocol dictates that the transfer itself be 'confirmed' between peer transport entities.

In classes 3 and 4 the acknowledgement of TPDUs is effected by the transmission by the receiving transport entity of an AcKnowledge (AK) TPDU, known as the *AK variant*. In class 1 the AK variant may be used but instead, subject to negotiation during TC establishment, the network data acknowledge service element may be invoked by the receiving transport entity (by use of N-DATA-ACKNOWLEDGE request). The use of the network service to this end is clearly dependent on the availability of this service in the underlying network. This is known as the *confirmation of receipt variant*. The two variants are demonstrated in Figure 7.5.

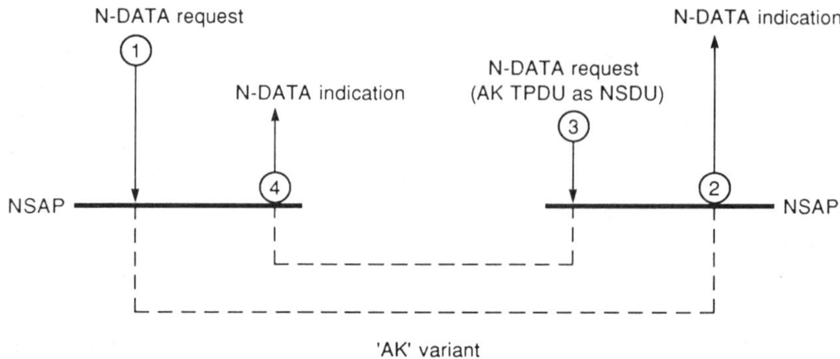

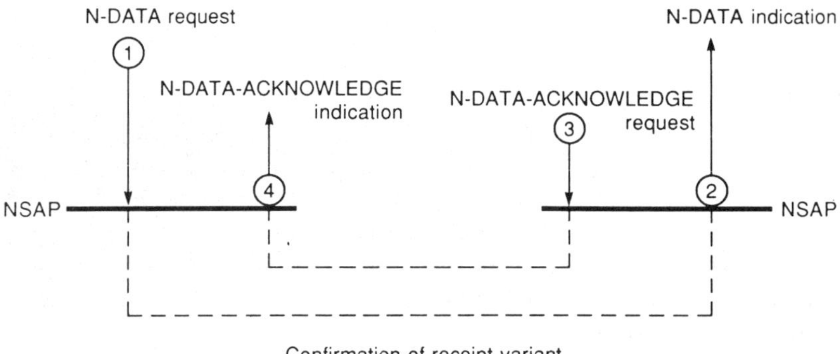

Fig. 7.5 — The two variants of confirmed data transfer.

Of course persistent loss of TPDUs will cause the QOS to fall below the negotiated acceptable level and, potentially, the TC to be terminated and the TS users informed.

7.2.3.14 Resynchronization

This is a procedure available to classes 1, 3 and 4. After a signalled event from the NS provider which indicates a (temporary) problem in the NC (an N-RESET indication), or after reassignment of a TC after NC failure, this procedure is used to restore the TC to 'normal'.

Resynchronization is only attempted by the transport entity which was the initiator of the TC in question, its peer taking only a passive role in the resynchronization process. The aim of the resynchronizing transport entity is to resume the activity on the TC that was outstanding at the time of the triggering event. One of the peer transport entities must take a passive role in this, since both entities will be aware of the need for resynchronization, given the nature of the cause, and for both, almost simultaneously, to attempt to initiate it would result in unnecessary 'event collision' resolutions being undertaken. The passive entity simply sets a timer and awaits resynchronization related TPDUs to 'arrive' from the TC initiator. Should the timer expire then the entity considers the TC released and the reference frozen.

The protocol defines the actions that must be taken to achieve a resynchronized TC in all possible cases. This may involve, for instance, the retransmission of unacknowledged TPDUs. Should resynchronization fail the TC is considered released and the transport reference frozen.

As part of resynchronization the ReJect (RJ) TPDU is conveyed between peers, partly in order to resynchronize, to the value it carries in a parameter, the 'next expected' DT TPDU sequence number (see *TPDU numbering*.)

The general nature of class 4, the most 'complex' class, means that in practice the mechanisms by which the aims of this procedure and that of the reassignment procedure are achieved will be somewhat different in implementation, being more 'interwoven' with other procedures than in the case of classes 1 and 3.

7.2.3.15 Multiplexing and demultiplexing

This procedure is available to classes 2, 3 and 4. It allows more than a single TC to share a single NC. In effect a transport entity transmits or receives TPDUs 'belonging' to different TCs over the same NC. A transport entity receiving TPDUs in this environment must perform demultiplexing, the TC to which individual TPDUs belong being determined by invoking the *association of TPDUs* procedure.

Clearly use of multiplexing and concatenation, and both together where a single NSDU is transferred containing concatenated TPDUs for different TCs, makes for economical and efficient use of a network.

7.2.3.16 Explicit flow control

This is a procedure available to classes 2, 3 and 4. Flow control that is policed by the transport layer acts independently of whatever flow control may be available in the network. It regulates the flow of DT TPDUs between peer transport entities over a TC.

Explicit flow control is optional in class 2 (its use being negotiated as a part of TC establishment) and mandatory in classes 3 and 4. The initial credit parameter set during TC establishment acts as the initial value for the 'window' governing DT TPDU transmission. This window is subsequently manipulated by the receiving transport entity in order to control the flow into it from its peer. In general terms the window imposes a bound on the number of DT TPDUs that can be transmitted without further explicit acknowledgement. It is in an AcKnowledge (AK) TPDU that the receiver includes a parameter 'advancing' the window in the transmitter. A transport entity can, at any time, send an RJ TPDU to its peer to 'retreat' the window.

Clearly the imposition of transport flow control and the efficiency with which the transmitting transport entity responds to window adjustment may have a significant effect on throughput.

The precise mechanisms of flow control differ between classes, and once again the more inquisitive reader is recommended to consult the standards for greater detail.

7.2.3.17 Checksum

This procedure is only used by class 4 and is optional.

The checksum is a value calculated according to an algorithm defined in the protocol specification which has the octets comprising the TPDU with which it is associated as its arguments. This checksum is carried in the TPDU in a checksum parameter. After transmission over the network the checksum is recalculated (by the receiving transport entity) and compared against the value in the TPDU parameter. If the values differ then corruption is assumed, the TPDU discarded and no acknowledgement sent. This will result in the transmitting transport entity retransmitting the TPDU (discussed later as the *retransmission on timeout* procedure).

Although checksum is optional in this class, it is always used on the CR TPDU.

7.2.3.18 Frozen references

This is a procedure used by classes 1, 3 and 4 to ensure that a reference — the information relating to the 'identity' of a TC — is not reassigned to another TC after being 'frozen'. A reference is frozen because sequences such as the following can occur.

An NC has many assigned TCs (multiplexed) when a class 4 TC is released by the receiver. At the same time the sender retransmits unacknowledged TPDUs (using *retransmission after timeout* procedure). These are delivered by the NS provider to the releasing peer transport entity. Now, had that entity reused the reference in between release and receipt of these TPDUs then they would be incorrectly associated with the new TC and so cause problems.

References are frozen for an (implementation-determined) period to avoid such problems.

7.2.3.19 Retransmission on timeout

This is a procedure used only by class 4 to provide retransmission by the sender of TPDUs that appear to have become 'lost', the event causing this loss being unsignalled.

The transmitting transport entity detects lost (i.e. undelivered) TPDUs when it does not receive an acknowledgement during a fixed time period and when acknowledgements are known to be outstanding. On the occurrence of such an event, the first TPDU in the sequence (see the *retention until acknowledgement* procedure) of unacknowledged TPDUs is retransmitted and the 'timer' reset and left to expire. If acknowledgements are then received then all is, perhaps, well. However, after a certain number of retransmissions without acknowledgement the sending transport entity will invoke the *release* procedure and inform the TS user of the failure.

Note that a receiving transport entity may at any time send an RJ TPDU to invoke TPDU retransmission by the sender. This is not available in class 4, as its use there is incompatible with the receiver resequencing capability.

7.2.3.20 Resequencing

Used only by class 4, this procedure is used to sort any misordering of DT TPDUs by the NS provider. This is done so that each TSDU delivered to the TS user will have correctly ordered octets regardless of vagaries of the underlying network which may cause out of order TPDUs. Such misordering can occur when, say, a TSDU is segmented by the transmitting transport entity into many TPDUs, and where splitting — discussed in detail in the section on the *splitting and recombining* procedure — results in these TPDUs travelling between end-systems spread over a number of network connections. The possibility of a TPDU arriving in other than its transmission sequence in this case is clear.

This procedure also detects any duplicate DT TPDUs, and discards the duplicates. Duplication can occur, for instance, where there is heavy congestion on the network possibly resulting in the retransmission timeout expiring on the transmitting transport entity. This would result in the retransmission of a DT TPDU, even though the original was still in transit and would subsequently be delivered.

7.2.3.21 Inactivity control

Used only in class 4, this procedure deals with unsignalled termination of a network connection. It is invoked on the expiry of an inactivity timer maintained by the transport entity. This times the period over which no TPDU is received. It expires after a fairly lengthy interval and then invokes the *normal release* procedure. It must be a long interval since too short a one might result in a healthy, but congested, connection being timed out.

When no activity is underway over a TC the timer can be prevented from expiring by the occasional transmission of an AK TPDU.

7.2.3.22 Treatment of protocol errors

Used in all classes, this procedure is invoked when a TPDU is received that cannot be interpreted under the rules of the standard, when no error has been signalled and the checksum is consistent. The detecting transport entity will take one of the following steps:

(1) issue an ERror (ER) TPDU which will result in the transmitting transport entity invoking the release procedure appropriate to the class,
(2) invoke the release procedure appropriate to the class,
(3) reset or close the network connection.

The appropriate action is selected by the entity bearing in mind operational details. For instance, if the NC is shared by other TCs then (3) would be unwise with its knock-on effect on the other TCs. However, if it cannot associate the TPDU with a particular TC then it may not have any option but to take this course. Under certain circumstances it is possible to ignore the TPDU.

7.2.3.23 Splitting and recombining

This is a procedure used only by class 4 to enable a TC to make use of multiple NCs. The result of this can be increased throughput (to meet the required service level) or greater resilience against failure in particularly unreliable networks, or both. Once an association exists between one TC and many NCs, TPDUs of that TC can be transmitted over any of the NCs, and so the TPDUs may arrive at the peer transport entity out of sequence: the effect of this has already been discussed.

The initial TC establishment over a single NC will have established a class 4 transport service — for if not then splitting is unavailable. After this, either transport entity can assign the TC to a further new, or existing, NC, perhaps on detection of a fall in throughput.

7.2.4 Transport protocol data units

In examining the procedures that make up the transport protocol we have introduced all the TPDUs. They are summarized in Table 7.6.

Table 7.6 — TPDUs

TPDUs		Validity within classes				
		0	1	2	3	4
CR	Connect Request	★	★	★	★	★
CC	Connect Confirm	★	★	★	★	★
DR	Disconnect Request	★	★	★	★	★
DC	Disconnect Confirm	–	★	★	★	★
DT	DaTa	★	★	★	★	★
ED	Expedited Data	–	★	1	★	★
AK	data AcKnowledge	–	2	1	★	★
EA	Expedited data Ack.	–	★	1	★	★
RJ	ReJect	–	★	–	★	–
ER	TPDU ERror	★	★	★	★	★

–: not available in this class; ★: always available in this class; 1: not available if explicit flow control is not selected; 2: not available when confirmation of receipt variant is selected.

7.2.5 Use of network services

In achieving the transport service the peer transport entities make use of all or a subset of the network service elements shown in Table 7.7.

Table 7.7 — Network service elements

Service element	Type
N-CONNECT	confirmed
N-DATA	unconfirmed
N-DATA-ACKNOWLEDGE	unconfirmed
N-EXPEDITED-DATA	unconfirmed
N-RESET	confirmed
N-DISCONNECT	unconfirmed

7.2.6 Issues in connectionless operation

In Chapter 3 we introduced the concept of connectionless operation. Since then we have concentrated on connection-oriented operation simply because, for the higher layers, connectionless standards are under an earlier stage of development. Connectionless standards do however exist for the transport layer, and many existing subnetworks are connectionless in operation. It is therefore appropriate to look further at this topic. The reader can consider the implications, for connectionless operation in the upper layers, of the following two general points which round off our look at the interface to transport and the lower layers.

(1) A connectionless transport may offer only a single service, that of unconfirmed data transfer. In the connectionless standard this is provided by the T-UNITDATA service element, a service with four parameters:

    Called address
    Calling address
    Quality of service
    TS user data

(2) Connection-oriented transport service operation is possible over a connectionless network. In this case the network service is composed only of a single service, data transfer, provided by the N-UNITDATA service element, and so a transport entity operating over a connectionless network can transmit a CR TPDU immediately, there being no lower level connection to initiate and await.

7.3 EXPEDITED DATA

Here we finally examine expedited data. A general definition of the instances of this service in the higher layers is as follows:

Expedited data is a special form of data transfer. Data carried by an *n* expedited data service is guaranteed to arrive at the receiving *n* S user before any data subsequently transmitted by a call on any *n* data service. Indeed it is intended that data transferred by the use of *n* expedited data will, if possible, arrive *before* normal data already submitted for transmission by the *n* S user that has not yet been 'delivered'. It will not, however, arrive before any previously submitted, undelivered expedited data.

This service is made available to an application process by the P-EXPEDITED-DATA service element. In Chapter 6 we saw that the session expedited service was negotiable. The availability of the presentation expedited service depends upon successful negotiation of this. Session expedited data can only be successfully negotiated if the session FU is implemented in both peer session entities, and if the transport expedited data service is available.

It is at the transport layer that the mechanics of expedited data become visible. We therefore concentrate on this layer.

The service in the transport layer depends upon the class selection: if class 0 is selected then the service will not be available. In classes 2, 3 and 4 the expedited effect is provided entirely within the transport layer. Expedited TSDUs are sent as ED TPDUs over network normal data service. In class 1 the expedited effect will be provided by the expedited mechanism within the transport layer, together with the use of network expedited data service to convey ED TPDUs. If this network service is not available, then the network normal data service will be used.

7.3.1 Achieving the expedited effect

The transport layer provides flow control between transmitting and receiving end-systems, either by use of explicit transport activity or of the network data acknowledgement service (see the explicit flow control procedure). It is by examination of the effect of such flow control mechanisms that we shall see how the expedited effect is achieved.

Under the direction of flow control, managed by the receiving transport entity, the transmitting transport entity will be either (a) able to send data, or (b) blocked from sending data through flow control restriction.

Consider a transport entity in state (b). This state will be 'released' to state (a) by a flow control activity initiated by the receiving entity. An efficient use of the network for 'bulk' data transmission will only be achieved if a transport entity in state (b) continues to accept data requests from the transmitting TS user even though it cannot then service them. In this way, when state (a) is entered the transmitting entity will have a 'queue' of data requests ready to be effected, thus eliminating any delay inherent in managing a restrictive flow control mechanism over a TSAP in the transmitting end-system. Some flow control is necessary here since the transport entity will not have resource (i.e. buffers) to manage an infinite data request queue; but such flow control will occur in 'parallel' with that between peer transport entities instead of 'sequentially' which is inherently inefficient.

At the very least one TSDU should be immediately available for transfer when state (a) is entered. The size of the 'pending TSDU' queue is purely an implementation detail: what we are interested in here is how this reflects on the provision of expedited data.

Consider Figure 7.6. At the time that the first time sequence event (1) occurs, the transmitting end-system, A, is in a (b) state. This diagram demonstrates the simple aspects of queue management. If now we were to suppose that just before event (4), the flow control 'release', there was a T-EXPEDITED-DATA request, then we can see that, by the use of the following rule for TSDU queuing, the expedited effect would be achieved once (4) occurs.

> If there is nothing on TSDU queue then place the expedited TSDU at head. Otherwise if any expedited TSDU is already on the queue then place the new expedited TSDU after all existing expedited TSDUs. Otherwise place it at the head of the queue.

This rule ensures that the definition of 'expedited' is adhered to.

Clearly there will be resource-constrained end-systems whose implementations are such that queuing mechanisms are not available. In this case the provision of a real expedited capability may not be possible, even though the class demands that the service be offered. There is no conflict in this since the expedited effect is defined such that an expedited TSDU being handled as though it were a normal TSDU meets the definition of expedited data, that is, 'arriving at the receiving TS user before a subsequently submitted normal or expedited TSDU.

Now consider the possibilities in the receiving transport entity. Here it is possible that the rate of receipt of TSDUs is in excess of the capability of the TS user to accept them. Either flow control between peer transport entities will then be used to keep the rate of receipt in line with the capability of the receiving TS user, or the

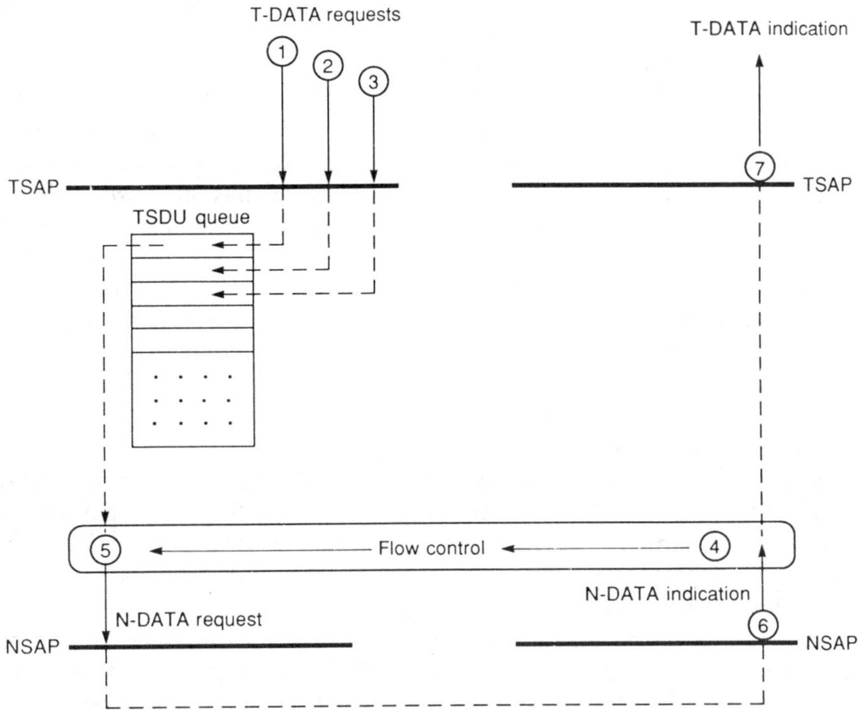

Fig. 7.6 — Flow control within the transport layer.

implementation of the receiving transport entity may invoke a received TSDU queuing mechanism. Considering this the reader should see how this also offers opportunities for the 'true' expedited effect to be realized.

7.4 QUALITY OF SERVICE

In the description of the presentation layer we saw a QOS parameter associated with the P-CONNECT service element which exists solely to give the application process access to the corresponding parameter of the session service element, S-CONNECT. Unlike the presentation layer, session-specific activity is implied by the QOS parameter; this includes monitoring and maintaining session services to a level agreed by negotiation between peers as part of connection establishment. There are also aspects of the QOS parameter of S-CONNECT that relate directly to the reliable data transfer environment required to service the session connection. These aspects are included in the QOS parameter of the T-CONNECT service element.

We now examine the QOS parameter of S-CONNECT, and its relationship to session layer activity and to the QOS parameter of T-CONNECT.

QOS can be expressed as a set of *performance criteria*. There are criteria covering each of the phases of the session service. They fall into two groups, speed and accuracy/reliability, shown in Table 7.8. The session QOS parameter is in fact a list of parameters, each related to one of the performance criteria.

The **session connection establishment delay** parameter puts a bound on the maximum acceptable time between the S-CONNECT request and the corresponding confirm. If this value is exceeded then the session entity initiating the connection will fail that connection attempt, inform the SS user of the failure, and 'clean up'—which may involve issuing a T-DISCONNECT request if the TC has been established.

The **session connection establishment failure probability** parameter is a bound on the maximum ratio of failures (of the 'delay' type) to establish a connection against the total requests over a measured sample. If this ratio is greater than the parameter value then the session entity will not attempt connection establishment. The session connection release parameters have similar meaning. The 'delay' in question is that between an S-U-ABORT request and the total release of the session connection. The release probability parameter dictates whether a connection is to be attempted, given the probability of release failure from a given sample.

Throughput gives the minimum acceptable rate of transfer of octets (SSDUs) between peer SS users over the session connection. It is specified for each direction of 'flow', initiator to responder and vice versa, and it relates only to normal and typed data transfer. This figure is negotiated between SS users and, perhaps, modified by the SS provider during connection establishment.

Transit delay gives the maximum acceptable delay, during the data transfer phase, between the servicing by a session entity of a service request and the issuing of the corresponding indication by the peer entity. It is specified for both directions of activity, the calculation being based upon some average size of SS user data associated with such service primitive 'pairs'.

Residual error rate gives the acceptable ratio of total lost, incorrect and duplicated units of SS user data to the total units presented over the SSAP over a measured period of the data transfer phase.

Transit delay, throughput or residual error rates falling below the acceptable levels result in the failure of the transfer and a 'failure' indication being given to the SS user (an S-P-ABORT or S-P-EXCEPTION-REPORT indication).

Transfer failure probability gives the maximum acceptable probability of total failure of the SS provider. If the actual observed total failure rates over a measured sample of transfers is greater than the value of this QOS parameter then the connection establishment requested by the SS user will not be attempted. A transfer, for sampling purposes, can generally be regarded as the duration of an individual session connection, and a failure of a transfer as an S-P-ABORT or S-P-EXCEPTION-REPORT indication that results from one of the last three criteria being infringed.

Session connection resilience is a maximum acceptable probability of total failure of the SS provider by non-SS user-initiated events, that is, those resulting in S-P-ABORT or S-P-EXCEPTION-REPORT indications, including the above data transfer-related failures. Again, if a measured sample indicates a greater probability then the session connection is not attempted.

Consideration of the QOS criteria shows that all have meaning not only to the session layer but also to the transport layer. For instance, the SS provider comprises peer session entities and the TS provider, and so aspects such as throughput are

Table 7.8 — Quality of service performance criteria

Phase	Speed criteria	Accuracy/reliability criteria
Connection establishment	Establishment delay	Establishment failure probability
Connection release	Release delay	Release failure probability
Data transfer	Throughput	Residual error rate
	Transit delay	Connection resilience
		Transfer failure probability

determined by the costs associated with the operaration of the peer session entities set against the potential throughput provided by the TS provider. Clearly then, the throughput required of the TS provider must be greater than that required of the SS provider in order to make up for the costs associated with the SS provider. It follows that in issuing a T-CONNECT request, a session entity must calculate an appropriate 'throughput' QOS parameter with respect to the transport layer. Generally, then, there is a set of QOS parameters associated with a transport connection for which the session implementation will determine values based upon those of the equivalent session QOS parameters.

We can now see that it is the QOS performance criteria related to the data transfer phase of transport that dictate the level of network service enhancement to be achieved by the transport layer; for example, splitting to achieve increased throughput.

There are other QOS criteria unrelated to performance which are associated with session and transport. **Connection priority** is concerned with the relationship of one connection to another and is a measure of relative importance. If, by some necessity, the general QOS of a connection is to be degraded, for example through loss of a network connection, then it will be the lower priority connections that suffer the effects first. If connections must be broken to maintain the general service level then it is this priority that determines which are broken. **Connection protection** is a security parameter which requests that a connection has a certain level of protection against monitoring or manipulation. There are four such levels: no protection; protection against passive monitoring; protection against monitoring, replay, addition or deletion; and the combination of the last two.

A transport entity determines equivalent QOS parameters for the NS provider based upon its 'experience' and capability, together with the constraining values put upon it by the T-CONNECT request QOS parameters. These NS provider QOS parameters will be included with the N-CONNECT request (connection-oriented operation), or with the N-UNITDATA request (connectionless).

8

File transfer access and management, FTAM

8.1 INTRODUCTION

The ISO application standard FTAM is defined in a five part document, ISO 8571. Part one is a general introduction to FTAM. Part two introduces the concept of a *virtual filestore*, which, as we shall see, is central to system-independent remote file manipulation. Part three is the file service definition. Part four is the file protocol specification. Finally, part five is a standard form that, once completed by an implementor, becomes the definitive description of the capabilities and limitations of a particular FTAM product. This part is called the *protocol implementation conformance statement proforma*.

In this chapter we shall look generally at the standard, at the services it makes available, and at the realization of these services. It is not possible to capture the scope of the standard and associated implementation issues in so short an examination, but the essence of the subject can be captured. It is hoped that the reader can progress from this, if necessary, to the standard itself.

FTAM offers three modes of file manipulation: *transfer*, *access* and *management*.

File transfer is the movement, over OSI, of a complete file between two filestores on different end-systems. File access is the reading, writing or deleting of selected parts (e.g. records) of a file residing in a filestore on one end-system, actioned over OSI by a user on some remote end-system. File management involves remotely reading or altering attributes (e.g. filename) that define a file within the filestore in which it resides.

Peer application FTAM entities, each as a part of peer application FTAM-based processes, provide services that make such activity possible. In this chapter we shall use the diagrammatic form introduced in Chapter 4 (Figure 4.1), which demonstrates the relationship between the application layer, an application entity and an application process. In that chapter we introduced the concept of the application process and suggested an architecture that had two components, entity and agent, interfacing via application service primitives. The purpose of introducing such a rigid model was to explain the relationship between the ISORM and the system on which an implementation of ISO/OSI is mounted. The actual implementation of an application process may not necessarily follow such an architecture — indeed it may be implemented as a single unit with no discernible boundary between the system-independent aspects (the entity) and the system-dependent (the agent). In this case there would be no 'exposed' interface on the end-system to the services presented in the service definition of the application standard. This is possible because the application service definition is a definition of an *abstract* interface: it defines the capability of the application but does not prescribe implementation of that interface. The advantage of implementing an application process in this way is efficiency: interaction between the protocol machine and real system resource would not have to go through an arbitrary interface mechanism.

In FTAM terms there might be no user access to the type of interface defined by the service definition on an end-system, but only access to a higher level 'command' environment that is, in effect, a synthesis of aspects of the service definition, for example, 'COPY File X to File Y at computer system Z'. Bearing this in mind we shall progress with FTAM while continuing to use the concept of distinct agent and entity for explanatory purposes.

Consider the case where a user on computer system A invokes an FTAM process with a request for a file to be transferred to his filestore from the filestore of some remote computer system, B. Before any FTAM-specific activity can be undertaken by the initiating FTAM process, an association must be established, by use of ACSE, between it and a peer process on the 'target' end-system. This peer process is invoked specifically to service such an association, having been identified by SAP addressing. Once the association is established the FTAM process will use FTAM services to realize the file transfer. Figure 8.1 summarizes the basic activity.

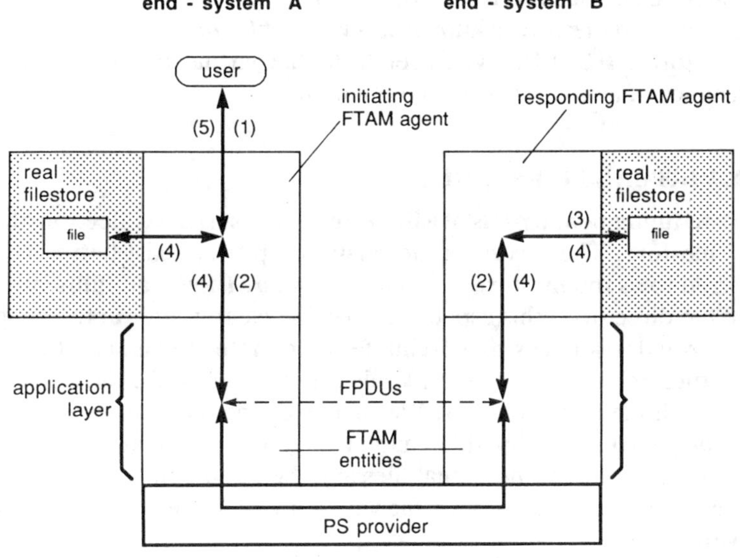

Fig. 8.1 — Use of FTAM.

(1) The user requests the file transfer which results in an association being established between peer FTAM processes.
(2) The initiating FTAM process uses a service whose function is to identify, to the responding FTAM process, the file in B's filestore which is to be the object of subsequent activity.
(3) The responding FTAM process successfully identifies the file in question.
(4) The FTAM process on A now uses another service to effect the transfer of the file contents at B into the specified file in A's filestore.
(5) The user is informed of the success (or otherwise) of his request.

Clearly, there is a master and slave relationship between two FTAM processes. The master, or *initiating* FTAM process is invoked by a local user request, and supplied with information about the local and remote files which are to be operated upon. The slave, or *responding* FTAM process is subsequently awoken on the remote end-system to become the cooperating peer; its activity is governed solely by the requirements of the initiating FTAM process.

Since the initiating FTAM process has immediate access to the filestore on its local end-system, we can assume that its agent fully understands the structure of its local filestore and of the local file identified by the initiating user. However, the responding FTAM process is not instructed by local user action, but by a remote peer process. The information presented to the responding agent with regard to the file and filestore on its own end-system will be conveyed over OSI in a PDU exchange between the peer FTAM entities.

Given the system independent nature of OSI, this filestore related information will not be presented in terms specific to the nature of the responding end-system but in terms of some 'generalized' filestore. The responding agent can then relate the FTAM 'generalized' filestore to its own real filestore.

This generalized filestore is known as a *virtual filestore* and effectively models all possible filestores. FTAM services relate to the virtual filestore and not to any specific instance of a real filestore (see Figure 8.2).

8.2 THE VIRTUAL FILESTORE

There are two fundamental parts of a filestore. The first is the collection of files stored within the filestore. The second is the relationships that exist between the files — often referred to as the filestore's *directory structure* (if you are unfamiliar with the concept of file directories this aspect will become clearer later in the chapter).

FTAM provides services that facilitate the remote management of a filestore's directory structure, e.g. creation and deletion of directories, moving (or copying) files from one directory to another. We shall examine these services in a section on *filestore management* later in this chapter. For now we concentrate on services related to manipulation of individual files and their contents.

In this context we can consider a file within a virtual filestore as being defined by the following:

(a) a single filename, allowing it to be identified without ambiguity;
(b) attributes expressing properties such as accounting information and history (for example, 'date and time of creation');

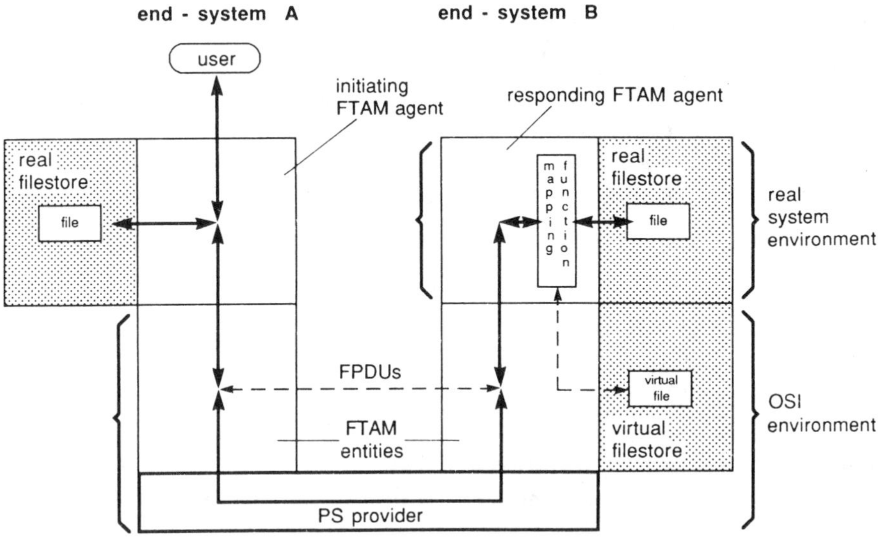

Fig. 8.2 — The virtual store.

(c) attributes defining the logical structure and dimensions of the information stored within the file;
(d) information units (if any) that make up the contents of the file, the relationship between information units being defined by (c).

The attributes (a), (b) and (c) above are known as *file attributes* and together they represent a file as it is actually 'stored' in the real filestore. File attributes remain constant throughout the lifetime of a file on a real filestore unless they are modified. Such modification can be performed either by a 'user' on the end-system on which the file is resident, or by an FTAM activity initiated by a remote user over OSI.

There is a second category of attributes known as *activity attributes*. These attributes describe the relationship between a file in a filestore on a (responding) end-system, and a remote (initiating) FTAM process. They only have scope whilst an FTAM dialogue is in progress as they are of no relevance to an end-system and its real filestore outside such a dialogue. They hold such information as 'identity of FTAM activity initiator' and 'current accumulated costs of this dialogue'.

The following is a list of the primary file and activity attributes relating to file manipulation.

File Attributes:

Filename	Permitted actions	Access control
Storage account	File availability	Contents type
Encryption name	Filesize	Future filesize
Legal qualification	Private use	

Date and time of: Creation

Last modification
Last read access
Last attribute modification

Identity of: Creator
Last modifier
Last reader
Last attribute modifier.

Activity attributes:

Current access request	Current initiator identity
Current access passwords	Current calling application entity title
Current account	Current responding application entity title
Current access context	Current concurrency control
Current location	Current processing mode

Many have obvious meanings while others have different degrees of obscurity. By the end of the chapter the meaning and use of most of them should have become clear.

8.3 FTAM FILE MANIPULATION SERVICES

The FTAM ASE offers a file service which is provided by a considerable number of component service elements. An association between peer FTAM processes is achieved by the use of ACSE (see Chapter 4). As in other standards the service elements of FTAM are grouped into FUs, each group containing the service elements related to a specific aspect of FTAM service.

The FTAM FUs related to general service provision and to file manipulation are:

Kernel	Read	Write
File access	Limited file management	Enhanced file management
Grouping	Recovery	Restart

Once an association has been established the next activity is the determination of the FTAM operational environment which is to exist over the association. This environment, known as an *FTAM regime*, is defined by the set of FUs available for use during the lifetime of the FTAM regime. The kernel FU must be available in all FTAM regimes; it contains the service element that determines, by negotiation, the FTAM regime itself. At least this and one other FU are required to make an FTAM regime productive; for example, kernel and write FUs together constitute an FTAM regime that permits the user on the initiating end-system to transfer a complete file to the responding filestore.

During FTAM regime establishment the peer FTAM processes negotiate the inclusion of FUs into the regime. If a FU is negotiated into an FTAM regime then *all* its associated services must be supported by both FTAM entities — an FU cannot be 'partially' supported.

Because there are a relatively large number of FUs, the possibility of disagreement in the negotiation of the FTAM regime is increased. To simplify negotiation, the standard defines a set of *services classes*. Each class defines a set of FUs designed to address a typical application requirement. In each class the presence of certain FUs is mandatory whilst others are optional. In negotiating the FTAM regime the initiating process proposes the use of a particular service class; the responding process may accept this proposal, or may offer a counter proposal. The negotiation of the inclusion of optional FUs of a negotiated service class is also a part of this regime establishment. The following service classes are defined:

The *transfer* class allows movement of files or parts of files between end-systems. It places emphasis on simple operation with a minimum of overhead, before and after information transfer.

The *management* class allows reading and modification of file attributes, but has no information transfer mechanisms.

The *transfer and management* class combines the features of the first two classes.

The *access* class permits the location of a specific part of a file (for example, record) in the responding filestore. The 'located' part can then be either read, written or erased by the initiator.

The *unconstrained* class leaves the selection of FUs open to negotiation by the peer FTAM processes. It is in effect a class with the mandatory kernel FU, and all other FUs optional.

The relationship between FUs and service classes is summarized in Table 8.1.

Note that the selection of enhanced file management entails selection of limited file management.

8.3.1 Service elements

An FTAM regime is established between peer FTAM processes by use of the F-INITIALIZE service element. This is in fact done in parallel with association establishment (more on this later in this chapter). Once the FTAM regime has been agreed, the service elements available during the regime will be known. An FTAM regime is terminated by the use of either F-TERMINATE or F-ABORT.

Throughout this section we shall use time diagrams to expand on the interrelationships of service elements. In these, time flows from left to right; use of a service element is indicated by a vertical line. For instance an FTAM regime is represented by Figure 8.3.

The kernel FU, which includes all three service elements in this diagram, is always included in an FTAM regime. F-INITIALIZE offers a confirmed service bringing about, by negotiation, an FTAM regime. F-TERMINATE offers a confirmed service only available to the initiator of the FTAM regime. It brings about an orderly closing of the regime and has a single parameter, used only by the responder in the response, to convey any details of 'costs' incurred by the initiator at the responding end-system during this regime. Either FTAM process can effect a disorderly closing of the FTAM regime by use of F-ABORT.

Now consider Figure 8.4. The first of the inner regimes, the *file selection* regime, is established to identify a specific file (in the filestore at the responder) which is to be the object of subsequent activity. The regime is established by use of either of two service elements. Using the F-SELECT service element (confirmed), the FTAM

Table 8.1 — Relationship between FTAM FUs and service classes

FU	Service classes					Services	Service elements
	T	A	M	TM	U		
Kernel	M	M	M	M	M	Regime establishment	F-INITIALIZE
						Orderly regime release	F-TERMINATE
						Disorderly regime release	F-ABORT
						File selection	F-SELECT
						File de-selection	F-DESELECT
Read	*	M	—	*	O	Read bulk data	F-READ
						Data unit transfer	F-DATA
						End of data transfer	F-DATA-END
						End of transfer	F-TRANSFER-END
						Cancel data transfer	F-CANCEL
						File open	F-OPEN
						File close	F-CLOSE
Write	*	M	—	*	O	Write bulk data	F-WRITE
						Data unit transfer	F-DATA
						End of data transfer	F-DATA-END
						End of transfer	F-TRANSFER-END
						Cancel data transfer	F-CANCEL
						File open	F-OPEN
						File close	F-CLOSE
File access	—	M	—	—	O	Locate	F-LOCATE
						Erase	F-ERASE
Limited file management	O	O	M	O	O	File creation	F-CREATE
						File deletion	F-DELETE
						Read attributes	F-READ-ATTRIB
Enhanced file management	O	O	M	O	O	Change attributes	F-CHANGE-ATTRIB
Grouping	M	O	M	M	O	Beginning of grouping	F-BEGIN-GROUP
						End of grouping	F-END-GROUP
Recovery	O	O	—	O	O	Regime recovery	F-RECOVERY
						Checkpointing	F-CHECK
						Cancel data transfer	F-CANCEL
Restart data transfer	O	O	—	O	O	Restarting data transfer	F-RESTART
						Checkpointing	F-CHECK
						Cancel data transfer	F-CANCEL

M: mandatory; O: optional; —: not available; *: at least one of read or write must be included.

regime initiator opens a file selection regime by identifying a file that already exists in the responder's filestore. The parameters associated with the request/indication carry, amongst other things, the authority by which the initiator requests access to this file. The use of F-CREATE has a similar effect, except that a new file is created in the responder's filestore. A file selection regime is closed by use of either of F-DESELECT or F-DELETE service elements, the latter causing the file in question to be destroyed. As with F-SELECT, there are authority parameters associated with all the file selection regime services. Once a file selection regime has been established all subsequent activity, until the regime is closed, is assumed to be directed at the specified file.

Consider Figure 8.5. We see that the atomic activities associated with file

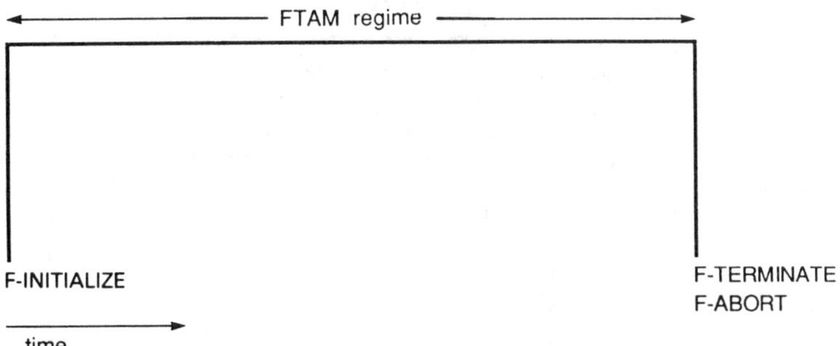

Fig. 8.3 — FTAM regime.

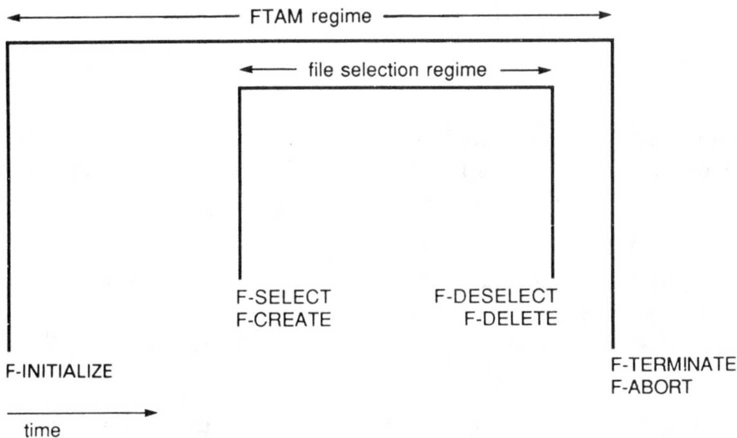

Fig. 8.4 — Within the FTAM regime.

management can be undertaken during a file selection regime when no further inner regime is in force. These activities are achieved by use of the service elements F-READ-ATTRIBUTE and F-CHANGE-ATTRIBUTE, both being confirmed. Clearly these activities are directed at the file identified with the file selection regime in the responder's filestore

The successful establishment of a file selection regime implies that a file has been identified in the responder's filestore and that authority for the initiators right of access has been confirmed. Before the 'contents' of the file can become the object of activity, the file must be 'opened' — a *file open* regime must be established. It is opened by use of F-OPEN and closed by use of F-CLOSE, both confirmed. Only one file open regime can be in force at any time. In order to understand what is achieved

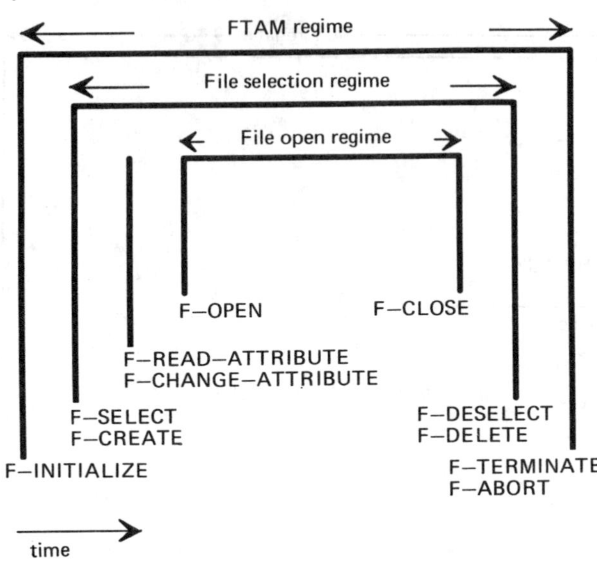

Fig. 8.5 — File open regime.

in establishing this regime we have to consider the selected file's contents in terms of structure and syntax (not semantics). We saw in the section on the virtual filestore that a file is defined by four elements, two of these, (c) and (d), being concerned with contents:

(c) Structural attributes defining the logical structure and dimensions of the information stored within the file.
(d) Information units (if any) that make up the contents of the file, the relationship between the information units being defined by (c).

In this chapter we shall henceforth refer to an 'information unit' as a 'data unit', as it is the term used in the standard.

Associated with every data unit (DU) is an abstract syntax; note the tie-in with presentation layer terminology (Chapter 5). All the DUs which comprise a file may have the same abstract syntax or there may be a wide range of abstract syntaxes associated with one file. File structure is defined in terms of DUs and of their positional relationships. For the purpose of structural expression a general hierarchical model has been included in the FTAM standard. We shall examine this model later.

Once a file selection regime is established, and if file activity involving the transfer of DUs of that file is required, then it is essential that the structure of the file at the responder be understood by both initiator and responder. Such understanding is in terms of the virtual filestore. Now consider the case where an initiator is to write DUs to a newly created file (F-CREATE) in the responder's filestore. At this stage the responder will not know the intended structure of the file. Similarly, where the initiator is to read DUs from, or write DUs to, an existing file at the responder, it does not at this stage have any knowledge of the structure of the file; that information being contained within the responder's filestore. One purpose, then, of the confirmed F-OPEN is to convey the structural information between FTAM processes in the appropriate direction, initiator to responder or vice versa. This is done by use of the F-OPEN **contents type** parameter. Another function of this service element is to establish the presentation service requirements of any data transfers which are to occur during this file open regime; i.e. a statement of the abstract syntax(es) associated with the file. Once a file open regime has been successfully established, the presentation service provider will have established a negotiated defined context set for the abstract syntax(es) in question; use of the presentation service is discussed later.

A DU is the smallest identifiable file element, so far as FTAM is concerned. It is the basic unit of data transfer between peer FTAM processes within a file open regime. The abstract syntax associated with each DU determines the action required by the presentation layer to ensure a common representation during transfer. The relationship between the DUs which comprise a file, the *file access structure*, is defined in the framework of the general hierarchical model, which represents the file as it appears within the virtual filestore. The mapping between the real file, and the virtual file with its file access structure is performed by the local FTAM agent. Figure 8.6 is an example of an hierarchical file structure in the virtual filestore.

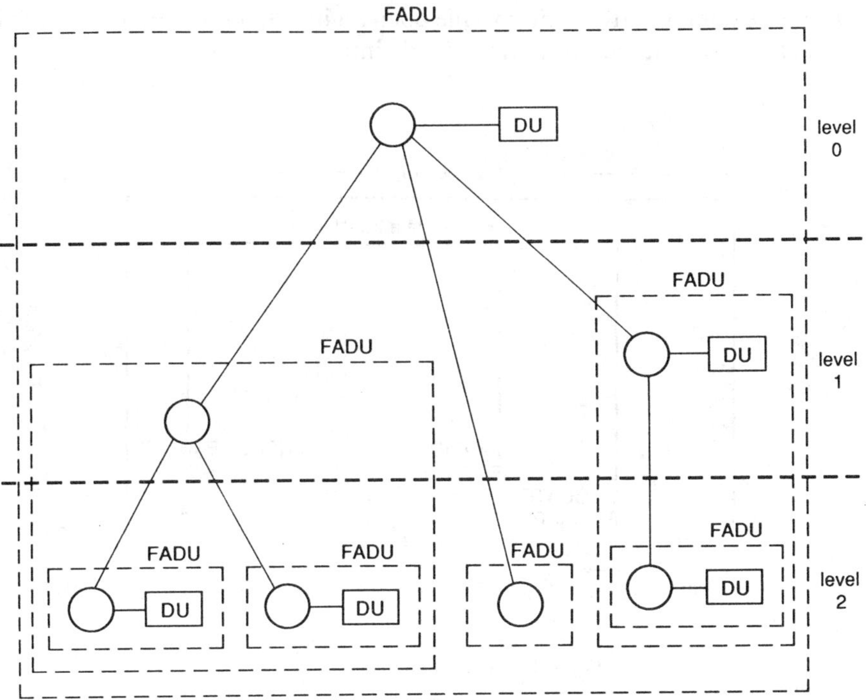

Fig. 8.6 — Virtual file structure.

Each node of the file access structure may have associated with it zero or one DU. It may also point to further nodes at lower levels of the structure. A *file access data unit* (FADU) is defined as a node together with all nodes at lower levels for which this particular node is a 'root' node. Clearly, then, each node at level 1, for which the node at level 0 is root, is a part of that FADU but is also, in this case, the root of another (subordinate) FADU. A 'terminating' node is a node which does not point to any nodes at a lower level; it may, like all other nodes, have an associated DU.

Now, whereas DUs are the object of data transfer, FADUs are the object of data *location* within the file open regime. A reference to a particular FADU is also a reference to all subordinate FADUs, and thus to all DUs associated with these FADUs. Each FADU can be assigned a 'name'. It is the responsibility of the responding FTAM process to relate the file access structure of the virtual file to the actual file structure in the real filestore, and the names of FADUs to actual indexing within the real file.

Some common forms of real file together with their representation within the FTAM virtual filestore are as follows:

- Unstructured file: a single FADU and its associated DU.
- Sequential flat file: a single level 0 FADU (with no DU) as root node to unnamed FADUs at level 1, each of which is a terminating node with an associated DU. This models Fortran sequential I/O.
- Ordered flat file: as above, with all level 1 FADUs named.

We can now examine activity within a file open regime. Consider Figure 8.7. Services concerned with activity in this regime divide into two groups.

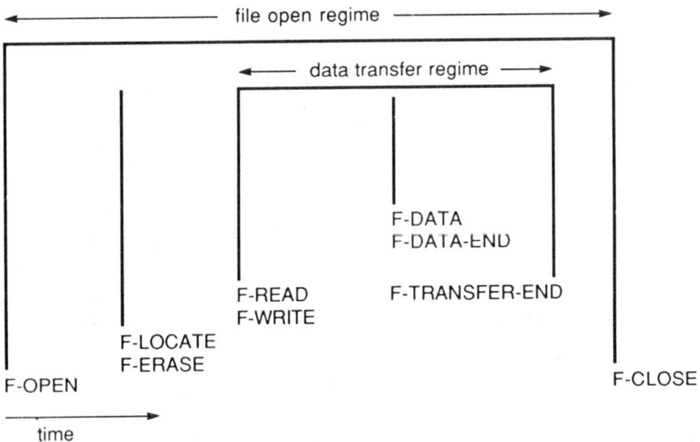

Fig. 8.7 — Within the file open regime.

The first group is concerned with providing management services to the initiator. In this group there are two service elements, F-LOCATE and F-ERASE. The first allows the initiator to locate a specific point in the file at the responder by reference to a FADU in the virtual file. As a result of using this confirmed service, the initiator knows that subsequent activity undertaken by it will be understood to relate to this FADU. F-ERASE also offers a confirmed service and results in a specific FADU being identified. It causes the FADU in question to be erased from the file structure, the DUs contained within it being destroyed.

The second group of services is concerned with the transfer of data between end-system's filestores, from initiator to responder or vice versa. These services can operate only within a regime, the *data transfer* regime, established by use of either of the F-READ or F-WRITE service elements. Which of these is used determines the subsequent direction of flow of DUs: F-READ implies responder to initiator, and F-WRITE initiator to responder. Until such a regime is created DUs cannot be exchanged between peer FTAM processes. The regime is terminated by use of F-TRANSFER-END. The F-READ and F-WRITE services also convey, in parameter form, the identity of the FADU that is the object of subsequent DU transfer within the regime. If F-READ is used then no physical change of the file contents can occur at the responder. However, certain file attributes may be altered: for example, 'identity of last reader'. If F-WRITE is used then a further parameter is included to specify the actual form of write activity that is to take place on the file in the responder's filestore (for example, 'replace', 'extend', etc.). Once the data transfer regime has been established, the transfer of DUs can commence. The data transmitting FTAM process uses a separate instance of the F-DATA service (unconfirmed) to transfer each DU associated with the FADU. The order in which the DUs associated with an FADU are transmitted is defined by the 'FTAM virtual filestore hierarchical file structure traversal algorithm'. For example, consider the sequential flat file represented by Figure 8.8. Here, the FADU transfer will result in three calls on F-DATA, one for each for DUs (a), (b) and (c), and in that order.

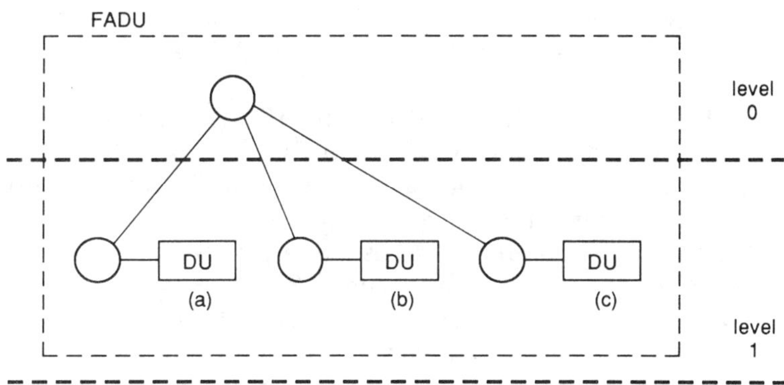

Fig. 8.8 — Ordered DU transfer.

When all the DUs associated with a FADU are transferred the following occurs:

Read: The responder issues F-DATA-END request to signal the end of the data transfer; it is unconfirmed. On receipt of the indication the initiator issues an F-TRANSFER-END request (confirmed) to close the data transfer regime.

Write: The initiator issues an F-DATA-END request to indicate that all DUs have been transmitted, followed by an F-TRANSFER-END request to terminate the regime. The responder will not issue the F-TRANSFER-END response until all data has been secured.

Within a file open regime, any number of consecutive data transfer regimes can be established, each associated with a (root) FADU. Furthermore, any number of consecutive file open regimes can be established within a file selection regime and any number of consecutive file selection regimes can be established within an FTAM association regime.

We have covered the primary services of FTAM and the reader should have a feel for the scope of the standard. There are, however, other services that appeared in the summary table but which have not yet been discussed. We shall examine these briefly, now.

In the Read and Write FUs there is a service, provided by F-CANCEL, for the cancellation of a data transfer. This can be used only within a data transfer regime by the initiator or responder. It is a confirmed service that abruptly terminates the regime.

The Grouping FU is provided by a pair of service elements, F-BEGIN-GROUP and F-END-GROUP. It is used by the initiator only, to allow more than a single regime to be established or closed in a single exchange between peer FTAM processes. F-BEGIN-GROUP indicates to the responder that the initiator is about to activate a set of 'grouped' service elements. It includes, as a parameter to the F-BEGIN-GROUP request, a threshold parameter which tells the responder how many responses it may defer (but only if the individual grouped activities are each successful) before it need take responsive action. F-END-GROUP conveys the end of such a grouping to the responder. The use of grouping reduces the number of interactions between end-systems over OSI and so potentially increases efficiency, especially in the case where small and regular file transactions occur between the end-systems.

The checkpointing service, provided by the F-CHECK service element, is only required if either of the recovery or restart FUs, or both, are selected over the association regime. This service element provides a facility for the insertion of check points in the flow of data in the data transfer regime. It is a confirmed service. On receipt of an F-CHECK confirm, the transmitting process knows that the data up to a specific point has been received and secured. Should some failure in data transfer subsequently occur, use of the restart FU will enable the data transfer to be restarted without having to retransmit data which has been transferred and secured. The transmitting FTAM process may continue to transmit data and further checkpoints without waiting for an F-CHECK confirm, but only until the point where a certain number (i.e. window) of checkpoints remain without response. The size of this checkpoint window is a subject of negotiation between FTAM processes during FTAM regime establishment. The F-RESTART service element, providing a confirmed service, is reliant on F-CHECK. It can be used by either FTAM process to interrupt a data transfer in progress and, by negotiation, agree a point in the secured data at which the data transfer can be restarted. The F-RECOVER service element provides for a file open regime to be re-established after failure, so that activity can be resumed from some point which can be identified from records of the failed regime. If the recovery FU is selected over a regime, then both initiator and responder will store regime records in a docket associated with that FTAM regime.

8.4 FTAM FILESTORE MANAGEMENT SERVICES

Before looking at the filestore management services provided by FTAM, we need to examine the virtual filestore a little further.

The inclusion of filestore management facilities, and the definition of a virtual filestore model, was a later (1989) addendum to the FTAM standard and this work introduced refinements to the original ISO 8571 view of the world. These refinements will unfold as this section of the chapter progresses.

Throughout the remainder of this chapter we shall no longer talk of a file as being a complex object composed of (potentially) structured information elements; instead we shall regard a file as a single indivisible unit which can be the object of filestore management activity (e.g. moved from one directory to another). Indeed within the standard, in the context of filestore management, a file is talked of as an *object*.

There are also two other types of virtual filestore object: *file-directories* and *references*. Each of the object types has an associated set of attributes. We have already discussed those of the file object type — file attributes — earlier in the chapter.

We shall give a precise definition of both file-directory and reference, and, by use of an example, introduce the scope of the virtual filestore model.

The **virtual filestore** is defined as being capable of containing an arbitrary number of objects. The absolute minimum is one, i.e. a *root* object that can either be a file-directory or, where the virtual filestore consists only of a single file, a file. There is only ever one root object (i.e. an object without a parent) in a virtual filestore. A **file-directory** is an object that maintains a parenthood relationship with zero or more subordinate objects, i.e. with other file-directories, files, or references. A **reference** maintains a link to precisely one other object which must be either a file-directory or a file. An object in a virtual filestore is identified by a *pathname*, which itself comprises a series of objects.

File-directories give an hierarchical structure to a virtual filestore that has at its root a single file-directory. As will become clear in the following example, references provide a simple tool for allowing objects to appear in more than a single place in the virtual filestore without the implicit necessity for file duplication.

Consider Figure 8.9. here we see the root file-directory with three subordinate file-directories A, E, and G. File-directory A has three subordinate objects, two files, B and C, and a reference, D. File-directory E is parent to a single object, file F; and so on. In this example the file object F has a primary pathname of E, F. However, it also has a number of other pathnames:

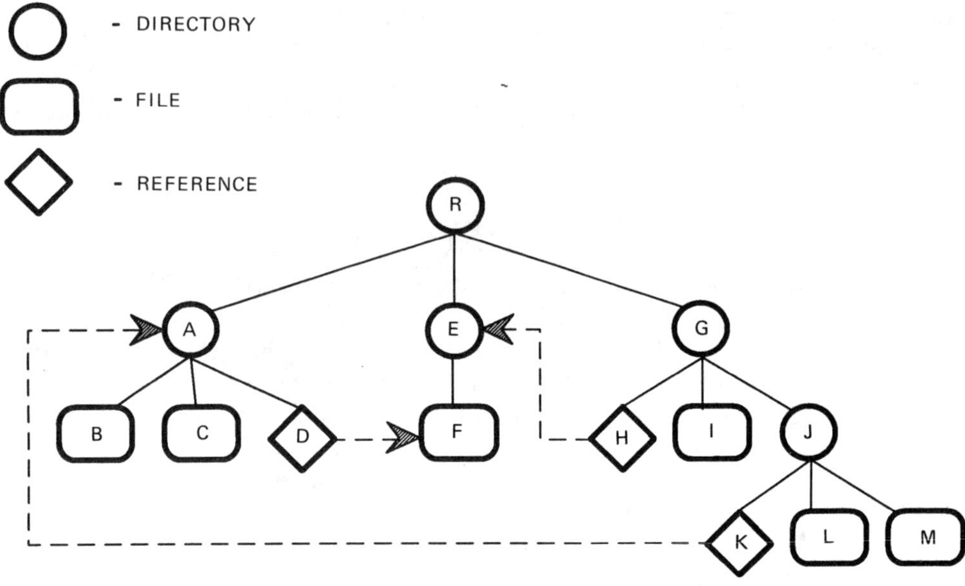

Fig. 8.9 — An example file directory.

(1) A,D
(2) G,H,F
(3) G,J,K,D

Notice that, when constructing a pathname, if a reference lies in the path then the reference to an object replaces that object in the pathname. The apparent structure of the filestore defined in this example is illustrated in Figure 8.10.

8.4.1 Object attributes

In section 8.2 we introduced a number of file attributes. Some of these, together with others not yet introduced, can be applied not only to file objects, but also to both file-directory and reference objects. Within the standard this group of attributes are referred to as *generic object attributes*.

These generic attributes are as follows:

Object name	Object type	Primary pathname
Storage account	Legal qualifications	Access control
Permitted actions	Object size	Future object size

Unique permanent identifier
Identity of: Creator
Last attribute modifier
Date and time of: Creation
Last attribute modification

The generic attribute *primary pathname* holds a complete pathname for the

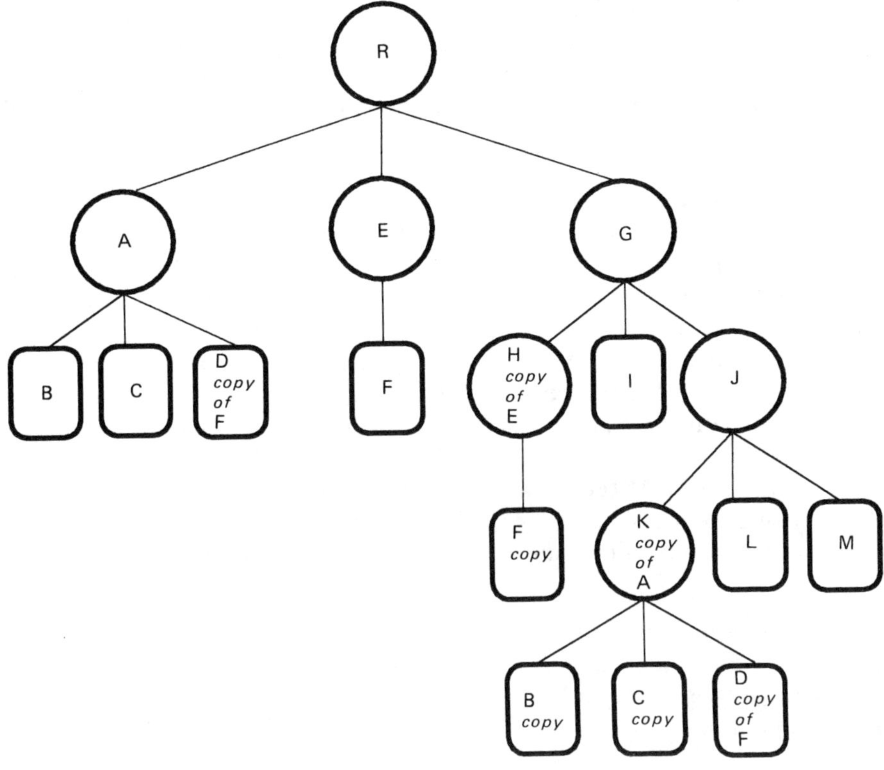

Fig. 8.10 — Apparent filestore structure.

object defined from the root. Implicit in such an hierachical structure is the uniqueness of this pathname for each object within a virtual filestore.

Clearly, in the context of file object type, the generic attribute *object name* is the same as the file attribute *filename* introduced in section 8.2. The generic attribute *unique permanent identifier* is intended to permit the assignation of a name to an object at the time of its creation which cannot be modified at any future time. There are also attributes specific to file-directory and to reference object types. For file-directory these are:

Path access control
Date and time of last read access
Identity of last reader
Date and time of last modification
Identity of last modifier

and for references are:

Path access control
Linked object
Linked object type

The *path access control* attribute stipulates the conditions under which objects may be accessed if the pathname by which they are identified includes this particular file-directory or reference object. The *linked object* attribute names the object to which a reference is maintained; it is the complete primary pathname of the referenced file or file-directory.

8.4.2 Object selection

In section 8.3.1 we introduced the concept of *selection*. Indeed we introduced a *file selection regime* initiated by the use of the F-SELECT service element (see Figure 8.4). Once an existing file is selected in this way, specific activity can be undertaken with respect to that file. This type of regime is clearly also required to encompass filestore management activities which act upon file-directory and reference objects. For this reason the F-SELECT service element is defined to create a selection regime for any one of the three types of object. The file selection regime as we have defined it is actually known in the standard as the *object selection regime*. At any one time there can exist within a FTAM regime a single object selection regime which has scope over an instance of one object of type file, file-directory or reference.

Filestore management introduces a number of additional FUs to FTAM. These are:

Limited filestore management
Enhanced filestore management
Object manipulation
Group manipulation

The relationships between FUs and the service classes were introduced in section 8.3 and summarized in Table 8.1 We can now revise this table to include all aspects of filestore management. Table 8.2 shows the enhanced kernel FU, whilst Table 8.3

Table 8.2 — Amended kernel FU and service class relationships

FU	Service classes					Services	Service elements
	T	A	M	TM	U		
Kernel	M	M	M	M	M	Regime establishment	F-INITIALIZE
						Orderly regime release	F-TERMINATE
						Disorderly regime release	F-U-ABORT
							F-P-ABORT
						Object selection	F-SELECT
						Object deselection	F-DESELECT

gives the additional FUs — limited filestore management, enhanced filestore management, object manipulation, group manipulation. Notice that, as indicated above, the services *file selection* and *file de-selection* within the kernel FU are now known as *object selection* and *object de-selection*.

We shall now examine the services offered by filestore management, at the same time reassessing FUs and service classes where the addition of filestore management has necessitated modification.

In this second edition we have intentionally chosen to discuss the addition of

Table 8.3 — Additional FUs and their service class relationships

FU	Service classes					Services	Service elements
	T	A	M	TM	U		
Limited filestore management	—	O	O	O	O	Change current name prefix List file-directory	F-CHANGE-PREFIX F-LIST
Enhanced filestore management	—	O	O	O	O	File-directory creation Refrence creation Reference deletion Read reference attribute Change reference attribute	F-CREATE-DIRECTORY F-LINK F-UNLINK F-READ-LINK-ATTRIBUTE F-CHANGE-LINK-ATTRIBUTE
Object manipulation	—	O	O	O	O	Move object Copy object	F-MOVE F-COPY
Group manipulation	—	O	O	O	O	Generalized selection Generalized deselection Group move Group copy Group list Select another	F-GROUP-SELECT F-GROUP-DESELECT F-GROUP-MOVE F-GROUP-COPY F-GROUP-LIST F-SELECT-ANOTHER

O: Optional; —: not available.

filestore management to the standard in this way, i.e. making minimal alteration to the chapter as presented in the first edition and, in an additional section, describing the changes as well as the concepts introduced in the addendum. In this way we hope that the reader will experience something of the process of evolution of a standard.

8.4.3 Service elements

Specification of filestore management services has spawned a number of additional regimes within FTAM. Figure 8.11 is the complete FTAM regime diagram, which we shall examine in time order, left to right, indicating enhancements to already introduced components, and describing in detail the filestore management components.

F-INITIALIZE remains the same, except that there are now a number of additional FUs to be included in the initial negotiation.

F-LIST provides a service for the remote listing of a specified file-directory. The listing of objects subordinate to this file-directory can be selective, such selection being based upon object attribute values. For instance, it is possible to ask for a list of only those file objects whose contents have been modified since a certain date. Since it requires a response it is a confirmed service, and it has as one of its optional parameters **access passwords**. The responding filestore may require this parameter to be set and it is the basic security mechanism for this and many other filestore services. It is a complex parameter and is used to establish both the permission to read attributes of the objects being listed, and also permission to read the file-directories containing them. The use of F-LIST produces, for each object, a primary pathname and a list of values for each of the requested attributes.

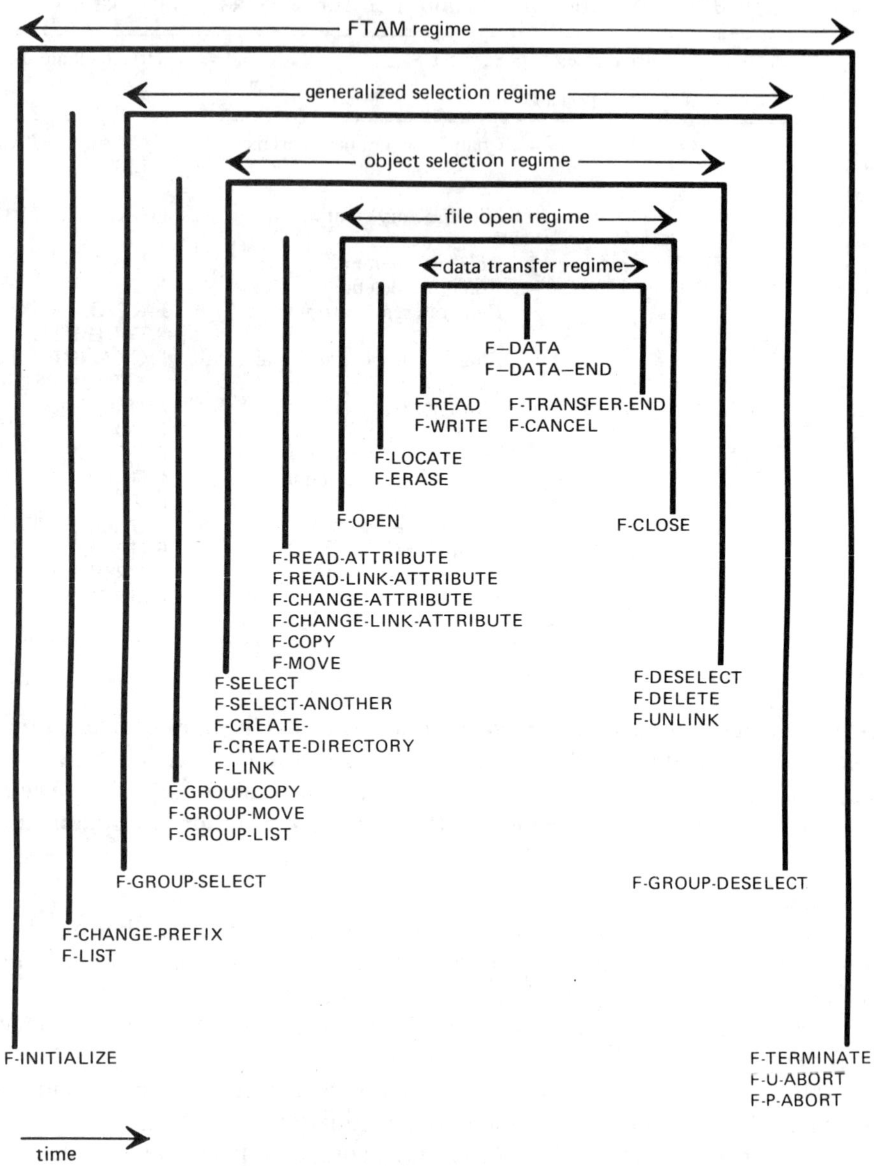

Fig. 8.11 — The complete FTAM regime diagram.

Identifying an object by use of a full primary pathname can become very clumsy when that object is buried deep in a comlex hierarchy. This can become especially frustrating if one considers interactive remote filestore manipulation involving many objects subordinate to some file-directory deep in such a hierarchy. FTAM provides a simple tool to ease such frustration in the form of the *current name prefix*. This global prefix is assigned as a part of the FTAM regime initialization and can be altered at any time when selection is not in force by use of the F-CHANGE-PREFIX service element. When set to the primary pathname of a file-directory, this prefix facilitates the use of simpler pathnames by the initiator when referencing objects subordinate to that file-directory.

Notice that neither F-LIST nor F-CHANGE-PREFIX initiate a regime — they are simple atomic actions.

There are some filestore management activities that may need to be invoked in a repetitive manner in order to realize a particular task. This task may simply be to move all the files from one file-directory to another, or it may be to make a copy of all files in a particular file-directory that have been changed since a certain date (backup). These examples could be achieved by repetitive calls on move or copy services (which we examine later), but a more efficient method would be to be able to identify these file objects as a group by virtue of common attributes, and then to utilize a single service that results in the same effect as the repetitive calls, e.g. 'copy all'. FTAM has just such features which are based upon the creation of an optional regime, the *generalized selection regime*.

This optional regime is established by use of the F-GROUP-SELECT service element, and terminated by F-GROUP-DESELECT. Use of access passwords is an optional feature of the establishment of this regime. Only file objects and reference objects that point to file objects can be 'group selected'. Both service elements offer a confirmed service. The confirmation of group selection is simply a statement of the success or failure (perhaps due to no matching objects, or access denial) of the activity. No list of the files actually selected is returned with the confirmation — this, if required, must be requested explicitly by use of F-GROUP-LIST. Use of this service results in a list of the pathnames of all the objects in the select group at the responder, together with the selected attributes of each object.

The two service elements F-GROUP-MOVE and F-GROUP-COPY provide the initiator with the capability to act, in a single service call, on all the objects in the current group selection regime. Here an entire group of files or file referencing reference objects can be moved or copied from one part of the filestore to another. In both instances, there is a service parameter **destination file-directory**, wherein the destination in the filestore hierarchy is identified.

The object selection regime can by initialized by the use of any one of five service elements. Two of these, F-SELECT and F-CREATE, we looked at in section 8.3.1. F-SELECT-ANOTHER can only be utilized when a generalized selection regime exists (an optional regime). Use of this service simply results in the selection of the 'next' object within the set of objects identified in the generalized selection regime that has not yet been selected. Should all objects have been selected then the responding filestore will indicate this in its response, at the same time resetting the status of all the objects to 'not yet selected'. This gives the initiator the facility to multi-cycle through groups of objects.

Use of F-CREATE-DIRECTORY causes a new file-directory to be created in the responding filestore. The file-directory is then automatically selected, i.e. bound into an object selection regime. Similarly, F-LINK causes a new reference object to be created and bound into an object selection regime. In this case a mandatory parameter is **target object**, which is the pathname of the file or file-directory object that is to be referenced by the new reference object.

There is one additional service element the use of which terminates an object selection regime, F-UNLINK. This service can only be used if the object that is selected in the regime was identified by a pathname that terminates in a reference object (i.e. not the primary pathname). In this case the deselection procedure includes the deletion of that reference object. Of course, the object that was linked by the reference will continue to exist but the pathname by which it was identified during the object selection regime no longer remains valid for the object. The definition of F-DELETE is extended in filestore management to act in a simlar manner. If the access to a selected object was by a reference object, then both the referenced object *and* the reference object are deleted. When applied to a file-directory object, the deletion will only succeed if the file-directory is not maintaining parenthood relationships, i.e. is currently an empty leaf on the hierarchical tree. Notice that, regardless of the result of the 'deletion' aspect of the service, the deselection always succeeds.

The F-READ-ATTRIBUTE and F-CHANGE-ATTRIBUTE service elements already encountered earlier, provide a mechanism for reading or amending the values held in the responding filestore for a range of attributes associated with a selected file or file-directory object. The F-READ-LINK-ATTRIBUTE and F-CHANGE-LINK-ATTRIBUTE service elements give the same facility for a reference object when a file or file-directory object is selected via a non-primary pathname that terminates at this reference object. Whenever a modification activity of this kind is undertaken, the responding filestore will automatically reset the values of 'date and time..' and 'identity of..' modification attributes.

We have already met F-MOVE and F-COPY in their group guises. Here the atomic activities refer to a single selected object. Use of F-MOVE results in a change in the primary pathname of the object as its position within the filestore is altered. It is in effect a three-part activity:

adding a parenthood relationship into the target file-directory object;
removing the parenthood relationship in the old file-directory object;
amending the object's primary pathname.

Should the object selection regime have identified a reference object (and hence the object referenced by the reference), then the move will not affect the referenced object whose primary pathname remains as it was; it is the reference object that is moved.

F-COPY is simlar to F-MOVE, but results in the original object remaining in place, and with a copy being made in the filestore as instructed.

The remaining inner regimes are concerned with file manipulation and not filestore activity and so remain as presented earlier in the chapter.

8.5 FTAM PROTOCOL AND THE USE OF LOWER LAYER SERVICES

The convention adopted for the naming of FTAM PDUs (FPDUs) is slightly different from that used in the lower layers. Here the FPDU associated with an activity is named after the associated service primitives; for example, the FPDUs associated with the F-OPEN service element are F-OPEN REQUEST FPDU and F-OPEN RESPONSE FPDU. The structure and contents of FPDUs are defined in part four of the standard.

8.5.1 ACSE

The FTAM regime is established as follows:

- The initiating FTAM process (agent) issues an F-INITIALIZE request.
- The FTAM entity constructs an appropriate F-INITIALIZE request FPDU on the basis of parameters supplied on the request.
- Other parameters of the request are used by the FTAM entity ACSE component to construct an AARQ APDU; the process places the FPDU in the user data field of this APDU.
- The association is then progressed as developed in Chapter 4; an example is given in Chapter 9. The result is a receipt of the AARE APDU by the initiating FTAM process. The peer FTAM processes will have negotiated the FTAM regime as a part of association acceptance, and the F-INITIALIZE response FPDU will be in the user data parameter of the AARE APDU.

Other FPDUs are conveyed in the user data field of associated APDUs; these are: F-TERMINATE REQUEST FPDU, F-TERMINATE RE-SPONSE FPDU, F-ABORT REQUEST FPDU. With some exceptions, other FPDUs are conveyed using the presentation normal data service (P-DATA service element).

The F-CANCEL REQUEST FPDU and F-CANCEL RESPONSE FPDU are conveyed in the user data of the P-RESYNCHRONIZE (abandon) service element, if it is available. This would possibly result in the by-passing of any lower layer data 'blockage' (see Chapter 6). If not available then presentation normal data is used.

F-RESTART REQUEST and RESPONSE FPDUs can only be conveyed in user data of the P-RESYNCHRONIZE (restart) service element. Restart is not available if the session synchronize minor service is not available.

The F-CHECK and F-DATA service elements are such that they have no associated FPDU since their intent can be conveyed to the peer solely by the indication of the appropriate lower layer service used. In the case of F-DATA, the transmitting FTAM process, on being requested to transfer a data unit, includes the data and an indication of its abstract syntax as a parameter of a P-DATA request. This presentation service eventually results in an indication being presented to the receiving FTAM process and the data is transferred. In the case of F-CHECK, the activity is implicit in the use of the P-SYNC-MINOR service element. The only parameter is the 'check point', which in fact is the SPSN (see Chapter 6); this is managed by the session layer. For these two services an FPDU exchange would be superfluous.

8.5.2 Presentation layer

As we have seen, presentation layer functionality is provided by two presentation FUs, namely kernel and context management. Use of the context management FU by FTAM is optional, and subject to availability in the peer presentation entities. We have seen that FTAM establishes the presentation requirements of data transfer activity within a file open regime as a part of the regime establishment. These requirements are based upon the abstract syntax(es) defining the DUs within the file in question. We saw in Chapter 5, that defined context set manipulation can occur either (i) at presentation connection establishment time, or (ii) at any time during the life of the presentation connection, by use of the context management FU.

If, as part of FTAM activity, the peer FTAM processes are to define the abstract syntax(es) at the time of file open regime establishment, then it can do so only if the context management FU of presentation is available for use. If it is not, then all the abstract syntax(es) that will be used during a FTAM regime must be established and made available to the presentation layer at the time of presentation connection establishment; that is, with the P-CONNECT request.

8.5.3 Session layer

As in the case of presentation, FTAM can function over a session connection even if only the kernel FU is available. However, two other FUs of the session layer are optionally used by FTAM if they are available: resynchronization and minor synchronization.

FTAM restart FU cannot be provided unless both of these session services are available. The recovery FU requires that the minor synchronization session service be available.

Notice that, in the course of FTAM regime establishment, the user data field of a CN SPDU carries the CP PPDU, AARQ APDU and F-INITIALIZE request FPDU.

9

Consolidation by example

This chapter is intended to illustrate the use of individual layer standards outlined in the preceding chapters. For the purpose of demonstration we shall use the diagrammatic 'skeleton' shown in Figure 9.1.

9.1 EXAMPLE ONE

The first example is of association establishment. For this we are assuming that a network connection already exists between the two end-systems, and that the transport connection yet to be established will be assigned to this connection. Also assumed is that the transport connection will be Class 2 with no explicit flow control. Example one is worked through in three diagrams, time sequence events being numbered 1 to 27.

Notes for time sequence events:

(1) An association establishment request.
(2) The ACSE of the initiating application entity makes a presentation service request. The ACSE PDU associated with association establishment, the AARQ APDU, is included in the user data parameter of this primitive.
(3) The resultant connection establishment PDU, the CP PPDU, which contains the proposed presentation context definition list and the user data provided by ACSE, is included in the user data parameter of the session service request.

Neither ACSE nor presentation wait for a lower layer connection to be established before transmitting their associated establishment PDUs. They use the user data parameters of the next lower layer 'connect' service requests to convey their PDUs.

(4) The session entity initiates a transport connection.
(5) The transport entity assigns the potential transport connection to an existing, suitable, network connection. It builds a connect request PDU, CR TPDU, and transmits it to its peer on the responding end-system over the network connection.
(6) The network data transfer is indicated to the addressed transport entity.
(7) The responding transport entity interprets the TPDU and, on finding the proposed connection acceptable, issues an indication to the addressed session entity. Had the transport entity found the proposed connection unacceptable, it

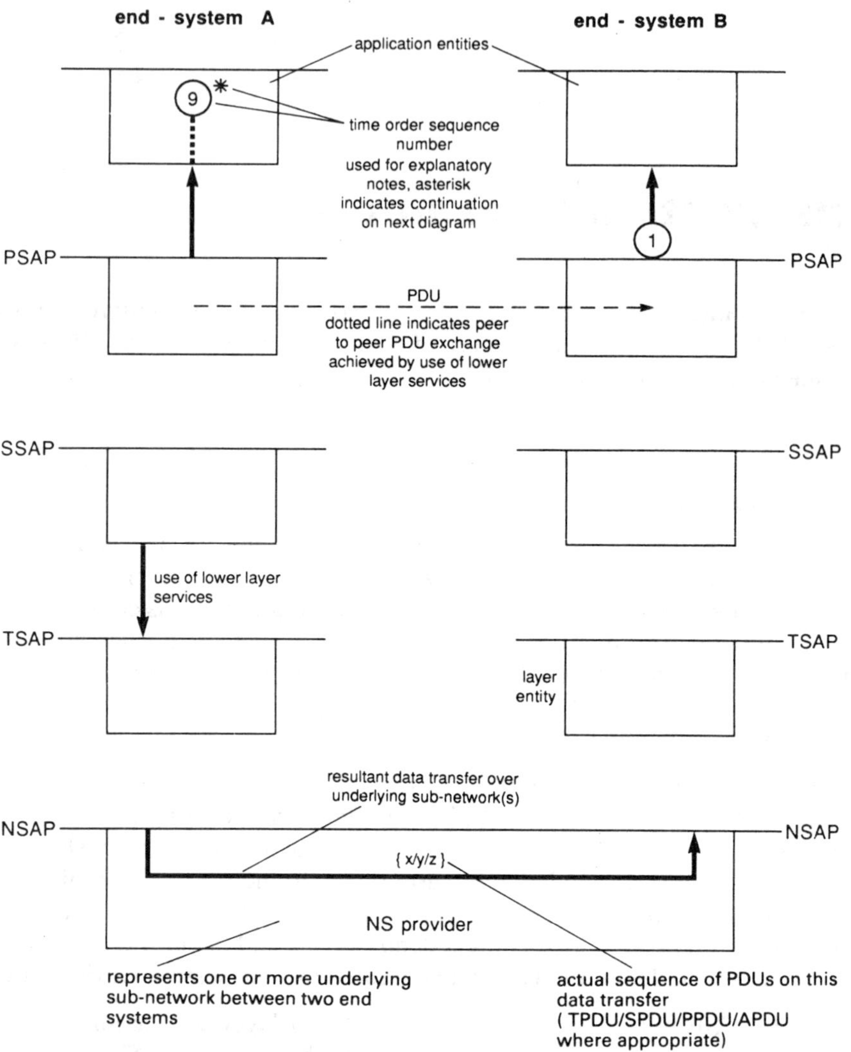

Fig. 9.1 — Diagrammatic skeleton.

would have had two possible courses of action. It could either refuse the connection (by transmitting a Disconnect Request, DR, TPDU) or it could modify the parameters of the connection and proceed to issue the indication; such a modification would be transmitted to the initiating transport entity in the subsequent transport connect confirm TPDU, and the initiator would then determine whether the connection remained viable.

(8) Given adequate resources (buffers etc.), the session entity indicates its ability to manage a (further) session connection by issuing a response.

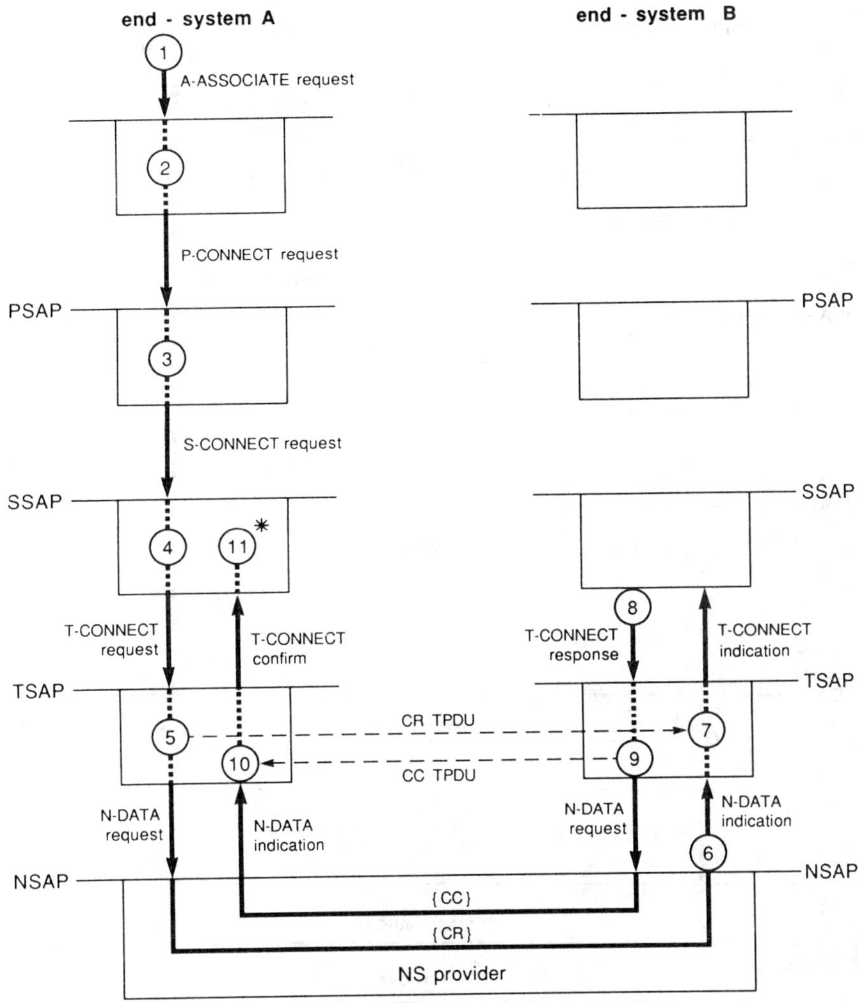

Fig. 9.2(a) — Example one (a).

(9) The transport entity builds and transmits a Connect Confirm (CC) TPDU, thus accepting the transport connection.

(10) The CC TPDU is interpreted by the initiating transport entity and, if within bounds of acceptability (QOS etc.), the entity issues a confirm to the initiating session entity. If the parameters of the CC TPDU were unacceptable, because of modification by the peer, then the transport entity would, via network normal data, send a Disconnect Request (DR) TPDU to the peer and issue a T-DISCONNECT indication to the initiating session entity, thus failing the connection attempt.

(11) Having waited for a transport connection, the session entity now sends a

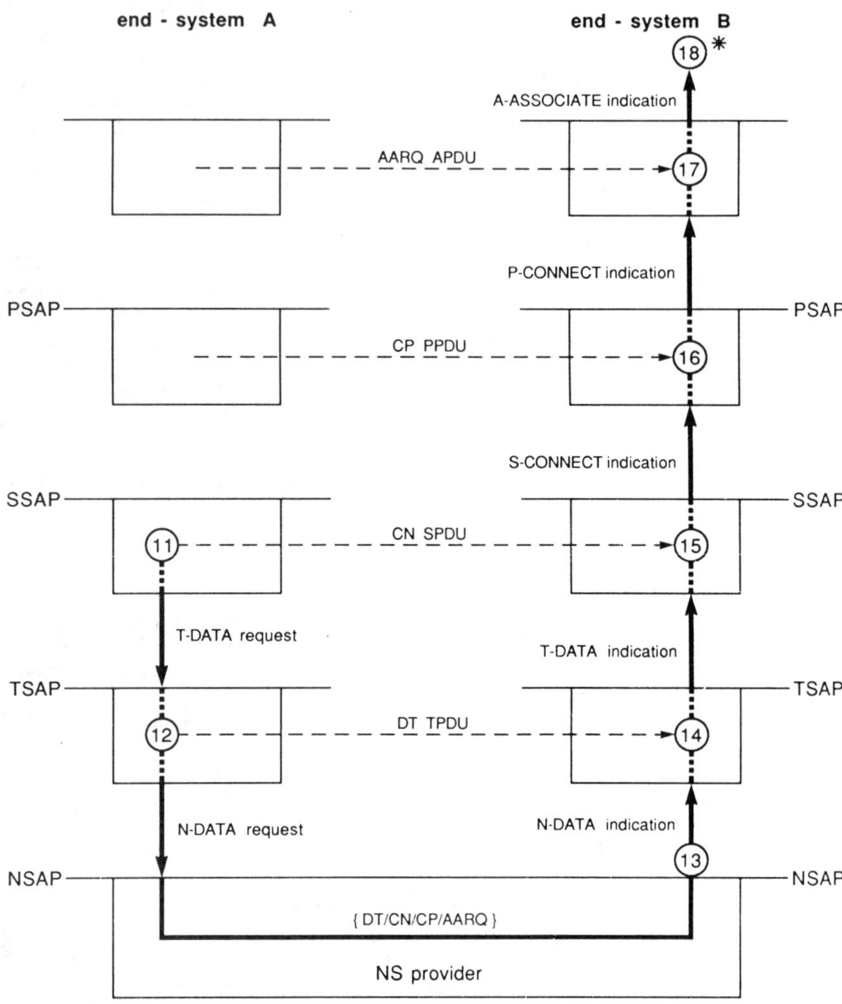

Fig. 9.2(b) — Example one (b).

Connect (CN) SPDU to its peer using transport normal data service. This SPDU has a user data parameter containing the CP PPDU and AARQ APDU.

(12) The CN SPDU is a TSDU which is conveyed in a normal data (DT) TPDU. The TPDU is sent as network normal data.

(13) The NSDU is indicated to the receiving transport entity.

(14) The DT TPDU PCI is decoded and the 'residue', the TSDU, is presented to the responding session entity. If the TSDU was segmented it would only be presented if it was complete, that is, if a TPDU had been received with the EOT parameter set.

(15) The CN SPDU (the received TSDU) is interpreted and, if the connection can be accommodated, appropriate selections are made as part of the connection

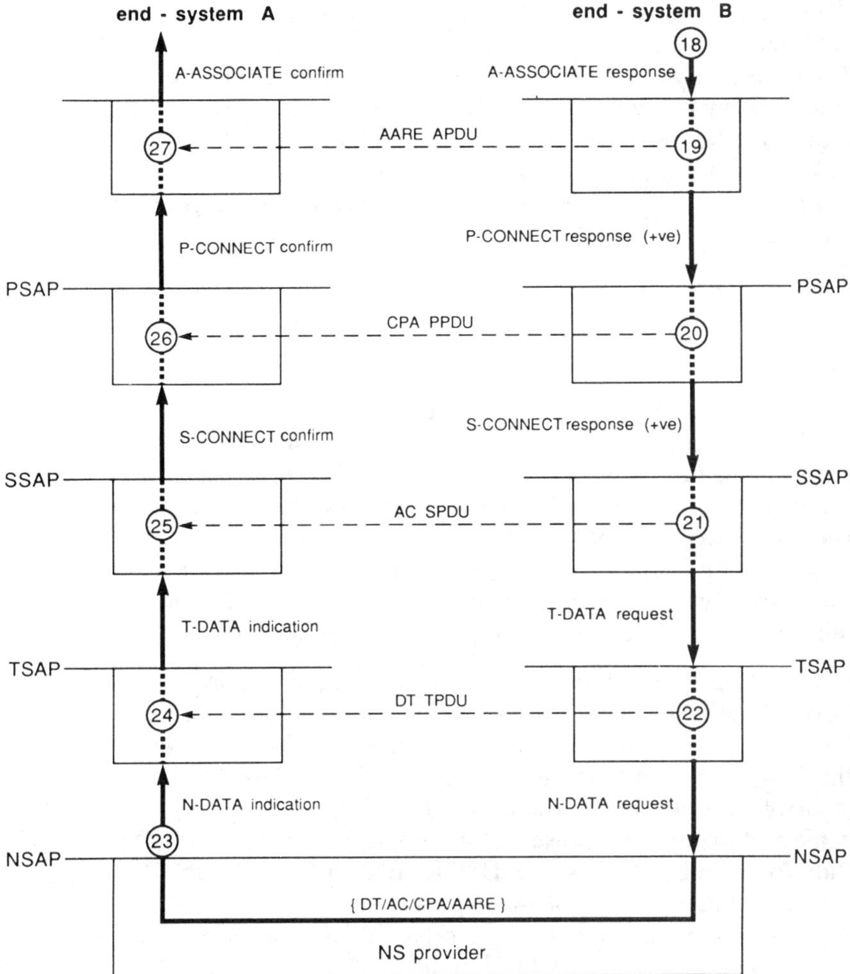

Fig. 9.2(c) — Example one (c).

negotiation procedure (FUs, use of transport expedited etc.). An indication is issued to the addressed SS user, a presentation entity.

(16) User data is expected to accompany this indication and is interpreted as a CP PPDU by the presentation entity. It progresses presentation context negotiation by appropriate transfer syntax selection and, having determined that the connection is viable, indicates the connection attempt to the application process, which in this instance is represented by the ACSE component of an application entity.

(17) Again, user data is expected with this indication and is interpreted as a AARQ APDU by the entity, resulting in an 'indication' to the appropriate ASE component of the application process.

(18) The association is accepted and a response issued.

(19) The AARE APDU, like the AARQ, is conveyed as user data on the P-CONNECT response.

(20) The presentation connection accept CPA PPDU parameters include a presentation connect definition list and user data (carrying the AARE APDU). It is conveyed by use of the user data parameter of the S-CONNECT response.

(21) The responding session entity generates the appropriate Accept (AC) SPDU with the CPA PPDU as user data, and sends this on transport normal data service.

Steps (22) onwards should now need no further comment.

9.2 EXAMPLE TWO

In this example we consider peer FTAM processes involved in remote file update on a record-by-record basis. We assume that an established association exists between the peer FTAM processes and that a point in activity has been reached where the FTAM process to receive an data unit (a record) has established the position in the file where the record will be written; i.e. a data transfer regime has been established, and hence the location of the root FADU determined. The information transfer is then initiated by the sending application agent, by use of the F-DATA service element of FTAM. Figure 9.3 illustrates the resulting activity.

(1) The sending application agent issues a request to its partner FTAM entity.

(2) Given that the peer FTAM processes are in the data transfer phase and therefore have already established the precise nature of the DU transfer(s) about to occur, there is no necessity for a specific FPDU to be exchanged since no further 'control' information is required. It is sufficient for the DU transfer to be achieved solely by the use of presentation data service. The FTAM entity therefore simply passes the DU to presentation (a PSDU) together with identification of its associated abstract syntax.

(3) The appropriate transfer syntax is selected, by reference to the defined context set, and any necessary transformation is performed on the information unit. The resultant encoded information unit will be regarded as transparent user data by the lower layers. This encoded information, together with an indication of the associated presentation context, is packaged in a TD PPDU which is transmitted by use of session normal data service, that is, as an SSDU.

(4)–(7) Session, transport and the network service provider ensure delivery to the peer presentation entity.

(8) The receiving presentation entity performs whatever transformation is necessary on the received SSDU: that is, from the transfer syntax to the local representational form of the abstract syntax. An indication, together with the PSDU (DU) and the identity of its abstract syntax, is issued to the receiving FTAM process which subsequently 'secures' the DU as agreed.

9.3 EXAMPLE THREE

This example covers the normal release of an association. Since the release of the session connection is implicit in this action, the application process initiating the

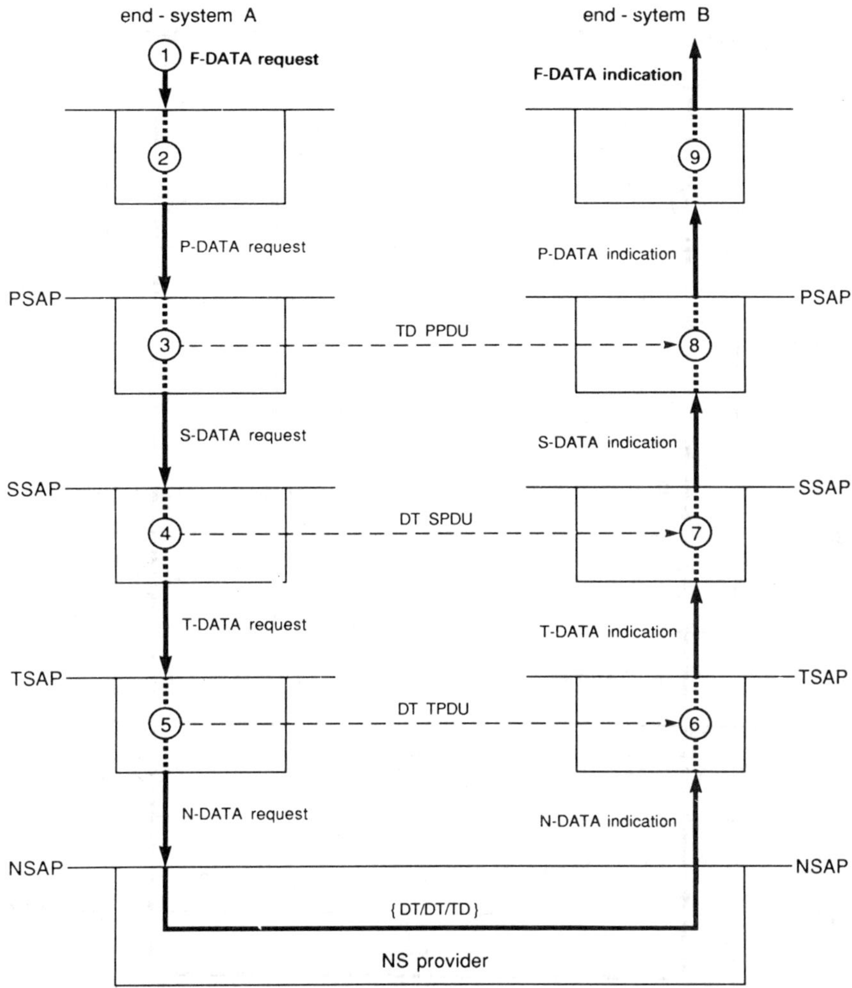

Fig. 9.3 — Example two.

association release must obey the token restrictions outlined in Chapter 6. In this example we assume that the release is accepted by the responding application process, but in extra notes we also consider the implications of a rejection.

(1) An application agent initiates a normal release.
(2) A Release Request (RLRQ) APDU is generated by the ACSE component which is included as the user data parameter of the presentation service request.
(3) As we saw in Chapter 5, there are no representational issues involved in this activity, which falls into the 'mirror' category of services with no associated PPDUs. All that is required of a presentation entity is that it notes the change

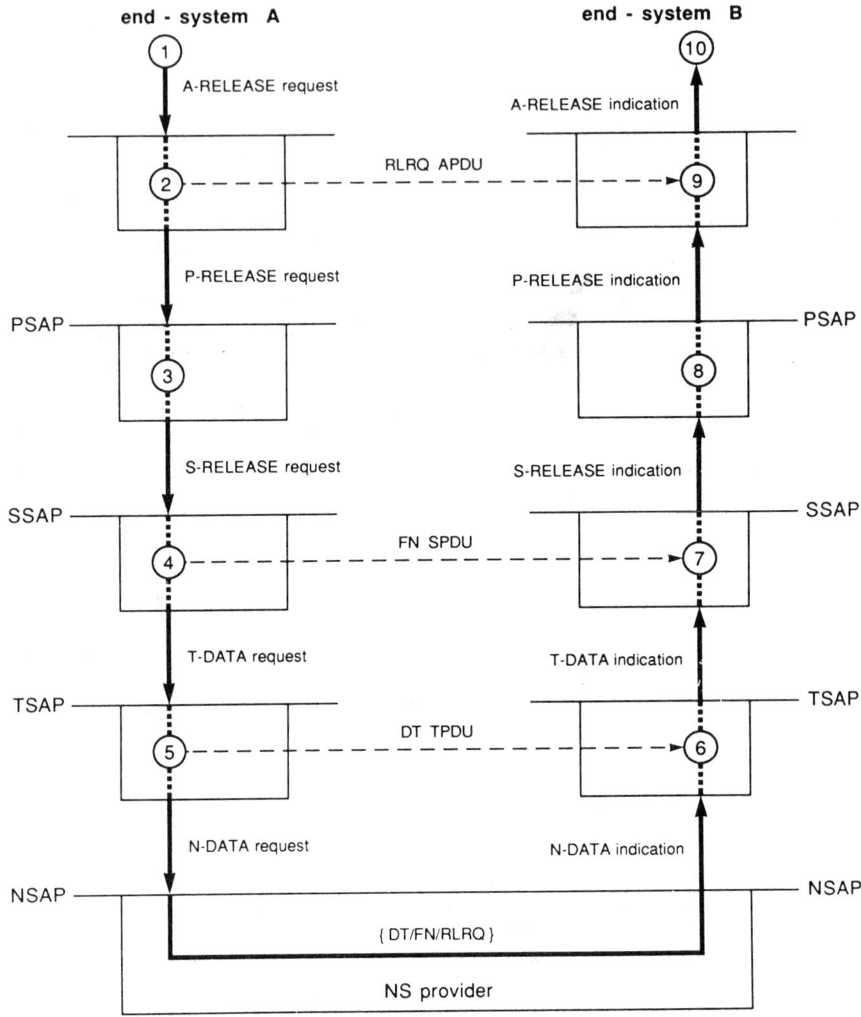

Fig. 9.4(a) — Example three (a).

of state of the presentation 'connection' implicit in receipt of presentation and session release primitives.

(4) The session entity constructs a Finish (FN) SPDU, including the RLRQ APDU passed on by the presentation entity as user data. It then uses transport normal data service for the SPDU transfer to the peer. Notice that the transport layer is not yet entering a release sequence as the upper layers are, because transport connection release is not negotiable. It cannot therefore be invoked until such time as (possible) session release negotiation is completed, that is, until such time that no further TSDU transfers are required. Indeed,

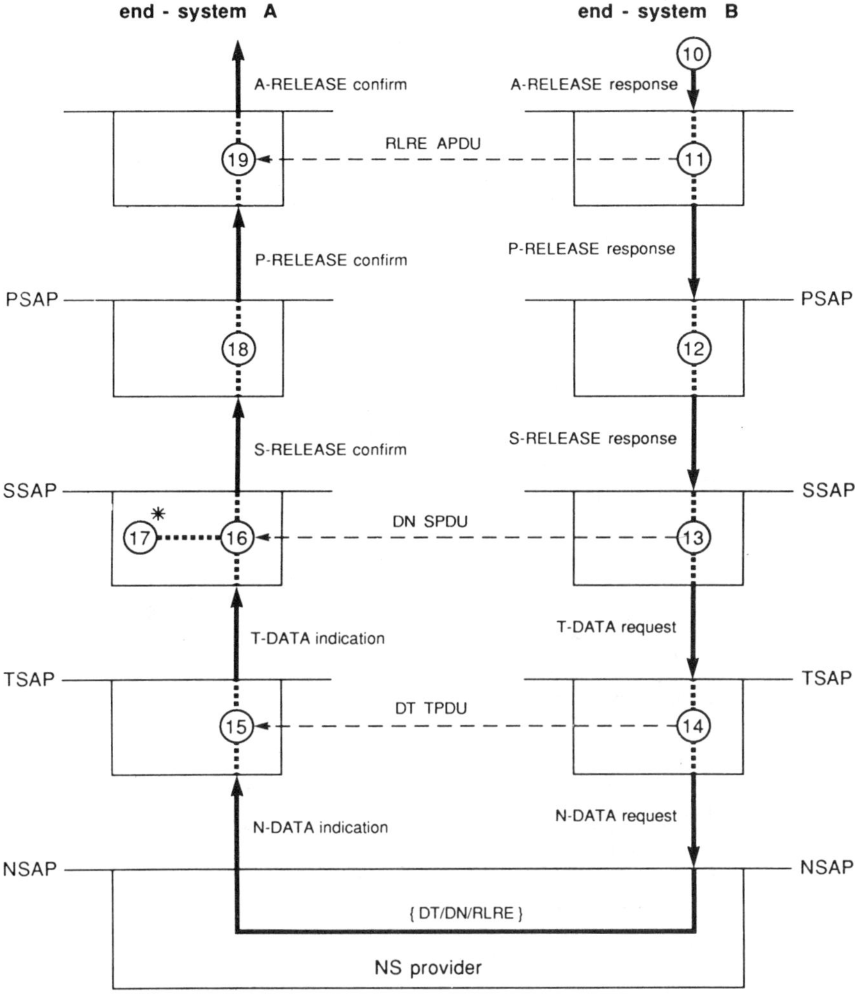

Fig. 9.4(b) — Example three (b).

even when the session connection has been released, the session entity which initiated the transport connection may choose to re-use it rather than release it.

(5)–(6) This is a TSDU transfer.

(7) Interpreting the TSDU as an FN SPDU, the responding session entity performs the required protocol consistency operations, such as token ownership checks. It then issues an indication, including the user data carried on the SPDU, itself containing the RLRQ APDU.

(8) As discussed, the presentation entity notes a change of state of its 'connection' and issues an indication, passing on the user data.

(9) The ACSE component interprets this user data as a RLRQ APDU, resulting in an indication to the appropriate ASE component.

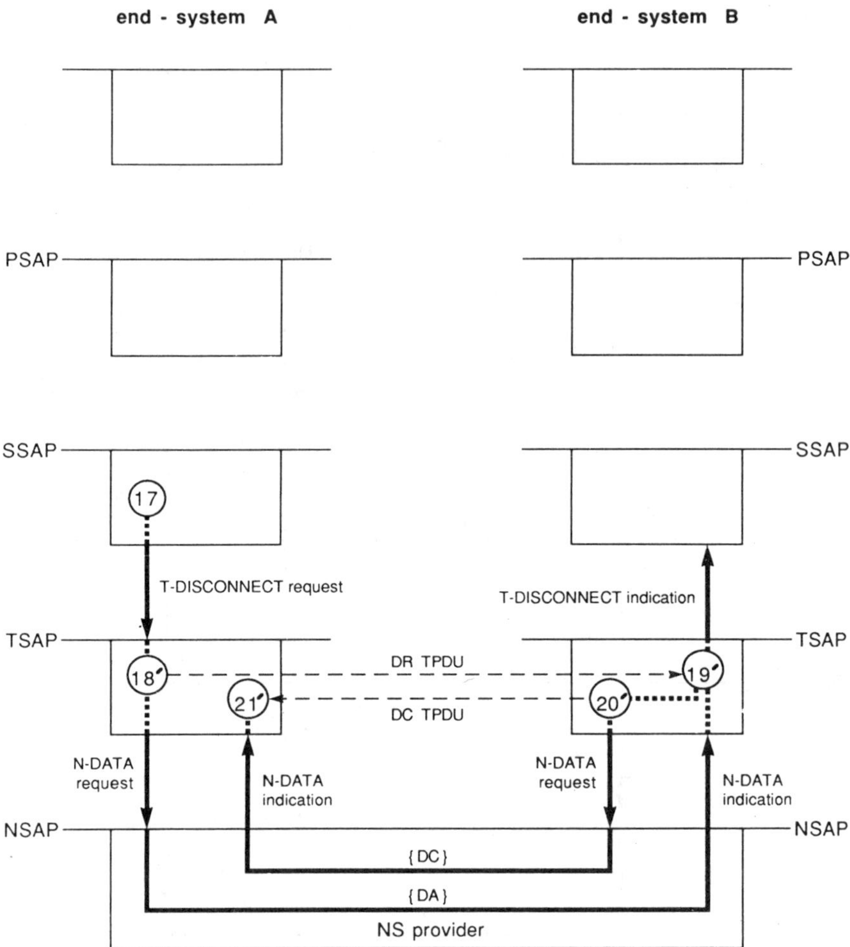

Fig. 9.4(c) — Example three (c).

(10) If the association is no longer required (or if negotiated release is not available) the ASE component issues a positive response.

(11) A Release Response (RLRE) APDU is constructed carrying, as a parameter, the nature of the response, in this case positive. This is supplied as a user data parameter with the positive P-RELEASE response. The application process now regards the association as ended.

(12) The presentation entity simply passes on the user data to session in the S-RELEASE response which also has a parameter indicating the nature of the response, positive or negative, gleaned by the presentation entity from the corresponding parameter in its own service response. If the response is positive, the entity now regards the presentation 'connection' as released.

(13) The session entity, on seeing a positive response, builds a Disconnect (DN)

SPDU, including the supplied user data (i.e. the RLRE APDU), which it transmits by use of transport normal data service. It now regards the session connection as released but its responsibility has not yet ended. It is aware, as a result of the negotiation during session connection establishment, of any possibility of transport connection retention. Assuming that this connection was not initiated by this end-system (the responder to the release), there are then two possibilities: first that re-use was negotiated. In this case the session entity responsibility ends, apart from remaining available to service a future T-DATA indication (whose TSDU would contain a CN SPDU). In the second possibility, where the transport connection is not available to be re-used, the session entity must 'police' the transport release; this release will be initiated by the session entity on the end-system that initiated the association release when it is in receipt of the DN SPDU. If, however, the transport connection is not released, that is, the policing session entity does not receive a T-DISCONNECT indication within a certain period, then that entity will initiate a transport connection release itself. This prevents a possible proliferation of transport connections between end-systems due to a malfunctioning session entity.

(14)–(15) Transport normal data is achieved.

(16) On receiving the DN SPDU, the release initiating entity finds itself with two responsibilities. First it must issue a P-RELEASE confirm, the result of which is the sequence (17)–(19). This completes the release as far as session, presentation and the application process are concerned. Secondly, if the transport connection is not to be kept, it must release it by issuing a T-DISCONNECT request, (17′).

(18′) We have based these examples on transport Class 2 over a network connection without explicit flow control and which we assume is to be retained. In this instance, then, the explicit transport connection release variant must be invoked. A Disconnect Request (DR) TPDU is transmitted over network normal data service.

(19′) The responding transport entity issues a T-DISCONNECT indication, the receipt of which enables a 'policing' session entity to stop the timer and become idle. It constructs a Disconnect Confirm (DC) TPDU which it transmits to the initiating peer.

(20′) The DC TPDU completes the required handshake removing the association between the network connection and this transport entity.

10

Message handling systems, ISO 10021/X.400

In the earlier chapters which covered the individual ISORM layers, we were able to examine each layer in detail and provide a relatively complete technical study. However, the application layer standards are altogether more complex and it becomes necessary to be selective in the aspects of the standards examined. Consequently, in examining the standards for *message handling systems* (MHS), this chapter does not provide a complete technical picture of those aspects of the standards which provide peripheral support, but concentrates on the areas which are central to message handling. One difficulty for the student of MHS arises from the complexity of the subject: it may be fairly clear what a particular feature of the service will do, but not easy to understand why such a feature is thought desirable and how it will be exploited. For this reason, some historical background is included to explain the service requirements which underlie the development of MHS. As we shall see, the standards have had a long development history, and expression of them in ISORM architectural terms has occurred only recently. Wherever the description in this chapter appears to be inconsistent with the concepts encountered earlier in the book the reader should assume that the simpler view of the model encountered earlier is extensible to the more complicated instance.

The aim of the MHS standards is to provide an international service for the exchange of electronic messages. Two organizations are involved in the production of standards for MHS: CCITT and ISO. In 1984, CCITT published a set of recommendations, known as X.400 (1984). Since then, the two organizations have agreed to harmonize their activities, and produce parallel standards with almost identical text. These later standards are called, respectively, X.400 (1988) and ISO 10021 (MOTIS). The differences which do exist between the two versions of the standards arise from the differing areas of authority of the two organizations. CCITT members comprise telecommunication administrations and other commercial partners; ISO members are the national standards authorities of each participating country. This chapter will concentrate on the 1988 versions of the standards.

10.1 INTRODUCTION

The basic activity performed by MHS is the conveyance of electronic messages through a communications system. The users of this service are, primarily, individuals who wish to exchange interpersonal messages, but the medium may also be used for other applications such as the exchange of orders and invoices between commercial organizations.

A simple model for MHS is shown in Figure 10.1. This model outlines the basic

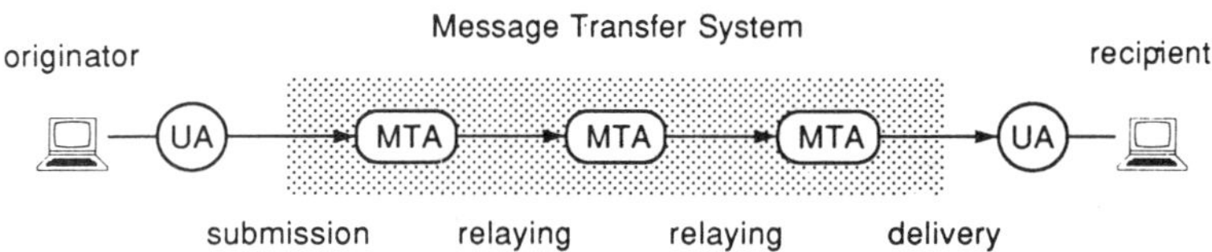

Fig. 10.1 — Simple messaging model.

components involved when one user, the *originator*, sends a message to another user, the *recipient*. The originator makes use of a *user agent* (UA) to compose a message and submit it to the *message transfer system* (MTS). A UA is similarly involved when the MTS delivers the message to its recipient. After delivery, the recipient uses the services of his UA to process the received message. Within the MTS, a set of *message transfer agents* (MTAs) cooperate in conveying messages to their intended recipients. Together, the collection of UAs and MTAs comprise the *message handling system* (MHS).

The 1988 standards identify two further functional entities: the *message store* (MS), which provides services to UAs for the storage and management of delivered messages, and the *access unit* (AU), which provides a port to another communications system, such as a postal system.

A principal feature of MHS is that it operates in a store-and-forward manner. This means that the originator of a message need not wait until the recipient indicates willingness to accept delivery before he can send the message. Rather, the originator can submit a message at any time convenient to him, and equally, the recipient can choose the time when he will actually read it. This contrasts with some other forms of electronic communication such as facsimile or telephony where the sender and receiver must be linked in a simultaneous 'connection' before communication can begin. It can be time-consuming for the sender to establish this link, as well as disruptive for the receiver to switch his attention to deal with it. One source puts the success rate for telephone dialling attempts in the US as low as 28%. The reasons for failure include mis-dialling, failure to connect, number engaged, not answering, or answered but the person required is unavailable. In practice, the failure rate for a properly addressed electronic message is close to zero.

A further feature of the store-and-forward basis of operation is that it does not require the originator's computing system to become attached, in any sense, to the recipient's system. Instead, the message may be routed via some intermediate system which is capable either of attaching to the recipient's system, or of performing a further transfer to another intermediate system still closer to the destination. The activity of transferring a message through the MTS by store-and-forward operations is known as *relaying*; this should not be confused with network relaying which is discussed in Chapter 1.

An important service provision of MHS is the ability to send a message to multiple recipients; little extra effort is required for a user to send his message to many recipients rather than to a single recipient. The ease of use of MHS, and facility for communicating with many users, encourages a level of communication which would not otherwise occur. A further essential service provision promotes confidence in the reliability of the messaging system: if a message cannot be delivered, then MHS guarantees to return a report to its originator advising him of the reason for non-delivery.

We shall revisit the MHS model later in this chapter. First, it is useful to examine the history of MHS to understand the problems which the new standards are intended to solve.

10.2 HISTORICAL DIGRESSION

The earliest *computer-based messaging systems* (CBMS) were located in time-shared computers, and allowed local users to exchange messages with each other. Earlier still, services like Telex provided messaging services based on the use of the telephone network to link geographically dispersed users. The synthesis of these services, one providing the users of an isolated computer system with messaging, the other offering networked services, was first demonstrated on the ARPA computer network.

The ARPA project itself was based on the development of packet-switched technology, which allowed resource-sharing over dispersed computing facilities. To support this, communications protocols were developed to provide for remote terminal access, file transfer, and other applications related to distributed computation.

By 1972 these services were well established, and it was realized that they could provide the basis of a new service — communication between individuals. The first user programs to exploit this capability provided simple facilities for message composition and dispatch, and for displaying received messages. The messages were transported using the existing network file transfer services. From the beginning, the message service was a success, and soon accounted for a considerable proportion of the total network traffic.

Initially, messages were regarded as unstructured units of text. This allowed the message creation and display software to be very simple, but made for very limited functionality. Since messages both originate and terminate on computer systems, it seemed clear that there were many possibilities for introducing message processing tools. But before this could happen, a standard form for messages would have to be agreed so that processing software could interpret messages according to the same rules as those which had been used to create them. A simple example of this is the *reply* function, which assists a user in composing a response to a message by automatically abstracting from it the address of its originator.

The first of the ARPA standards concerned with this issue introduced the distinction between message headers (the first few lines of a message, which resemble the header of an office memo), and message body (the text of the message). Certain standard headers were defined to indicate such details as the recipients, the originator and the date and time of sending of a message. A formal syntax for these headers was defined, which made their contents readable by humans but also capable of interpretation by message processing software. Thus it was intended that processing software on one system would be able to interpret messages created on any other system. As message processing software continued to develop, new requirements of message format were identified and a number of further standards were published to address these.

Today, most user-level message processing programs provide facilities for message creation and editing, the manipulation of individual message fields, message selection by key (e.g. 'all messages from Smith'), message filing into named subgroups, message forwarding and formatted message display. Although of great importance to the end-user, these facilities are regarded as matters of local concern to each end-system and are not subject to any standard.

Considerable experience in computer-based messaging was gained in the ARPA environment and by 1979 a new forum was established to promote the development of the next generation of standards: IFIP Working Group 6.5. A starting point for the new standards was to address the shortcomings of the prototype ARPA message service. The following issues were of concern:

— The limitation of text-only mail. The industry is currently enjoying considerable growth in the use of facsimile. It would be desirable to be able to include facsimile components in messages as well as graphics and voice components.
— The lack of structure in the message body. One operation that is commonly performed is to encapsulate an existing message or messages within the body of another; this happens when a message is forwarded. When this occurs, the original structure of the encapsulated message is lost and the message cannot be easily extracted for further processing. In addition, some method of partitioning message content is necessary to support multiple data types where they appear within one message.
— A consequence of basing protocol elements on labelled text strings has been that these were too readily misused by human intervention or by poorly constructed message processing software. Binary encoding is preferable, since it entails a more precise definition, and requires a higher degree of conformance from software.
— The lack of status reports. When the delivery of a message is not possible because of an addressing error, the destination host system is expected to create a non-delivery report and return this to the message originator. These reports have no defined format and cannot readily be related to the message originally sent. There is a requirement for a distinctive message type for these reports.
— Existing protocols fail to make a proper distinction between envelope and content. As a result, the event-trace details describing the progress of a message through the system are added to the message content. On occasions where it is necessary to examine this trace information, for accounting or authentication

purposes, we find that agents other than the recipient's have opened and examined the content of the message. For reasons of privacy and security the information required to transfer a message from its source to its destination should all be confined to an enclosing envelope; the content of the message should be neither examined nor altered.

— The common means of addressing a recipient is to supply his user account ID (which may be his surname) and the name of the host he uses (or, more generally, its domain name). There has been some progress in existing messaging systems beyond this simple approach, but it is still predominant. It is not easy to discover either of these pieces of information unless you have been explicitly told them. Moreover, it is a simple matter to address a message such that it reaches someone other than the intended recipient (the ambiguous 'Jones'). Nor is it possible to determine when this erroneous delivery to an ambiguous name has occurred. The originator should be able to specify information about the intended recipient which is readily known and does not suffer from the problem of ambiguity. Such information would consist of a series of attributes such as given name, surname and organization name. Both the end-user and the MHS require a Directory Service to map names of this kind to addresses.

In many ways, a message originator cannot fully express his intentions concerning the disposition of his message. Consider the following cases:

— If a message arrives at its destination organization and is found not to be deliverable because of an addressing error in the recipient name, should it be redirected to a person responsible for rerouting such messages at that organization or should it be returned to its originator? The originator should be able to specify in advance the action taken.

— Before going on holiday, a user might set his mailbox to automatically forward all messages it receives to a colleague for him to deal with. A message originator should be able to indicate that the sensitivity of a message is such that it should not be subject to auto-forwarding.

— On occasions where a message is sent to a large number of recipients, the originator may not be concerned about successful delivery in every case. He should be able to indicate that non-delivery reports for the message should be suppressed. Further, where non-delivery reports are to be allowed, the originator should be able to specify whether or not the content of the message should be returned along with the delivery report.

— As the physical characteristics of user's equipment varies widely, the message created by the originator may have quite a different appearance when displayed on the recipient's output device. The originator should be able to specify the logical structure of his document, free of detailed layout instructions. The recipient's message display software should interpret the logical structure with knowledge of the characteristics of the local output device and generate an appropriate layout. In this way, the form of presentation intended by the originator can be preserved.

These points were identified as problem areas that the new standards should address. A further, and pressing reason for the development of new standards was the proliferation of commercial messaging services all operating to different standards. These have been characterized as 'electronic islands': separate populations of users, each of whom can communicate only with users on the same island. An important goal of the new standards is to bridge these islands.

10.3 MESSAGE STRUCTURE

Three distinct types of message are distinguished in MHS. The *user message* is the basic message type, used to send information between one user and another. The *probe message* allows a message originator to test the viability of sending a message of given characteristics to some recipient or recipients. A probe might be sent to verify that some address is correct, where this cannot be checked locally, before sending some large and costly message to it. The *delivery report* message type is originated by the MTS to inform a message originator of the outcome of an attempt to deliver a previously submitted user message or probe message. Each message type is discussed further, below.

The structure of the three message types is shown in Figure 10.2. All consist of

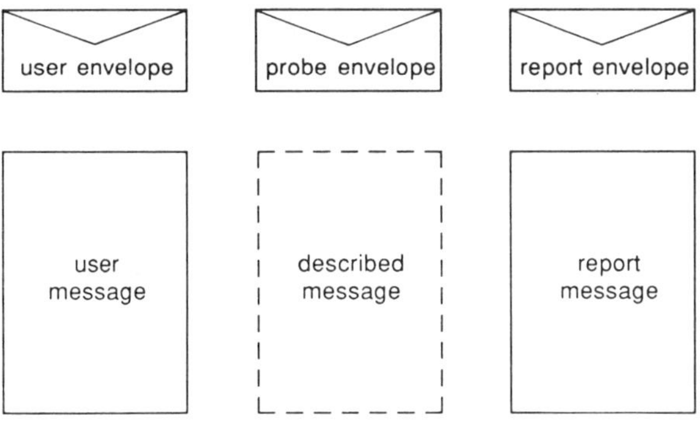

Fig. 10.2 — Basic structure of the three message types.

two parts: envelope and content. The *envelope* contains all the information required by the MTS to convey the message to its intended recipients. The *content* consists of the substance of the message itself, supplied by the message originator (or, in the case of a report, by the MTS). The MTS confines its attention to the envelope and neither examines nor alters the message content, except where conversion is requested, before delivering the message to its recipient. The distinction between envelope and content persists throughout the lifetime of a message.

This is best illustrated by the basic message type, the **user message**, which fulfils the primary purpose of MHS, the exchange of information between end-users. The main business of the end-user in constructing a message is to specify its content. The UA acting on his behalf will create a submission envelope to contain it. After submission, the MTS confines its attention to the envelope in progressing the message through the MTS to its recipient, and treats message content as transparent data. Upon delivery, the message content is presented to the recipient UA with its delivery envelope. While in transit, the envelope contains such information as the name of the recipient, the originator, and various characteristics of message content which the MTS must know to deal appropriately with the message. The envelope also bears an item of trace information for each occasion on which the message was relayed, and so bears an audit trail of its passage through the MTS.

For a user message, the envelope also records the *content-type* of the message it encloses. This identifies the syntax and semantics of the message content. Once the message has arrived at the destination MTA, the MTS confirms that the destination UA is capable of interpreting the particular content-type of the message before proceeding to deliver it. Only one content type has been defined for inclusion in user messages: the *interpersonal message* content-type. This is examined in detail in section 10.11.

Again, to enable the MTS to determine whether delivery is possible, the envelope also contains details of the *encoded information types* (EITs) of distinct parts of the message body. The types defined include IA5 text, Teletex and G3 facsimile. Where a recipient UA is unable to handle a particular EIT, the MTS may be able to perform conversion of that part of the message body to an encoding acceptable to the UA. Thus the MTS can be given a message which includes content encoded in one format, and deliver it with the content converted to a different format, so improving the possibilities for users with terminals of different capabilities to communicate. In performing conversion, the MTS is violating the general rule that message content is transported without inspection or alteration. It is permitted in this case solely for the pragmatic purpose of enabling communication to occur between users of otherwise incompatible equipment. Some conversions are of course impractical — facsimile to text, for example — and indeed, a message originator may specify at the outset that conversion is prohibited. Whenever conversion has been performed, the message recipient is informed of the original EITs of the message. The conversion of EITs is an activity which would appear to belong properly to the presentation layer. However, in MHS, there is only token use of presentation, and these conversions are performed within the application.

The structure of a **probe** differs from a user message in that it consists of envelope alone, with no content. The purpose of sending a probe is to determine whether some particular user message is deliverable. In effect, the probe embodies a *description* of the message whose deliverability is being tested. The probe envelope closely resembles the envelope which the described message would acquire if it were actually submitted, but in addition, includes the length of the described message content. The MTS treats a probe in the same way as it would the described message, except that delivery is not performed nor is the probe subject to redirection. Rather, the normal outcome of a probe is the generation of a report by the MTS, indicating whether or not delivery is possible for the described message. This delivery report is returned to the probe originator as soon as the deliverability of the described message has been established.

The **delivery report** is a distinct message type, with its own delivery report envelope and delivery report content definition. Reports are generated by the MTS, and may be sent to the originator of a user message or probe when the MTS determines the deliverability of the message. The report may indicate that delivery has taken place (or, for a probe, could take place), or that delivery was found to be impossible.

By default, the originator of a message will receive a report only in the event of non-delivery. However, the originator may instruct the MTS to return a report both in the case of successful delivery and of non-delivery. Conversely, he may indicate that non-delivery reports are to be suppressed. Different conditions controlling the generation of reports may be attached to each recipient of the message. For the message as a whole, the originator can indicate whether the content of the message should be included in any reports generated by the MTS. This wide set of control mechanisms illustrates the philosophy of the standards, in providing the message originator with the fullest possible control over the disposition of his message within the MTS.

10.4 MHS FUNCTIONAL MODEL

We now examine the MHS model in more detail. A functional view is given in Figure 10.3. As noted at the beginning of the chapter, the purpose of the MHS is to provide a

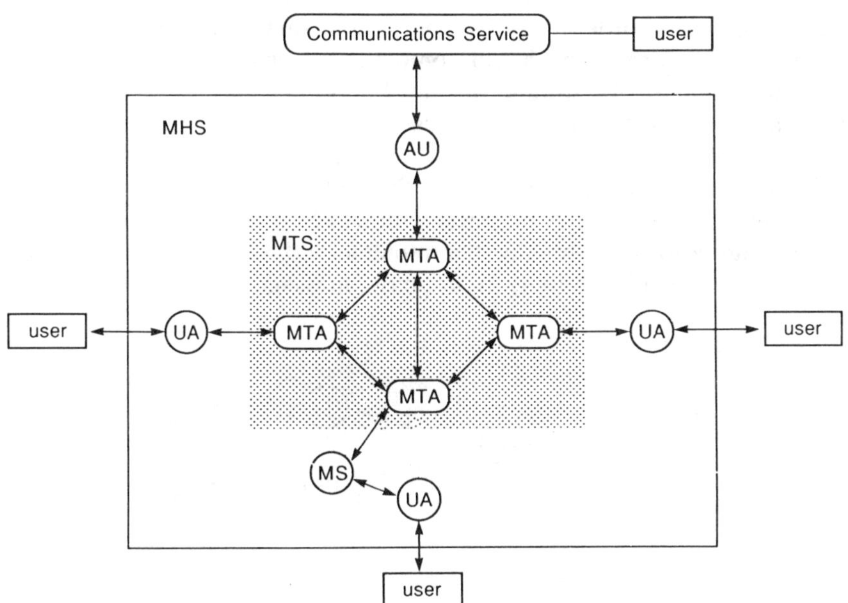

Fig. 10.3 — Functional model of MHS.

medium for the exchange of messages between communicating users. A *user* is a person, or an application program which originates or receives information objects. *Direct users* interact directly with the MHS. *Indirect users* participate in message handling through another communications system (e.g. a postal system) which is attached to the MHS.

This single model actually embodies two distinct services. The message transfer service operates as a general purpose carrier of messages across the message transfer system. Messages are conveyed regardless of content (as transparent data), and without alteration. Using message transfer as the underlying carrier, the interpersonal messaging service provides users with facilities to assist in communicating with one another; effectively, it defines the encoding and interpretation of message content exchanged end-to-end between user agents.

The functional entities which cooperate to provide the user with message handling services are described below.

10.4.1 The user agent (UA)

The *user agent* provides access to the MTS for its client user. The minimum functionality required of a UA is that it can perform the submission interaction and the delivery interaction with the MTS. In practice, the UA will sustain a range of other capabilities to provide its user with additional services for message composition and manipulation. In preparing a message for submission, the user may exercise a variety of locally-provided tools, including editors, word processing packages, spelling checkers and document formatters. The user will also expect the UA to provide facilities for retrieving and processing messages previously received, for the purpose of review or in order to perform operations such as replying and forwarding to other users. Thus the UA should combine text processing facilities, message database management (for storage, retrieval and keyed search of messages), and message manipulation (to build new messages from parts of old ones). The precise operation of these local UA functions lies beyond the scope of the standards although they are of immediate interest to the end-user.

The manner in which a UA interacts with its MTA will vary according to their physical configuration. Both may be implemented as processes on the same computer system (see Figure 10.4). In this case, message submission and delivery is

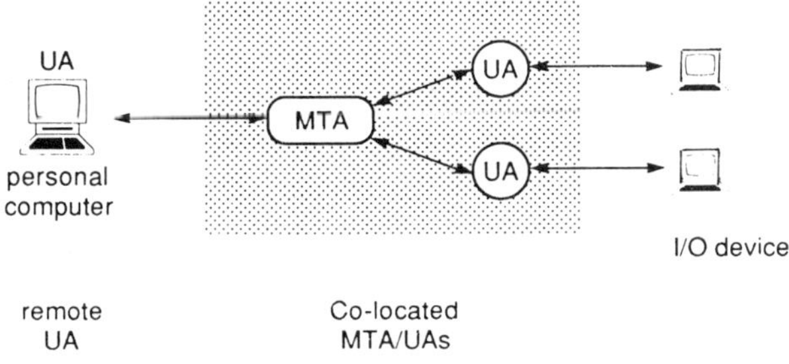

Fig. 10.4 — Remote UAs and co-located MTA-UAs.

performed by direct interaction between the two. As this is a local function, it is not subject to standardization. The user would typically access his UA using a keyboard/ display device.

Alternatively, a user may employ a UA implemented on a personal computer, remote from the MTA. As this involves non-local operation, the access mechanisms are subject to OSI standardization. The services required include UA log-on to the MTA, which may involve the presentation of a name and password, and formally defined message submission and delivery operations. The MTS may also perform delivery autonomously by initiating the access procedure which establishes an association with the personal computer. This MTA-initiated delivery may be subject to restrictions placed by the UA on acceptable message size, message type and message priority. A UA can employ the *hold for delivery* service to instruct the MTA to refrain from attempting delivery of some or all messages until the UA lifts the restriction. A set of management functions is also defined to allow the remote UA to effect changes in its registration parameters with the MTA: name, password, acceptable message size, etc. The X.400 (1984) Recommendations define these operations in the 'P3' protocol.

It was found that P3 did not satisfy all the messaging requirements of users working with personal computers. For example, when a UA becomes attached to its MTA using the P3 protocol, it is obliged to take delivery of unexamined messages in an unselective fashion. Consequently, time may be spent in taking delivery of unwanted messages by transmission over relatively slow communication links. The quantity of backing store available on these small systems is also seen as a limiting factor. The message store facility was introduced in the 1988 standards to address these problems (see section 10.4.4).

UAs are grouped into classes, according to the content-type of the messages which each is capable of processing. Each user message submitted by a UA contains an indication of its content-type and hence the class of UA which originated it. Only a recipient UA of a similar class is capable of interpreting the message content correctly. The P2 content-type defines the syntax and semantics of the message content-type used in the message handling application known as Interpersonal Messaging (IPM). This service provides a user with the capability to communicate with other users of the IPM service. The service uses the infrastructure provided by the MHS for submitting, relaying, and delivering messages, but is itself concerned only with the message content exchanged between the end-users. This is discussed in detail in section 10.11. To date, IPM is the only message content-type which has been standardized. It is likely that further content-types will be defined, to support communication between new classes of cooperating UAs. The first of these is likely to be the Pedi content-type (edi stands for electronic data interchange), which addresses the communication requirements of businesses, in the exchange of purchase orders and invoices.

10.4.2 The message transfer agent (MTA)

The *message transfer agent* is a functional entity which, in cooperation with similar entities, conveys messages through the message transfer system. It performs activities in response to service requests from two sources:

— submission requests made by a client UA.
— messages received by transfer from a remote MTA.

An MTA in receipt of a message from either source undertakes responsibility, on behalf of the whole MTS, for the correct handling of the message. The nature of the responsibility varies according to the message type: user message, probe or delivery report. Typically, an MTA's responsibility for a message ends with its successful local delivery, or, where the message is addressed to a non-local recipient, with its transfer to a remote MTA.

When a message is submitted, its submission envelope is validated and some items of red-tape are dealt with, such as recording submission time and generating a message identifier. The next stage of processing can be regarded as being aligned to the treatment of an incoming message received by transfer from a remote MTA.

The actions which result from the arrival of an incoming message are described below. The message (user message, probe or report) is examined and its recipients extracted. For each recipient for whom delivery is still outstanding, three possibilities exist:

Case 1. *The recipient is a client of this MTA*
The action taken varies for each message type. For a user message, the message is delivered if this is possible. If the originator requested confirmation of delivery, then a delivery report is prepared and transferred back to him. If delivery is not possible, and the level of reporting requested by the recipient includes non-delivery, then a report containing the reason for non-delivery is prepared and transferred back.

If the incoming message is a delivery report then different actions are required. For the purposes of charging, or statistics collection, the MTA may employ a policy of requesting delivery reports for all messages which it originates. So, a received delivery report is matched with the corresponding subject-message (i.e. the original message which is the subject of the report), and the charge or statistic is recorded. If the level of report requested by the originator of the subject-message was sufficiently high, then the delivery report is delivered to him. Alternatively, the MTA may delay delivery of individual reports until all reports expected for a particular subject-message have been received, and then deliver a single combined report to the originator.

If the incoming message is a probe, and a message with characteristics similar to those described by the probe envelope could be delivered, then the report generation consistent with that event is performed. Otherwise, non-delivery is reported.

For simplicity, this description of events has not included the possibility of message redirection. The circumstances under which redirection can occur are discussed in section 10.8. A further possibility which has been omitted is that conversion of message content may be required. See section 10.8 for details of conversion options.

Case 2. *The recipient is associated with a remote MTA*
Again, the actions taken depend on message type. For a delivery report, the trace information detailing the report's progress through the MTS is checked for loops. If the report is found to be looping, then it is deleted. Otherwise it is transferred to the remote MTA. Since a delivery report has a single recipient, only one transfer is required.

For a user message or probe, again a check is made for loops, and if found, a non-delivery report is generated. Otherwise, a process of message replication is followed. The position to be reached once all recipient names have been processed is that a distinct copy of the message should have been created for each distinct MTA, which will then become responsible for the next stage of processing. Therefore, if the current recipient is the first to require relaying to a particular MTA, then a copy of the message is made, with the envelope amended to indicate that the remote MTA is held responsible for dealing with this recipient only. If a copy has already been made, then its envelope is amended to indicate that the remote MTA is held responsible for progressing delivery to this additional recipient. All copies of the message destined for different MTAs are identical except for the flags stored against each recipient name, which indicate to the receiving MTA the recipients for which it is held responsible.

Case 3. *An error is detected in the recipient name*
A delivery report is normally generated. Depending on the nature of the error, message redirection to an alternative recipient may be possible. Redirection is discussed in section 10.8.

10.4.3 The message transfer system (MTS)

The *message transfer system*, comprising all the individual MTAs, is a distributed system providing international message transfer services. It effectively constitutes the backbone communications system of MHS. The MTS conveys messages regardless of their content-type. It neither examines nor alters the content of messages in transit, but confines its attention to the message envelope.

The MTS is partitioned into a number of *management domains* (MDs). Each MD contains at least one MTA and zero or more UAs. The purpose of dividing the MTS into domains is to devolve the responsibility for the organization and management of the system to authorities capable of undertaking this task. Each domain is responsible for its own internal management, in particular for the correct routing of messages and their reliable delivery. A message which enters a domain remains its responsibility until either it is delivered internally, or it is relayed to an external domain.

Where the MD is managed by a CCITT Administration (i.e. a PTT, or national telecommunications body), it is known as an *administration management domain* (ADMD). Where the MD is managed by a private organization it is known as a *private management domain* (PRMD). The X.400 (1984) recommendations are principally concerned with the interworking between ADMDs; PRMDs are regarded as existing strictly within national boundaries and subject to the authority of the associated ADMD, which have a role in overseeing their correct operation. Communication between PRMDs located in different countries should take place via the ADMDs in each country. Furthermore, direct communication between PRMDs in the same country is considered to be beyond the scope of the recommendations.

The ISO view of MDs is rather different. Here the main concern is to standardize the interconnection of open systems, not just those managed by Administrations. Hence ISO 10021 allows for the interconnection of PRMDs both domestically and internationally. Many countries have taken steps to deregulate the telecommunications industry, abolishing the role of the monopoly PTT which acts both as service provider and regulating authority. Consequently, responsibility for the regulation of service providers has fallen to other national authorities, which have refined the International Standards according to national policy. Figure 10.5 illustrates one possible configuration of ADMDs and PRMDs from the ISO viewpoint.

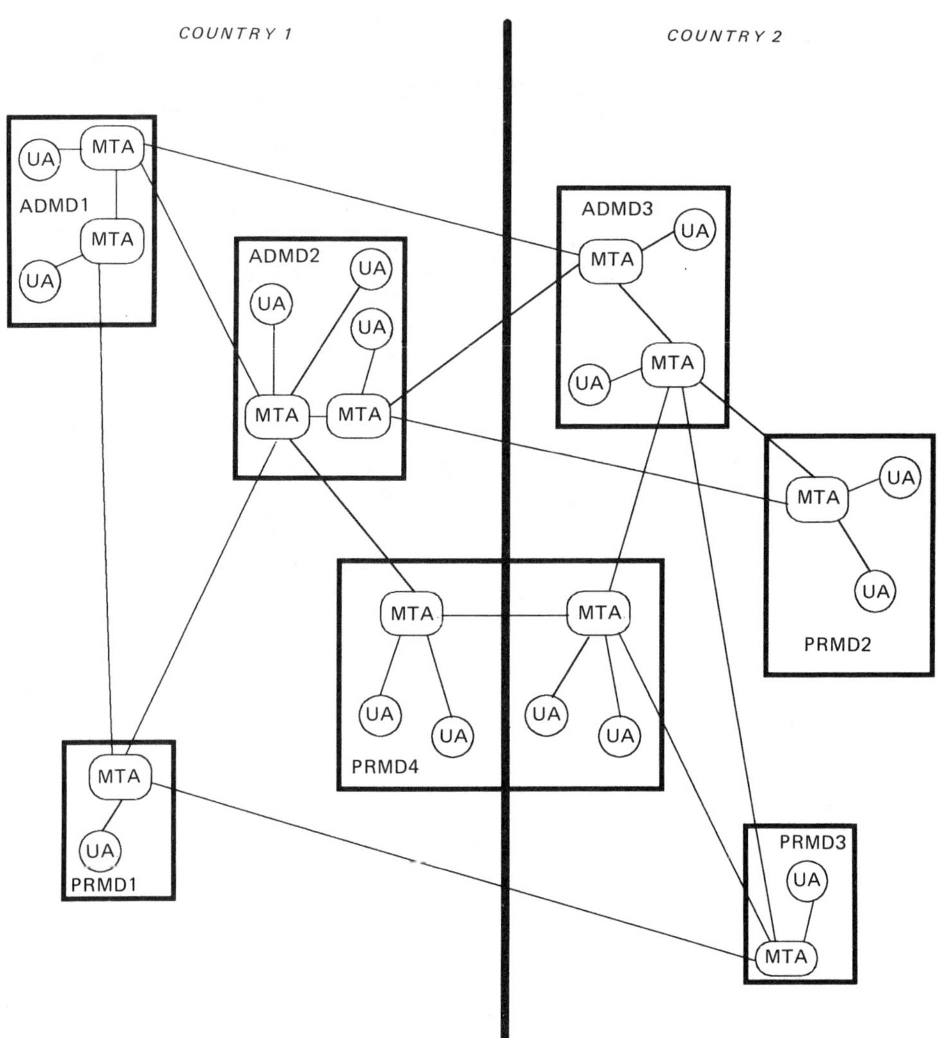

Fig. 10.5 — Administration and private management domains.

MHS is distributed globally, linking many organizations in many countries for the purpose of message transfer; the organizational configurations of MDs constructed on this scale will clearly be complex.

10.4.4 The message store (MS)

Section 10.4.1 indicated that X.400 services could be provided using a wide range of equipment, configured in a variety of ways. In particular, personal computers (PCs) will have an increasing role to play as stand-alone UAs, and the 1984 recommendations did provide a mechanism to allow remote UAs to perform submission and delivery interactions with an MTA by use of the P3 protocol. However, this mode of operation suffers from a number of problems due to the restricted capabilities of these isolated devices.

The first difficulty suffered by PC UAs is that the MTA must hold for delivery all messages addressed to a remote UA until that UA makes itself available for delivery. If the UA remains incommunicado for a given time, possibly as little as 24 hours, then the MTS may declare the queued messages to be undeliverable and return non-delivery notifications to their originators. If the PC is powered-down for an extended period, then the recipient may lose messages. Even if the recipient can anticipate a down-time for his PC, he cannot take steps to arrange that his messages will be auto-forwarded to another UA for the period during which the PC is not available. Auto-forwarding is only possible if the UA first takes delivery of a message then itself performs forwarding to another recipient. The 1988 standards do include another service for message redirection, *recipient-requested redirection*, which could be employed where down-time was anticipated. However, this is still not a very satisfactory solution.

A second area of difficulty lies in the storage capabilities of PCs. A UA must be able to provide facilities for the storage of delivered messages. A basic requirement is that the quantity of store available should be sufficient to hold all the user's messages: the user should not have imposed on him the drudgery of constantly purging messages, sooner than he would otherwise wish, in order to make room for new ones. A second basic requirement is that the integrity of the store should be preserved from corruption or accidental loss, by the adoption of a backup regime. This entails placing copies of messages on an alternative storage medium at regular intervals. Many PCs are not equipped to satisfy either of these requirements. A further problem arises if the user wishes to access his message database from a location remote from his office; messages locked-away on a PC are not accessible remotely.

For these and other reasons, there is an apparent need for an additional functional entity, placed between the UA and MTA. This entity, introduced in the 1988 standards, is known as the *message store* (MS). It provides facilities for taking delivery of messages from the MTS, storing them reliably, allowing UA retrieval of individual messages, and performing message deletion under UA instruction. To allow the user to make an informed choice on which messages are to be retrieved at any one time, the MS can provide a synopsis of the messages it holds. This might include details of various message attributes, such as originator, size, submission date, and subject.

The MS may also be authorized by the UA to perform various functions automatically, such as auto-forwarding of delivered messages (or only of those which satisfy some criteria), generation of receipt notifications (see section 10.11.3), and automatic deletion of time-expired messages. The stand-alone UA accesses the MS by means of the MS-access protocol (P7). The P3 protocol defined in the 1984 recommendations is retained, but operates between the MS and MTA rather than between the UA and MTA.

As currently defined, the MS provides an 'in-tray' for the short-term storage of delivered messages. Extensions to the functionality of the MS to equip it to satisfy a broader set of requirements are at present under consideration with the standards organizations.

10.4.5 The access unit

The *access unit* (AU) provides a gateway between MHS and an external communications service. Three types of AU have been defined, providing MHS access to physical delivery systems (i.e. the postal system), telematic agents, and telex agents. An MHS user who specifies that a particular recipient should receive a message by physical delivery may also specify a variety of parameters to control the disposition of the message within the physical delivery system. If such a message is found to be undeliverable, a non-delivery report may be sent back to the originator by post. For the teletex and telex systems, messages may be both originated and received on these terminals.

10.5 NAMING AND ADDRESSING

When a user submits a message, he must inform the MTS of the identity of the intended recipients. Both originators and recipients are defined by *O/R name* (where 'O/R' represents 'originator/recipient'). Every user of MHS has one or more O/R names, which are equivalent in the sense that they all identify the user unambiguously. An O/R name has two components, at least one of which must be present:

— directory name
— O/R address

As its name suggests, the O/R address contains information which an MTA can readily transform into instructions for routing a message to its destination; this process is described below. By contrast, a directory name is intended to fulfil a much broader function.

The *directory name* is defined in the context of the *Directory service* (see Chaper 11). This is an ambitious project, intended to provide a global, interconnected directory service for all types of OSI entities: individuals, distribution lists, application entities, MTAs; in general, all agents involved in OSI communication. MHS has a clear need for directory services, and in recognition of this the directory name is included as a component of the O/R name. The directory name is intended to be a more user-friendly and more stable form of name than the O/R address, which may be subject to change, reflecting the changing physical configuration of MHS. If a user originates a message addressed to an O/R name which consists solely of a directory name, then the MTS is expected to consult the Directory to discover the corresponding O/R address. If an originator supplies an O/R address in the O/R name, then the MTS will use this directly to route the message to its recipient. As the Directory becomes established, it is intended that users will become known to each other by directory name, with the use of O/R addresses confined to internal operations within the MTS. Until this time, O/R addresses must be supplied by users of MHS: every O/R name will simply consist of an O/R address.

The Directory may also be consulted by a user to verify that a given address is valid, or to discover an address given some other details of the intended recipient: "There are two Bob Smiths in Marketing. What is the mail address of the one with telephone extension 2642?"

The *O/R address* is modelled as an ordered list of attributes, each of which consists of a type and a value. For example, the attribute type *country-name* could in one instance have the attribute value 'Spain'. A number of standard attribute types are defined, as described below:

country-name	identifies a country
administration-domain-name	identifies an ADMD within the country named by country-name
private-domain-name	identifies a PRMD, within the context of the ADMD or the country
organization-name	identifies an organization within the context of the ADMD or the PRMD
organizational-unit-name	identifies a division of the named organization, or identifies a sub-unit of a previously named organizational-unit
personal-name	identifies an individual within the context of another entity (e.g. organization), and consists of surname, and optionally, any of given name, initials (excluding surname initial), and generation qualifier (e.g. 'Jr').
common-name	identifies a user or distribution list, within the context of another entity (e.g. organization).

A number of other standard attributes are defined for specialized access to MHS. These are *numeric-user-identifier*, *network-address* and *terminal-identifier*. A further kind of attribute is allowed, the *domain-defined attribute*. This provides a bridging mechanism to allow MDs which already employ a private addressing convention to continue to use this for an interim period. Their use should eventually be replaced by the use of standard attributes.

Given that a variety of standard attribute types are available, how are they assembled to construct O/R addresses? The standards define a series of *O/R address forms*, each adapted to serve a distinct mode of access to MHS. For each form, a different set of attributes is allowed, some of which must be present in all addresses, and others which may be present dependent on the rules adopted by the ADMD within which the address is located. The forms defined include the following:

mnemonic O/R address	for user-friendly naming of individuals or distribution lists.
numeric O/R address	for identifying a user by means of a numeric keypad.
terminal O/R address	for identifying a user by means of a network address (e.g. a Telex user).

postal O/R address for identifying a user capable of receiving a message by means of the postal system.

The *mnemonic O/R address* is the most important O/R address form in present MHS systems. It is intended to provide a user-friendly style of naming until the Directory service becomes established. It identifies a user or distribution list relative to an MD. The MD is identified by country-name, ADMD-name, and optionally PRMD-name. The user or DL is identified relative to this MD by a combination of organization-name, organizational-unit-name, and personal-name or common-name. In addition, one or more domain-defined-attributes may be present.

It should be noted that MHS simply provides the framework for the construction of O/R addresses; the allocation of actual values for the names and addresses used in MHS is devolved to the responsible naming authority (i.e. the management domain or organization).

While an O/R address specifies where the delivery point of a message is located, an MTA must be capable of devising a *route* which enables it to relay the message to that point. This process has not been formally standardized, but some guidelines have been drawn up. The optimal approach is to transfer the message directly to the MTA with which the recipient's UA is registered. There are several reasons why this may not be practical: it may be necessary to route the message to an intermediate MTA to access a conversion service; the cost of acquiring and maintaining routing information may limit the quantity of information available; certain MDs may wish to restrict disclosure of their internal structure, and only allow connection through nominated MTAs; the need to control costs may favour the use of 'trunk' links, even where this introduces additional relaying steps; where available, a high-bandwidth link may be preferred to a more direct but ultimately slower route.

An MTA must first determine whether the recipient belongs to the same MD as itself, by examining the country-name, ADMD-name, and PRMD-name attributes. If the recipient is located within this MD, the remaining attributes of the O/R address are used to discover if the UA is registered with this MTA, in which case local delivery occurs. Otherwise, unless another MTA can be identified capable of progressing the transfer of the message to its destination, the message is declared undeliverable. If the recipient is located in a remote MD, then the MTA may have knowledge of a route to that MD. If the external MD is unknown, then transfer to an ADMD is appropriate. ADMDs possess the capability to relay to all other ADMDs, and so provide a backbone service through which all PRMDs may be reached.

An important service offered by the Directory is the provision of *distribution lists* (DLs). Each DL has a name, and an associated list of member O/R names. MHS makes use of DLs by providing a *DL expansion service*, which allows an originator to send his message to a group of recipients by citing the name of the group, rather than by naming each member of it.

Since an O/R name which denotes a DL is not readily distinguishable from an O/R name belonging to an individual, an originator may submit a message, not realizing that it addresses a DL O/R name which is then subject to expansion; to prevent this unintended consequence, a service is provided which enables a message originator to prohibit DL expansion of a submitted message.

A DL's O/R address specifies the point (i.e. the MTA) at which expansion occurs. A message which contains a DL recipient name is conveyed to this expansion point, where the set of member names of the DL are added to the list of recipients of the message. A member of a DL may itself identify another DL. In this case, the message is routed to the next expansion point. If two DLs each contain the name of the other, then the possibility of a closed loop arises, within which a message might circulate indefinitely. To prevent this, a *DL expansion history* field is added to a message each time it undergoes expansion. By inspecting this field, an MTA about to perform expansion of a DL can check whether expansion of this DL has already been performed; if so, the expansion is abandoned. The DL expansion history field also informs a recipient that he has received a message by virtue of his membership of a given DL.

After DL expansion, delivery to one of the DL members might cause the generation of a delivery report, or non-delivery report. This report is returned to the DL which performed the expansion. Depending on the policy adopted by the DL, the report will normally be forwarded to the DL owner (the person responsible for its maintenance), but may also be forwarded to the message originator.

10.6 MHS APPLICATION LAYER MODEL

The individual components of the MHS system have been described in earlier sections. This section examines how these components fit together within a common framework. MHS employs an *abstract model* to describe how its activities are performed in a distributed environment. This model uses the concepts of *objects*, (UAs, MSs, MTAs), *ports*, (points of connection between objects), and *services* (capabilities that one object offers to another by means of its ports). Figure 10.6

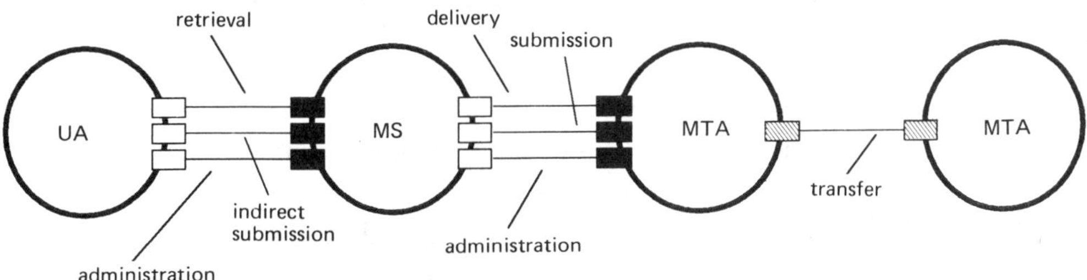

Fig. 10.6 — MHS ports.

shows the objects and ports defined in the MHS model. This approach assists the process of standardization by providing a mechanism to describe the activity of an application in abstract terms independent of any particular concrete realization. Thus a *service definition* can be developed which specifies precisely what the task is intended to accomplish without regard to the *protocol* details. In earlier standards, where service definition and protocol definition were not delineated, implementors were occasionally obliged to attempt to deduce the intended service provision from a reading of the protocol. A further reason for making this separation is that several concrete realizations may all satisfy the same service definition: a distributed system may contain some components which operate using proprietory means while others employ OSI communication. So long as the overall functionality of the task is maintained, the objective of OSI is satisfied.

Interaction between objects can occur only after a *binding* has been established between a pair of corresponding ports. The performance of a service occurs between paired ports where one object invokes an operation which is then executed by its paired object. Three types of port are shown in Figure 10.6. The open boxes represent ports which consume a service, closed boxes represent ports which supply a service, and hatched boxes represent ports which are capable of operating in either mode. The nature of the application task, and the definition of the operations performed, determines the mode of behaviour of each port. In a typical application, the bind operation establishes an application association by connecting one or more pairs of ports for the duration of the association; a corresponding operation, unbind, releases the association.

Given a description of a distributed processing task expressed in terms of an abstract model relating objects, ports and services, it is necessary to specify the manner in which the concrete realization of the model is constructed. As we have seen, in OSI, objects are realized by application processes which communicate with peer processes within an application context. The application context determines the binding, use and unbinding of sets of paired ports. In turn, an application context is defined as the cooperative activity of a group of application service elements. Thus the link between the abstract model discussed here and the application layer architecture discussed in Chapter 4 lies in defining an ASE for each port of the model. Consequently, the MHS standards contain protocol specifications which define ASEs for each of the ports shown in Figure 10.6. This correspondence is shown in Table 10.1. (As a detail it can be noted that the MS and UA employ the

Table 10.1 — Mapping of ports to protocol elements

Protocol	Application context	ASEs	Ports
P1	mts-transfer	Message-transfer (RTSE, ACSE)	transfer
P3	mts-access	message-submission message-administration message-delivery (ROSE, ACSE)	submission administration delivery
P7	ms-access	message-submission message-administration message-retrieval (ROSE, ACSE)	submission administration retrieval

same ASEs for submission and administration; the MS simply propagates operations invoked by a UA to the MTA.)

A further correspondence between the model and its concrete realization in protocol terms is provided by the use of remote operations (ROS). ROS provides a set of services (through the remote operations service element, ROSE), which support the invocation and execution of operations in interactive applications. ROS supplies a notation for the specification of application contexts and ASEs, and a set of macros (BIND, UNBIND, OPERATION, ERROR) which constitute an operation interface to the application context. By providing a framework for the specification of a ROS-based application protocol which corresponds exactly to the framework used to specify services within an abstract model, ROS provides a straightforward mapping of abstract services to application protocol.

A number of features of Table 10.1 deserve further comment. Each of the protocols P1, P3, and P7 is shown with a single corresponding application context. In fact, each protocol includes several application contexts which accommodate different modes of operation. The primary source of these variations arises from the use of the reliable transfer service element (RTSE) in place of ROSE. Reliable transfer was defined in the 1984 standards to support the transfer of PDUs between application entities. At that time the standards for presentation and session were not complete, so reliable transfer included certain capabilities which have since become the concern of presentation and session. In addition, with the development of ROS, with its general solution for the support of the request/response mode of interaction between entities engaged in interactive applications, RTSE may be regarded as largely obsolete. However, to preserve the existing base of implementations which rely on the use of RTSE, it has been retained within the P1 application contexts. Given the small number of P3 implementations developed before 1988, support for the RTSE-based P3 application context is optional while support for the ROSE-based P3 application context is mandatory. Similarly the P7 protocol favours the ROSE-based approach over the RTSE-based application context.

The absence of a ROSE-based P1 application context is a curious omission perhaps owing more to expediency than to consistent modelling. Since 1984, RTSE has been developed to make proper use of session services, and so exists in two versions: 1984-mode and 'normal' mode. For the historical reasons indicated RTSE may persist for some time within P1 application contexts. However, it is a doubtful candidate for adoption in the application contexts of any other standard; in particular, the Directory protocols are ROSE-based.

Table 10.1 does not include P2 among the protocols described. The reason for this is that within the current application model (containing objects, ports, and services) message content is encapsulted as transparent data in the protocols used to convey it, and holds meaning only for the end-users between whom it is exchanged. Consequently, P2 is not relevant in the definition of ASEs and is not regarded as a true protocol, but rather as a convenient label for a particular content-type.

10.6.1 MHS ports

This section briefly examines each of the ports illustrated in Figure 10.6. The **transfer port** enables MTAs to exchange messages, probes, and reports, in order to convey these message types from originator to recipient. These operations are internal to the

MTS and do not concern MHS agents which lie beyond the boundary of the MTS. The operations available at the transfer port are described in section 10.7.

The **submission port** enables the MTS-user (a UA or MS) to submit a message or probe to the MTS for transfer, and, in the case of a message, delivery to other MTS-users. This activity may be performed directly by a UA (using the P3 protocol), or indirectly where the UA employs an MS to convey the submission request on its behalf to the MTS (using the P7 protocol). The submission-control service enables the MTS to temporarily restrict the range of submission operations which the MTS-user may invoke.

The **delivery port** allows an MTS-user to accept delivery of messages or reports from the MTS. Since this port optionally enables the MTS to initiate delivery, further services are provided to enable the MTS-user to place temporary constraints, based on factors such as message size, content type, and priority, upon the use of this port by the MTS.

The **administration port** enables both the MTS-user and the MTS to change the information it uses to authenticate its identity to the other when establishing an association. A further service enables the MTS-user to register details of its ability to process various message encodings and content types; the MTS will deliver only those messages which satisfy the registered constraints.

The **retrieval port** provides services which enable the UA to perform a variety of selection and retrieval operations on the set of delivered messages which the MS stores on its behalf. The role of the MS in the 1988 standards is to act as a short-term repository for messages. However, the requirement exists for a facility which will provide UAs with a complete message storage and retrieval service. The standards may accommodate these additional requirements in a future extension.

10.7 THE MTS TRANSFER PROTOCOL (P1)

The MTS provides the backbone service of MHS in transporting messages from orginator to recipient in a manner which treats message content as transparent data. The MTS consists of a collection of MTAs which cooperate to supply message transfer services to MTS-users. MTA communication is modelled as the performance of operations which take place at the transfer ports of paired MTAs. As we have seen, communication between application processes (in this case, MTAs) is defined by an application context which specifies the behaviour of the application entities which perform the interactions.

The application context for message transfer enlists three service elements to accomplish its purpose. The principal activities are undertaken by the message transfer service element (MTSE), with RTSE and ACSE acting in supporting roles. The MT application entity contains an additional element, the *user-element*, which coordinates the activities of the other service elements in performing the application task (see Figure 10.7).

The MTSE provides a set of services for message transfer to the service user. The three services offered are concerned with the transfer of distinct message types:

— *message-transfer* to transfer a user message
— *probe-transfer* to transfer a probe

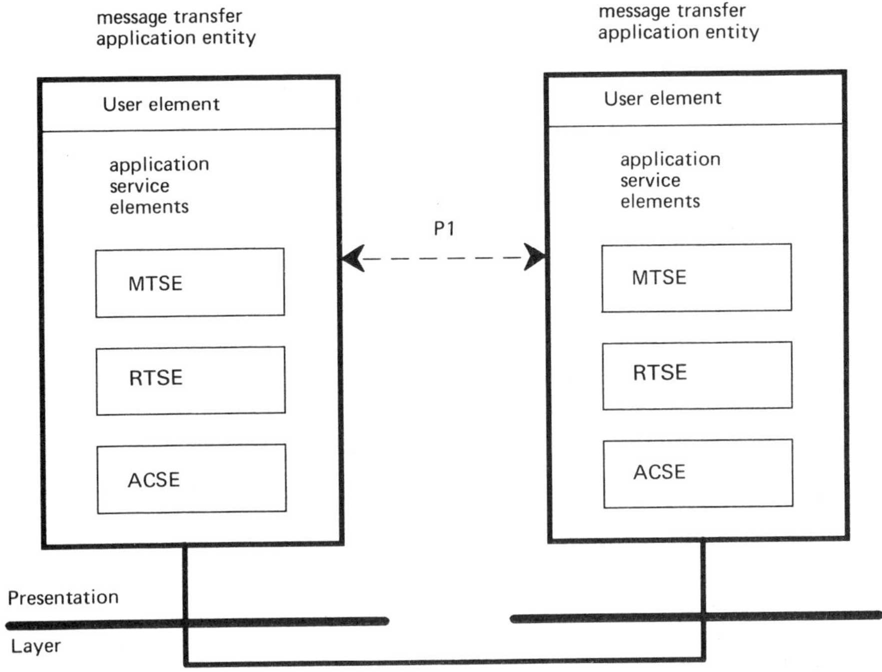

Fig. 10.7 — MTS transfer protocol model.

— *report-transfer* to transfer a delivery report

Each of these services is examined in the following sections.

There are two additional application contexts for message transfer, both designed to enable interworking between 1988 implementations and 1984 implementations. One of these contexts operates purely as a 1984 system; the other includes the 1988 extensions, but communicates with a 1984 system using the 1984 RTSE. Neither of these additional application contexts is mandatory in ISO 10021 though both are in X.400.

10.8 THE MTS MESSAGE-TRANSFER SERVICE

We now consider the MTS message-transfer service in more detail. It is concerned with a central activity of MHS: the transfer of a message through the MTS. This service enables one MTA to transfer a user message over an application association to a remote MTA.

The reader is reminded that the MTS confines its attention to the envelope of the message, except in the special case of conversion. The content of the message and its type (e.g. interpersonal message), is not of concern here. The envelope details are modelled as a set of parameters to the MTS message-transfer service, presented by the MTS-user when it invokes the service. As a reminder of the context of the discussion so far, Figure 10.8 indicates that we have focussed on the parameters of the MTS message-transfer service, which is one of the services of the MTSE, which in turn is a service element enlisted by the message transfer application context. The parameters of MTS message-transfer are summarized in Table 10.2. In the following discussion, related parameters are grouped into several categories.

10.8.1 Routing parameters

This set of parameters is concerned with controlling the transfer of the user message through the MTS. The following routing parameters are defined:

Message-identifier distinguishes the user message from all other messages within the MTS. It is assigned by the originating MTA when the message is submitted, and is chosen to be different from that of any other message, probe or delivery report within the MTS. It consists of two parts: an identifier chosen by the originating MTA, and unique within its management domain, and a global-domain-identifier for the domain. Together, these provide an unambiguous identifier for the message. This identifier is used within the MTS to reference the message in any subsequently generated delivery reports. The user has a distinct identifier for his message which he may use to correlate delivery reports and the messages to which they refer.

Originator-name contains the O/R name (see section 10.5) of the originator of the message.

Priority specifies the relative priority of the message, as either *normal*, *non-urgent* or *urgent*. A message with a high priority may be transferred preferentially through the MTS, but at a higher tariff charge. Equally, a low priority message may be delayed for transmission before being sent at 'off-peak' rates.

Per-domain-bilateral-info carries information between the management domains involved in the transfer of a message through the MTS. Its purpose is to provide a mechanism for accounting and charging where several administrations are involved in message transfer.

Recipient-name contains the O/R name of a recipient of the message, and occurs once for each recipient. Associated with each recipient name is a **responsibility** flag which indicates to an MTA receiving the message whether it has been given the responsibility of progressing the delivery of the message to this particular recipient. The MTA discharges its responsibility by either delivering the message, if the recipient is known locally, or by transferring the message to an MTA closer to the recipient. Alternatively, if delivery is found to be impossible, then its responsibility ends with the generation of a delivery report, if this is consistent with the values of the delivery-report-request parameters. A further parameter, **originally-specified-recipient-number**, is also present, again with a distinct value for each recipient. The value is an integer; one for the first originally specified recipient name, and incrementing in steps of one to the last name. This parameter, combined with the message-identifier, unambiguously identifies the copy of the message delivered to each recipient.

DL-expansion-history contains the names of all the distribution lists which have been expanded, and whose members have been added to the list of recipients of the message. The parameter is generated by the first MTA to perform expansion, and is added to subsequently by MTAs performing further expansions.

DL-expansion-prohibited is specified by the originator, to control whether the

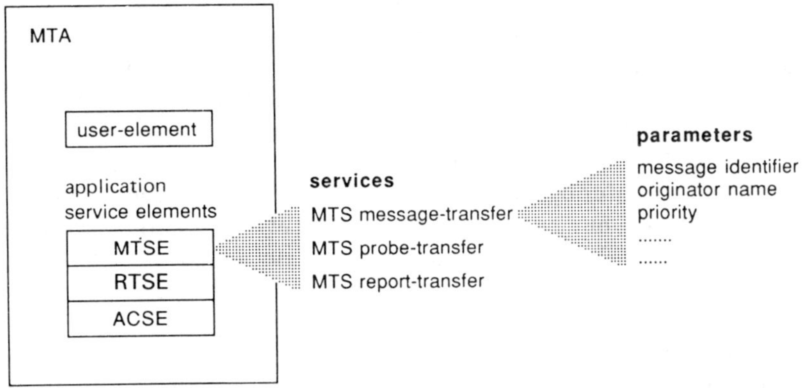

Fig. 10.8 — MTS message-transfer context.

Table 10.2 — MTS message-transfer parameters

Parameter	Description
Message-identifier	MPDU identifier
Originator-name	O/R name
Original-EITs	EITs before conversion
Content-type	If IPM, then 'P2' or 'P22'
Content-identifier	Conveyed to the recipient
Content-correlator	For use in subsequent delivery reports
Priority	Normal/non-urgent/urgent
DL-expansion-history	SEQUENCE of O/R name, Time
DL-expansion-prohibited	True/false
Disclose-recipients	To all recipients (true/false)
Conversion-prohibited	Of content's EITs (true/false)
Conversion-with-loss-prohibited	Of content's EITs (true/false)
Alternate-recipient-allowed	In the event of non-delivery (true/false)
Content-return-request	In the event of non-delivery (true/false)
Deferred-delivery-time	Date and time
Latest-delivery-time	Date and time
Per-domain-bilateral-information	SEQUENCE of country, ADMD, information
Security-parameters	See below
Recipient-redirection-prohibited	True/false
(SEQUENCE of recipient information)	For each recipient:
Recipient-name	To whom the message is to be delivered
Originally-specified-recipient-number	Integer value
Explicit-conversion	Requested at submission
Responsibility	True/false
Originator-requested-alternate-recipient	If intended recipient not available
Intended-recipient-name	If redirection has taken place
Redirection-reason	If redirection has taken place
Originator-delivery-report-request	Level of report required by recipient
MTA-delivery-report-request	Level of report required by MTA
Trace-information	Global domain identifier, trace info
Internal-trace-information	Global domain identifier, trace info
Content	User message (all other parameters constitute the envelope)

message may be sent to the members of a distribution list, i.e., whether a distribution list may be expanded, and its member names added to the set of message recipients. Since the message originator may not be aware that a particular O/R name identifies a distribution list, this parameter can prevent the unintended dispatch of a message to a set of distribution list members.

Trace-information records details of the conveyance of the message by each management domain through which it passes. **Internal-trace-information** similarly provides an audit trail, but is restricted to detailing events occurring within the local management domain. This information is not normally included when the message is transferred to an MTA belonging to a different management domain.

10.8.2 Redirection parameters

When a message cannot be delivered to its intended recipient because the specified recipient name does not match any UA known locally, it may be possible to redirect the message to an *alternate recipient*, or post-room facility run by the organization. (The term 'alternative recipient' might have been a better choice here.) Another cause for redirection is where a user instructs the MTS to redirect all messages addressed to him for delivery to another UA for some period. The following parameters control these activities.

Alternate-recipient-allowed may be specified by a message originator to grant permission to the MTS to deliver the message to an alternate recipient should it prove impossible to deliver it to its intended recipient. Often, an organization will nominate a UA to act as alternate recipient for messages correctly addressed to the organization, but where the personal name portion of the address does not match any locally known name. Messages received by the alternate recipient may then be manually forwarded, if the post-room personnel can deduce the correct recipient name.

Recipient-redirection-prohibited allows the message originator to control whether redirection, requested by the recipient, can take place. The originator may forbid redirection of the message if its contents are personal, or have some security sensitivity.

Originator-requested-alternate-recipient allows the originator to specify, for each intended recipient, one alternate recipient to whom the message may be delivered should delivery to the intended recipient prove impossible. The MTS will attempt this redirection only if the intended recipient name is correctly addressed at least as far as organization name.

Intended-recipient-name is added to the message by the MTA of the intended recipient when it undertakes redirection of the message. The parameter contains the recipient O/R name specified by the originator. This enables the recipient who actually receives the message to determine on whose behalf the message was redirected. It also provides a simple mechanism for preventing a message from looping endlessly through a circuit of redirecting UAs. For each recipient of the message, a different value of this parameter may appear (or several values if the message is redirected more than once).

Redirection-reason is added to the message by the MTA of the intended recipient when it performs redirection of the message. The parameter informs the actual recipient of the circumstances which caused the message to be redirected to him.

Again, for each recipient of the message, a different value of the parameter may be specified (or several values if the message is redirected more than once). The parameter takes one of the following values:

alternate recipient The recipient name was incorrectly specified, but judged by the MD to refer to a UA within the local organization. (In addition, the originator did not forbid redirection to the alternate recipient.) The actual recipient in this case is the UA nominated by the organization to receive such messages; if the identity of the intended recipient can be deduced, then the message can be forwarded manually to him.

originator-requested Again, the originator name was incorrectly specified, but the originator had nominated an alternate recipient to receive the message in the event that delivery to the intended recipient was not possible.

recipient-requested The intended recipient of the message had previously instructed the MTS to redirect all incoming messages intended for it to another UA. The intended recipient may have nominated a proxy UA to receive his messages because he anticipated a prolonged absence from the office.

10.8.3 Conversion parameters

As noted, the purpose of conversion within the MTS is to improve the possibilities for communication between users who possess terminals of different capabilities. Some conversions imply a loss of information, e.g. IA5 text to Telex, but where this loss is acceptable to the message originator, the conversion by the MTA makes possible communication between users which could not otherwise take place. The following conversion parameters are defined:

Originally-encoded-information-types indicates the encoded information types (EITs) of the content of the original message.

Conversion-prohibited indicates whether message content may be converted within the MTS. The message originator would use this parameter to prevent the MTS from performing conversion. This might be used if it was apparent to the originator that his message would not be meaningful unless it was presented to the recipient in the same form as it was submitted.

Conversion-with-loss-prohibited indicates whether a conversion which entails loss of information (e.g. IA5 text to Telex) is allowed. Coupled with the previous parameter, this parameter allows the originator to select whether conversion is allowed, or is prohibited, or is prohibited only in those cases where loss of information would result. If a particular recipient required a conversion which the originator had forbidden, then delivery would be abandoned, and a non-delivery report would be returned to the originator.

Explicit-conversion allows the message originator to request that a particular conversion be performed on the message before it is delivered. Use of this parameter might be indicated where the originator knows that a particular conversion will be required for several recipients, and so arranges that it is performed just once, on submission; it may also be used where the local MTA is known to be capable of performing the conversion, while the capabilities of the recipient MTAs are not known.

10.8.4 Delivery time parameters

These parameters allow a message originator to specify a time window during which a message must be delivered.

Deferred-delivery-time allows an originator to delay the delivery of a message, by specifying a date and time before which it should not be delivered. This facility is often used to send oneself, or others, reminders of some event. For example, it is possible to send out birthday greetings for the whole year on 1st January and have each delivered on the appropriate date.

Latest-delivery-time allows the originator to specify a date and time after which the message should not be delivered. Optionally, a non-delivery report would be returned if delivery did not take place before the time specified. This may be useful where the message is of short-term interest and lapses after a given time; in this case suppression of non-delivery notification might also be appropriate.

10.8.5 Disclose recipients parameter

Disclose-recipients allows a message originator to specify whether or not each recipient is informed, upon delivery, of the O/R names of his fellow recipients. This concerns disclosure of the set of names carried on the message envelope; the message content may also hold the full O/R names of all the recipients, or may only hold a free-form, or informal, version of each name.

10.8.6 Delivery report request parameters

These parameters control the circumstances under which delivery reports are generated by the MTS and the content of these reports.

Originator-delivery-report-request allows the originator to specify, on a per-recipient basis, the conditions which apply to the generation of delivery reports and non-delivery reports. The parameter indicates one of the following choices:

- No report (non-delivery report suppression). Even if the message cannot be delivered, no report should be returned to the originator.
- Basic (non-delivery report). Should it prove impossible to deliver the message, a non-delivery report is to be returned to the message originator.
- Confirmed. Both in the case of successful delivery and of non-delivery, an appropriate report is to be returned to the originator.

MTA-delivery-report-request allows the originating MTA to specify the level of report required. This must be at least the level of report requested by the originating UA. For the MTA, an additional level of reporting is defined, *audit-and-confirmed*, which requires the delivery report to contain all the trace information describing the message's journey though the MTS. For the purposes of charging or statistics collection, the MTA may specify a higher level of report than that requested by the originating UA. In ascending order, the reporting levels are no-report, basic, confirmed, and audit-and-confirmed. The parameter is specified on a per-recipient basis.

Content-return-request is selected by the originator to specify whether the content of the message is to be returned with any delivery report which may subsequently be created. If an originating UA is able to correlate a report with a local copy of the corresponding message, then it can make the economy of dispensing with return of content. Message size may also influence the setting of this parameter.

10.8.7 Security parameters

MHS has a number of security mechanisms designed to counter threats made to the integrity of the system. These threats take several forms: unauthorized access to MHS; one user masquerading as another; modification of a genuine message during its journey through the MTS; denial of having sent, or having received some message (particularly important where contracts are made by the exchange of messages).

Originator-certificate contains a verified copy (generated by a trusted source) of the originator's public encryption key. This may be required to enable recipients to validate the other security fields, in particular the message-token.

Message-token, in turn, may contain keys relevant to further security information. It may also convey a message-sequence-number which indicates the position of this message in a sequence of messages sent between the same two users; this allows the recipient to verify that the sequence has not been subject to message loss, reordering or replay (i.e. the receipt of the same message more than once).

Content-confidentiality-algorithm-identifier identifies the algorithm used by the message originator to encrypt the message content. The key required to perform decryption may be obtained from the message-token.

Content-integrity-check provides a means of verifying that the message content has not been modified, and also ensures that the originator cannot subsequently repudiate the message.

Message-origin-authentication-check provides the recipient, and any MTA through which the message passes, with the 'signature' of the message originator.

Message-security-label allows the message originator to attach to his message an indication of its sensitivity. This may be used by the MTS to guide its handling of the message; for example, it may refrain from delivering the message to a recipient with insufficient security clearance.

Proof-of-delivery enables the originator to request proof that the message was actually delivered to the recipient. This may be requested on a per-recipient basis.

10.8.8 Content parameters

Content-type defines the type of the content of the message, and is specified when the message is submitted. To date, only the interpersonal message content-type, 'P2', has been defined ('P22' identifies interpersonal messages which contain elements introduced in the 1988 version of the standard). However, a content-type of 'unidentified' may be specified, for private use between consenting management domains.

Content-identifier is conveyed to the message recipient and provides an identifier for the message content.

Content-correlator contains information which enables the originator to correlate the content of the message with any reports subseqently received.

Content consists of the message itself, supplied by the originator. All the preceding parameters belong to the message envelope. Message content is neither examined nor altered by the MTS, which confines its attention to the envelope parameters. The only exception to this is where conversion of the EITs of the content is either explicitly requested, or is allowed and is found necessary before delivery can take place.

A number of additional parameters are defined to control the treatment of the message when it is ported to a physical delivery system. These are not of central concern to OSI and are not considered further here.

10.9 THE MTS REPORT-TRANSFER SERVICE

The purpose of a delivery report is to inform the originator of a user message or probe, of the outcome of the attempt by the MTS to deliver it. In the case of a probe, the delivery report indicates whether or not the message described by the probe could have been delivered. By default, a report is sent only in the event of non-delivery; however, an originator may request a positive confirmation that his message was delivered. The message which is the subject of the report is referred to as the *subject-message*. Reports are generated by the MTS and are concerned only with events which occur within the MTS or at its boundary. Hence, successful delivery carries no implication that the recipient has actually seen the message, but rather that it is in some sense available to him. For interpersonal messages, a separate service is provided for receipt notification — see section 10.11.3. There are several possible reasons for unsuccessful delivery, e.g. transfer failure, conversion failure, invalid recipient address, time expired.

Delivery reports represent a distinct message type, with their own delivery report envelope and delivery report content definitions. These are summarized in Table 10.3.

Again, we can model the delivery report as a series of parameters to the MTS report-transfer service. These fall into three categories: envelope parameters, subject-message parameters and reported recipient parameters.

10.9.1 Delivery report envelope

The first three parameters constitute the delivery report envelope. The **delivery-report-identifier** distinguishes the report from all other messages, probes and reports within the MTS. The **originator-name** parameter identifies the originator of the subject-message, and hence the recipient of this report. The **trace-information** parameter records details of the report's traversal of the MTS.

10.9.2 Delivery report content

A single report may contain details of delivery and non-delivery concerning several recipients. Where an MTA determines the deliverability of a message to two recipients at the same moment, it is clearly preferable that it should return a single report rather than two distinct reports. To accommodate this, the parameters of the delivery report content are divided into two groups. The first group describes the message which is the subject of the report. The second group consists of one or more sets of *reported recipient information*, each of which describes delivery or non-delivery for a single recipient.

Table 10.3 — Structure of a delivery report

Envelope	
Delivery report identifier	— MPDU identifier
Originator name	— Hence, recipient of this report
Trace information	— For this report
Content	
Subject identifier	— Identifier for the subject-message
Content-type	— If IPM, then 'P2' or 'P22'
Content identifier	— Copied from the subject-message
Content correlator	— Copied from the subject-message
Returned content	— If requested in the subject-message
SEQUENCE of reported recipient information:	
Originator delivery report request	— No report/basic/confirmed
Originally specified recipient number	— Of the intended recipient
Subject intermediate trace information	— If audit-and-confirmed requested
Arrival time	— At the destination MD
Converted EITs	— The EITs after conversion
Recipient name	— The actual recipient of the message
Intended recipient name	— The originally specified recipient
Redirection reason	— If redirection occurred
Originator and DL expansion history	— DL trace
Reporting DL identifier	— DL containing the recipient name
Security	— Proof of delivery etc.
Delivery time	— If delivery was successful
Type of UA	— Public/private/physical
Non-delivery reason code	— For non-delivery only
Non-delivery diagnostic code	— Qualifies the reason code

10.9.3 Subject-message parameters

The **subject-identifier** parameter contains the message identifier of the subject-message, as generated by its originating MTA. The **content-type** identifies the type of content of the subject-message. For an interpersonal message, the value is 'P2' (or 'P22' for IPMs which contain any of the 1988 extensions); a type of 'unidentified' is also allowed. The **content-identifier** parameter contains an identifier for the content of the subject-message; its value was originally specified by the originator of the subject-message. The **content-correlator** parameter contains information provided by the message originator for the purpose of correlating any reports he receives with the subject-message. The **returned-content** parameter contains the complete content of the subject-message. It is present only if the originator of the subject-message selected content-return-request when the subject-message was submitted.

10.9.4 Reported recipient information

The following parameters constitute a single set, describing the outcome of delivery for a single recipient. There may be several such sets in one delivery report.

The **originator-delivery-report-request** parameter indicates the level of reporting requested in the subject-message for this recipient (no report, basic or confirmed). This may differ from the level of reporting actually used in generating the report, since the originating MTA of the subject-message may have requested a higher level of report-request, for its own purposes, than the user requested.

The **originally-specified-recipient-number** is a copy of the similarly named parameter contained in the subject-message which relates to this recipient.

The **subject-intermediate-trace-information** parameter is present if an audit-and-confirmed delivery report was requested by the MTA which originated the subject-message. It contains the accumulated trace information for the subject-message.
The **arrival-time** parameter indicates the date and time when the subject-message entered the MD within which the report was generated.
The **converted-EITs** parameter indicates the conversions performed on the subject-message before its delivery.
The **recipient-name** parameter indicates the recipient of the subject-message to whom this delivery report is related. If the message was delivered to an alternate recipient, then the parameter contains the name of this actual recipient, and a separate parameter, **intended-recipient-name**, indicates the name of the recipient originally specified by the originator of the subject-message. In the case of delivery to an alternate recipient, a **redirection-reason** parameter is present to indicate the reason for redirection (see the redirection parameters of section 10.8).

The **originator-and-DL-expansion-history** parameter contains a sequence of O/R names which describe the history of the subject-message. The first O/R name identifies the originator; the remaining names itemize each distribution list which has been expanded in progressing the subject message to this recipient.

Where some recipient of the subject-message is the name of a distribution list, then the member names of the list are added to the set of recipients for the message. If a delivery report is subsequently generated following an attempt to deliver the message to a member of the list, then it is normally sent to the list owner. (In some cases it may also be sent to the originator of the subject-message.) In order to identify which distribution list contains the recipient name being reported on, the parameter **reporting-DL-identifier** is present. This enables the owner to determine which of his distribution lists contains the recipient name to which the report refers.

A set of parameters concerned with the security features of MHS may also be present: **proof-of-delivery** guarantees that the subject-message was delivered; **recipient-certificate** may be required to verify the proof-of-delivery, using encryption techniques; **report-origin-authentication** guarantees that the report's origin is as stated; **message-security-labelling** prevents delivery of the report to a recipient with insufficient security clearance.

The **delivery-time** parameter indicates the date and time at which the subject-message was delivered to this recipient. The **type-of-UA** parameter indicates whether the recipient UA is public (i.e. owned by an administration), private, or is attached to a physical delivery service.

In the event of non-delivery, a **non-delivery-reason-code** is present to indicate why the transfer or delivery of the subject-message failed. Possible reasons include:

transfer-failure	a communications failure prevented the transfer or delivery of the subject-message.
unable-to-transfer	a defect of the subject-message prevented its transfer or delivery.
conversion-not-performed	a conversion of the EITs of the subject-message, necessary for its delivery, could not be performed.

A further parameter which qualifies the reason for non-delivery is given in the **non-delivery-diagnostic-code**. The values defined include the following:

unrecognized-O/R-name	the recipient O/R name was not recognized by the destination MTA.
ambiguous-O/R-name	the recipient O/R name matched more than one recipient.
MTS-congestion	owing to congestion in the MTS, the subject-message could not be transferred or delivered.
loop-detected	it was discovered that the subject-message was looping within the MTS.
maximum-time-expired	the latest-delivery-time allowed for delivering the subject-message expired.
conversion-prohibited	the originator of the subject-message prohibited conversion of EITs which were necessary before delivery could take place.

This section has described those delivery reports which arise from the delivery or non-delivery of user messages. Where delivery reports arise in response to a probe, the interpretation of some of the parameters changes slightly, in that the event being reported is the possibility of delivery, rather than delivery itself. For example, the delivery-time parameter indicates the time at which a probe's described message could have been delivered rather than the time at which a user message was actually delivered.

10.10 THE MTS PROBE-TRANSFER SEVICE

The purpose of a probe is to determine whether a user message of given characteristics (the described message) is deliverable. A probe consists of a probe envelope and no content. The probe envelope resembles the envelope which the described message would acquire if it was actually submitted. The differences between a probe envelope and a user message envelope fall into two areas: fields missing from the probe envelope which the envelope of the corresponding described message could contain, and fields which are specific to the probe envelope. There is only one item in the latter category: the probe envelope contains a field which indicates the content length of its described message.

In the former category are those fields which instruct the MTS on its treatment of a user message, but do not contribute to a description of it or to the evaluation of its deliverability. These are omitted since only descriptive fields are relevant to a probe. Five such fields, which may be present in a user message envelope, are absent in a probe. The **disclose-recipients** parameter is omitted since delivery of a probe can never take place. The two parameters which control delivery time, **deferred-delivery-time** and **latest-delivery-time** are omitted for the same reason. The **content-return-request** is omitted as a probe contains no content. The **priority** parameter is omitted as this does not influence the outcome of the probe. With these exceptions, the parameters of MTS probe-transfer resemble those of MTS message-transfer.

The result of a probe is that its originator is informed, by means of delivery reports, of the viability of actually submitting the user message which the probe describes. These reports indicate, for each recipient, whether delivery would succeed or fail if the described message was actually submitted.

10.11 THE INTERPERSONAL MESSAGING SYSTEM

In the discussion so far, we have concentrated on the capabilities of the message transfer system, which conveys user messages from originator to recipient without regard to message content. In this section, we turn to one particular content-type, the *interpersonal message* (IPM), known informally as P2 content-type. As outlined in section 10.4.1, UAs are grouped into classes of cooperating UAs according to a common ability to handle messages of a particular content-type. So far, P2 is the only content-type which has been standardized; it is designed to fulfil the requirements of person-to-person communication. Thus, P2 determines the encoding of message content exchanged end-to-end by IPM UAs, and defines the semantics of the information conveyed. The set of UAs which deal in IPMs constitute the *interpersonal messaging system* (IPMS).

Figure 10.9 illustrates the structure of an IP message, with reference to a typical

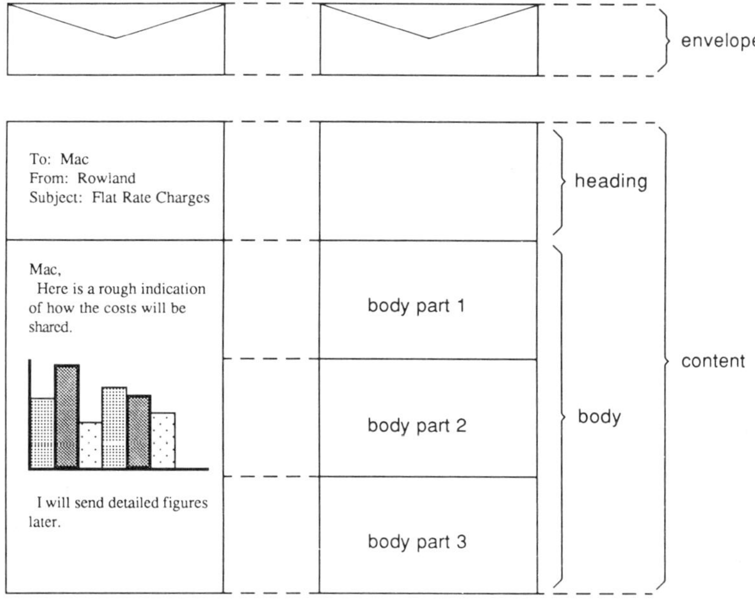

Fig. 10.9 — Relationship of an IP message to an office memo.

office memo. The nature of the envelope has already been discussed in section 10.8 — this is strictly a P1 issue. P2 content divides into two parts: heading and body. The heading of an IP message consists of a set of fields containing well-known, or 'standardized', items of information; in user interfaces, these are given labels such as 'from', 'to' and 'subject'. The body of a message contains the primary information object which the originator wishes to convey. This may itself consist of one or more body-parts, each of which may contain different types of encoded information. The memo example shows two text body-parts separated by a facsimile body-part. A variety of encoded information types is defined, any of which may be included in an IP message body. In addition, a body-part may itself consist of a complete IPM, notably in the case of a forwarded message, though the authenticity of such an encapsulated message is not guaranteed by the IPMS.

There is a subsidiary type of IP content, the *interpersonal notification* (IPN), which may be generated by a recipient UA on receipt of an IP message. Receipt notification should not be confused with delivery notification, which is generated as a result of P1 activity. Receipt notifications are created outwith the MTS by UAs or message stores, and are not guaranteed to contain authentic and verified assertions of the kind that delivery notifications embody. Note that in X.400 (1984), IPNs are termed *status reports*. IPNs are discussed further in section 10.11.3. The following section returns to the IPM and describes its heading in detail.

10.11.1 IPM heading fields

Certain IPM heading fields contain similar kinds of information; for example, the IPM heading fields which are often labelled 'to', 'cc' and 'bcc' in user interfaces, all contain 'recipient-specifier' components. Equally, the component type 'O/R-descriptor' may appear in several heading fields. These common component types are described first, before the headings themselves are examined in detail.

A *recipient-specifier* component identifies a single recipient of the IPM and may contain three sub-fields, the first of which is always present:

— O/R-descriptor
— notification requests
— reply requested

This grouping implies that the IPM originator may make notification requests or reply requests to individual recipients separately (rather than to all recipients or none). The O/R-descriptor is described below. The *notification requests* sub-field, if present, may take any combination of the following values, except that the first must be selected if either of the other two values is selected:

— non-receipt-notification is requested of the recipient in the event of non-receipt of the IPM.
— receipt-notification is requested of the recipient upon his receipt of the IPM.
— IPM-return is requested. The recipient is requested to return the content of the IPM with any non-receipt notification he generates.

The *reply requested* sub-field is a Boolean value, indicating whether or not the originator wishes this recipient to send a reply.

The *O/R-descriptor* identifies an MHS user and has the following sub-fields:

— O/R name. The formal name of the user, which provides an unambiguous identifier for him within MHS. See section 10.5 for a full definition of O/R name.
— free-form name. The name of an MHS user expressed in an informal style. This

name is intended as a user-friendly description, but is not in itself a name that can be used to identify the user unambiguously within MHS. At least one of O/R name or free-form name must be present.

— telephone number may be present as an optional sub-field.

Where an O/R-descriptor is used in a context where it may be extracted to address a message sent in response, the O/R name sub-field must be present. For example, the *reply recipients* heading field identifies the set of users who should receive replies to the current IPM, and so must contain O/R name sub-fields. Equally, where an R-specification contains a notification request or reply request, its O/R-descriptor must contain an O/R name sub-field. This is necessary to enable the recipient to recognize that this descriptor refers to him rather than to another recipient, and consequently to act upon the requests. Remember also that the message envelope bears the O/R names of the message originator and the recipients; whether these recipient names are disclosed to each recipient is controlled by the MTS message-transfer *disclose-recipients* parameter (see also *blind copy recipients* below).

Table 10.4 lists the heading fields of IPMs and gives an indication of their

Table. 10.4 — IPM heading fields

Field	Type
This IPM	IPM identifier
Originator	O/R descriptor
Authorizing users	SEQUENCE of O/R descriptors
Primary recipients	SEQUENCE of R-specifications
Copy recipients	SEQUENCE of R-specifications
Blind copy recipients	SEQUENCE of R-specifications
Replied to IPM	IPM identifier
Obsoleted IPMs	SEQUENCE of IPM identifiers
Related IPMs	SEQUENCE of IPM identifiers
Subject	Text
Expiry time	Time
Reply time	Time
Reply recipients	SEQUENCE of O/R descriptors
Importance	Low/normal/high
Sensitivity	Personal/private/company
Auto-forwarded	True/false
Extensions	Heading extensions

component types. Items marked 'SEQUENCE' can comprise several instances of the component type indicated. The fields are discussed in turn below.

The **this IPM** heading field identifies the IPM and contains an *IPM identifier* component. In its full form, the IPM identifier consists of two parts: the O/R address of the message originator and a user-relative identifier. Together, these unambiguously identify the IPM. The same IPM identifier may appear in certain heading fields of subsequently created messages, in order to refer to this message (for example, in receipt notification).

The **originator** heading field indicates the identity of the message originator to the recipient. It is defined as an O/R-descriptor, so might convey only a user-friendly, informal representation of the originator's identity. However, the MTS always provides an authenticated O/R address for the originator on the delivery envelope.

The **authorizing users** heading field enables the originator to inform the recipient of the one or more users who authorized the sending of the message. Typically, this might be used where a secretary sends a message on instruction from his manager, the authorizing user.

The **primary recipients** and **copy recipients** heading fields identify the intended recipients of the message. The distinction between the two is left open for the recipients to interpret. A copy recipient might be entitled to consider that no further action on his part was being requested. In an office memo, these fields would typically be labelled 'to' and 'cc' respectively.

The **blind copy recipients** heading field indicates an additional set of recipients for the message. However, the field is omitted from copies of the message received by the primary and copy recipients. Each blind copy recipient receives a copy of the message containing his own name in this field. Whether the other blind copy recipients are also disclosed to him in this field is determined locally and is not prescribed by the standard.

The **replied-to IPM** heading field identifies the message to which the current message is a reply. A reply is a standard IPM, with this additional field to indicate which message is being replied to. The presence of this field enables the UA which sent the original message to correlate it with any replies received.

The **obsoleted IPMs** heading field identifies the set of one or more IPMs, previously sent by the originator, that he now regards as obsolete. The present message can be taken to supersede the obsoleted messages. The action which should be taken by the recipient UA is not defined by the standard, but it would be reasonable to have it mark the obsoleted messages for deletion or remove them to an 'obsoleted' pigeon-hole. A user who subscribes to a message store service may employ the *auto-discard* facility which automatically deletes unread IPMs which become obsolete.

The **related IPMs** heading field identifies the set of one or more IPMs which are related to the current message, in the opinion of the originator. No definition of the nature of this relationship is given; this is left for the users of the service to determine. One possible use for this field is where a user is replying to a message which is itself a reply. In constructing the reply message, his user agent could copy the related IPMs field to the same field in the new message, and add to it the IPM identifier of the message being replied to. In this way, each new reply would accumulate the history of the correspondence to date.

The **subject** heading field is used to allow the originator to indicate to the recipient the subject of the IPM. It consists of a string of characters.

The **expiry time** heading field allows the message originator to indicate to the recipient the date and time after which he considers the message to be no longer valid. The action taken by the recipient UA when the expiry time is reached is not defined, but it would be reasonable to mark the IPM for deletion or remove it to an 'expired' category of message. A user who subscribes to a message store service may enable its 'auto-discard' facility, which automatically deletes unread IPMs whose expiry time has passed.

The **reply time** heading field enables the originator to indicate to the recipient a date and time after which a reply to the IPM would not be productive. In effect, it is a request to reply within a stated time. A recipient UA might make use of this field to issue reminders to its user of the impending deadline for replying.

The **reply recipients** heading field specifies the set of one or more users to whom the recipient wishes replies to be sent. If the field is omitted then a reply should be sent only to the originator. The field should not contain the originator name as its sole sub-field, since this is the default assumption made when the field is absent. (A reply-request can be explicitly made of a particular recipient in the R-specification component, described above).

The **importance** heading field allows the originator to indicate to the recipient the level of importance he attaches to the message. This is expressed as one of three values: low, normal or high. Use of this field does not affect the treatment of the message by the MTS (see the priority parameter of the MTS message-transfer service), though the originator may choose to engage high MTS priority whenever he selects high IPM importance. The presence of the field requires no specific action on the part of the recipient, though it is reasonable that his UA should favour the presentation of messages according to the value set.

The **sensitivity** heading field specifies the degree of confidentiality attached to the message by its originator. Three levels of sensitivity are defined. If marked *personal*, then the IPM is intended for a recipient as an individual rather than in his official capacity. If *private*, then the message should not be disclosed to any other individual. If marked *company-confidential*, then the message should not be disclosed to anyone outside the recipient's organization. The recipient's UA may adopt various policies in the treatment of sensitive messages; for example, it may prevent the operations of forwarding and auto-forwarding or refuse to list sensitive messages to a shared printer.

The **auto-forwarded** heading field indicates whether or not the IPM has been received as the result of a previous auto-forwarding activity. This occurs when the originally-intended recipient of a message has instructed his UA or message store to auto-forward all messages it receives to another recipient or recipients. A recipient can distinguish between manually forwarded messages and those received as the result of auto-forwarding by the value of this heading field: true or false. Auto-forwarding is suppressed in two cases: if the received message has itself been auto-forwarded then it is sensible for the UA to decline to auto-forward it again, to prevent the possibility of looping; secondly, if the message is marked as having a particular sensitivity then the UA should not compromise this by performing auto-forwarding. An auto-forwarding message consists of a set of IPM header fields, as specified by the auto-forwarding UA, with the auto-forwarded field set true, and the forwarded message itself contained as a single body-part. When a user sets auto-forwarding instructions he may also specify a text comment. If his UA subsequently performs auto-forwarding, this text comment is sent to the message originator as part of a non-receipt notification (assuming that interpersonal notification was requested by him).

The **extensions** heading field provides a mechanism for conveying information not carried by any other heading field. Two heading extensions have been defined. The *incomplete copy* extension field indicates that one or more body-parts are missing from this particular instance of the IPM. The *languages* heading extension identifies the languages used within the subject field of the IPM and within its body.

This completes the list of IPM heading fields.

10.11.2 IPM body-part types

The body of an IPM may consist of a sequence of body-parts, each encoded according to any one of a prescribed set of encoded information types (EITs). The following types are distinguished: IA5 text, Telex, Voice, G3 facsimile, TIF0, Teletex, Videotex, National, Encrypted, Message, SFD, TIF1, Bilateral, External. Not all of these EITs have been fully defined; for example, no standard has yet been agreed for the encoding of voice. The reader is referred to the standards themselves for precise details of the encodings. Other EITs clearly derive from communications standards defined outwith MHS; Telex and Videotex are obvious examples. Those which have been devised specifically for use within MHS are described here. The definition of EITs could be regarded as a proper concern of the presentation layer. However, MHS does not use presentation for this purpose, and operates on EITs wholly within the application layer.

The **IA5 text** body-part represents the most commonly found body part type, consisting of either the full IA5 character set or the ITA2 (Telex) subset.

An **external** body-part contains information whose semantics and syntax lie outside any MHS standard. It therefore provides the means for any group of cooperating IPMS users to exchange information encoded under the rules of a private agreement. The identification of each kind of private encoding relies on the use of *object identifiers* (see Appendix I), which may be obtained by individual organizations to tag their in-house object types. The **national** and **bilateral** body-parts exist purely for historical reasons. Their use has been supplanted by the external body-part, which is capable of distinguishing any number of distinct encodings, rather than an ad hoc set of national and bilateral encodings.

The **message** body-part has already been mentioned in the context of the forwarded message; it consists of a complete IPM together with its delivery envelope. Because a message body-part is created outside the MTS by an originator's UA, the IPMS cannot guarantee that it is a copy of a genuine message, rather than one which was created or modified by the originator.

An **encrypted** body-part contains one of the other standard body-parts held in an encrypted form. Included with the encrypted information itself is a set of attributes, which, in a manner not yet defined in the standards, will provide the recipient with the means to decrypt the body-part. (It is possible that this body-part type will be dropped as the security capabilities of MHS are realized in service operation.)

The **SFD** (simple formattable document) body-part contains text embedded in a revisable document structure. This includes a logical description of the document, sufficient to enable the generation of an appropriate concrete layout, suitable for display on an output device of given characteristics. The SFD body-part is available only in X.400 1984; it has been dropped from the 1988 standards.

10.11.3 Interpersonal notifications

The *interpersonal notification* (IPN) is a subsidiary class of message exchanged by IPMS users. It provides a mechanism for a message recipient to acknowledge receipt of an IPM or to report non-receipt; these notifications are sent to the message originator. The original IPM which is the subject of the notification is called the *subject-IPM*. The generation of an IPN only occurs following successful delivery of a subject-IPM, and takes place within the recipient's UA or message store.

The generation of a notification is dependent on actions taken both by the originator of the subject-IPM and by its recipient. The originator must have requested notification from the recipient when he submitted the message (refer to section 10.11.1 for a description of the Recipient-specifier heading component which contains such requests). Three request flags are defined which may be selected in any combination. The first must be selected if either of the other two is selected:

- non-receipt-notification is requested of the recipient in the event of non-receipt of the IPM.
- receipt-notification is requested of the recipient upon his receipt of the IPM.
- IPM-return is requested. The recipient is requested to return the content of the IPM with any non-receipt notification he generates.

Two types of event should be distinguished. The first concerns the circumstances under which a determination of receipt or non-receipt is made. The second concerns whether the recipient, or his UA, actually generates a notification to report this determination. Receipt of an IPM is declared when the recipient takes possession of the message in some locally-defined sense; typically, this would occur when the message is displayed on his terminal. Non-receipt arises from a wider set of events; before being displayed to the user, one of the following events might occur:

- the expiry-time of the message elapses.
- a new IPM is received, rendering the subject-IPM obsolete.
- the recipient's subscription to the message service is terminated.
- the subject-IPM is auto-forwarded.

When the determination of receipt or non-receipt is made, and the result coincides with the originator's request for notification, then the generation of a notification is appropriate. Whether this actually occurs depends on the policy in force at the recipient's UA or message store. The UA may honour the notification request automatically, or may invite the recipient to authorize its generation. Equally, the UA may have been instructed to ignore all such requests without even drawing them to the attention of the recipient.

It is important to distinguish receipt notification from delivery notification. The latter confirms that a message has successfully traversed the MTS to reach a recognized address. The former is concerned with whether the end-user has actually had the message made available to him. A further difference between the two is that delivery notification is a guaranteed service: where the level of notification requested by the originator requires the generation of a delivery report, then this will always occur and will always report authenticated information. By contrast, IPNs are generated only if the recipient so chooses, and are not guaranteed to contain valid information.

IPNs are constructed with a standard user message envelope. IPN content is summarized in Table 10.5.

Table 10.5 — Structure of IP notifications

Field	Description
Common fields:	
Subject-IPM identifier	— Subject of this notification
IPN originator	— Actual recipient of the subject-IPM
IPM preferred recipient	— If the intended recipient was not the actual recipient
Conversion EITs	— Of the subject-IPM at delivery
Non-receipt fields: (only present for non-receipt notification)	
Non-receipt reason:	
IPM discarded	— See 'discard reason'
IPM auto-forwarded	— See 'auto-forward comment'
Discard reason:	
IPM expired	— Subject-IPM's expiry time reached
IPM obsoleted	— A subsequent IPM obsoleted the subject-IPM
User subscription terminated	— So receipt can never occur
Auto-forward comment	— Text previously supplied by the recipient
Returned IPM	— If IPM-return was requested by the originator
Receipt fields: (only present for receipt notification)	
Receipt time	— When subject-IPM was received
Acknowledgement mode:	
manual	— Recipient authorized this notification
automatic	— Notification was automatically generated
Supplementary information	— Additional information

Four fields are common to both receipt and non-receipt notification messages. The *subject-IPM identifier* identifies the IPM which is the subject of this notification. The *IPN originator* identifies the originator of this IPN (and hence, the actual recipient of the subject-IPM). If the subject-IPM was received by an alternate recipient as the result of message redirection, then the *IPM preferred recipient* field is present to indicate the intended recipient. The *conversion EITs* field is present if conversion was performed on the subject-IPM before delivery, and identifies the final EITs of the subject-IPM.

10.11.3.1 Non-receipt fields

In the case of non-receipt, the following fields are present. The *non-receipt reason* indicates why the subject-IPM was not received by the originator of the notification following its successful delivery. Two possibilities exist: before its receipt, the subject-IPM was either discarded or auto-forwarded. *IPM discarded* can occur either because the recipient's subscription to the IPMS has terminated, or the subject-IPM was automatically discarded by the recipient's message store. This can happen only if the recipient has enabled the message store's auto-discard service; certain UAs may also offer this service as a locally-provided facility. This service causes the deletion of messages whose expiry time has been reached, or which have been rendered obsolete by the arrival of another IPM from the same user who originated the subject-IPM (see the obsoleted IPMs and expiry time heading fields in section 10.11.1).

Auto-forwarding is another message store service; a user may enable auto-forwarding, so that all IPMs subsequently delivered are immediately forwarded to another recipient or recipients. When he enables auto-forwarding, a user may specify an *auto-forward comment* to be included in each non-receipt notification sent to the originator of each IPM which is auto-forwarded.

10.11.3.2 Receipt fields

IPM receipt notifications may be generated explicitly by a user, or may be created automatically if the user has enabled the *auto-acknowledgement* service provided by his UA as a local function. This service generates a receipt notification message whenever an IPM is delivered which has requested receipt notification. Three fields are defined for receipt notification in addition to the common fields described above. *Receipt time* indicates the date and time at which the message was received. The *acknowledgement mode* field indicates whether the recipient explicitly authorized the sending of the notification, or whether this resulted from the automatic activity of an agent acting on his behalf. The *supplementary information* field is a text string conveying additional information concerning the receipt of the subject-IPM.

11

The Directory — ISO 9594/X.500

For several years ISO and CCITT have collaborated in the development of standards for the Directory. In 1988 this work resulted in the publication of technically aligned standards named, respectively, ISO 9594 and Recommendation X.500. The purpose of these standards is to assist the interworking of open systems by providing access to the information they require to establish communication. The Directory is intended to operate as a single integrated sytem over a global domain, and the standards define how individual systems interwork to achieve this effect.

The Directory can hold information about many different types of object: people, distribution lists, application entities. It may be consulted by a user to discover some information about another user, for example a telephone number, electronic mail address, postal address, or facsimile number. Equally, the Directory may be consulted by a computer process, in order to discover the PSAP address of a cooperating application process.

It is recognized in the standards that the Directory will be needed in a wide range of environments to manage the names of a wide range of objects. Since not all these requirements can be defined in advance, the standards have attempted to develop a general model, capable of accommodating virtually any naming regime. Of course, some of the areas of application for the Directory have already been identified, notably the naming of people and distribution lists in the MHS environment; services for these applications are now operating.

The individual systems which provide directory services cooperate in such a way that the Directory appears as a single integrated service (and hence is always referred to in the singular), capable of supporting naming regimes of international proportions. This would be impractical unless the management of the Directory was highly distributed, and its structure predominantly hierarchical. (A typical Directory application might be distributed firstly by country, then by organization within country.) So, while the Directory is capable of being distributed, as dictated by practical and organizational demands, it remains an integrated service by exercising a high degree of cooperation amongst its component parts.

11.1 PROPERTIES OF NAMES

Before considering the Directory in detail, it is useful to explore briefly the basis upon which it operates, in particular the concept of *naming*. A name can be regarded as a linguistic construct that denotes one particular object from amongst a collection of objects. A name derives meaning according to the *context* in which it is expressed and interpreted. Thus the string of characters 'John Black' may, in the context of a directory of textile manufacturers, identify the company, John Black, whereas in a directory of employees of that firm it might identify the boss's son.

An important property of names is that they must be unambiguous: a name denotes one, and only one object. However, a name need not be unique (i.e. be the sole linguistic construct which identifies some object). So long as no ambiguity is introduced, then the names 'John Black', 'J. Black', and 'Deputy Training Manager' might all denote the same individual.

The Directory does not consist solely of names; in order to fulfil its purpose, it will associate with each name a set of attributes which apply to the object being named. Thus a telephone directory contains the names of telephone subscribers and associates a telephone number with each entry. A closer look at a real directory shows that more than one subscriber may have the same personal name. (One particular telephone directory contains a dozen J. R. Browns.) In these cases, the personal name must be combined with a residential address to produce an unambiguous subscriber name. This illustrates the point that names may consist of a number of components, each of which describes some attribute of the object being named. (It is worth noting that telephone companies maintain directories where the entries consist of subscriber number, with subscriber name and address as associated secondary attributes.)

The Directory provides a very general naming framework and thus permits arbitrary variety in names. However, names may require further properties in order to be usable in the context within which they appear. In many contexts human users must deal directly with names, and consequently, criteria of user-friendliness will apply to the design of such names. The goal of user-friendliness dictates that names should be easy to deduce, remember, and understand, rather than be constructed for the convenience of computer processes. Thus a human user should be able to discover a business colleague's name given only the information acquired through routine business contact.

When a name is ambiguously specified, the Directory must recognize this case and avoid matching it against an entry which it only partly specifies. For example, if entries exist in the Directory for two people with the same surname, then the surname alone should not be taken as being adequate to identify either party. Rather, additional name components such as first name, initials, or residential address should be required to discriminate between the two entries.

11.2 THE DIRECTORY MODEL

The Directory acts as a repository of information about objects of interest in the realm of OSI communications. Its purpose is to facilitate communication amongst its users, both people and application processes, who may read, or in some cases modify, the information stored. Each user of the Directory interacts with it by employing the services of a Directory User Agent (DUA). This operates as an application process, capable of establishing access to the Directory by binding to one of its *access points* (see Figure 11.1). The various search, retrieval, and modification capabilities available to DUAs are described in section 11.4.

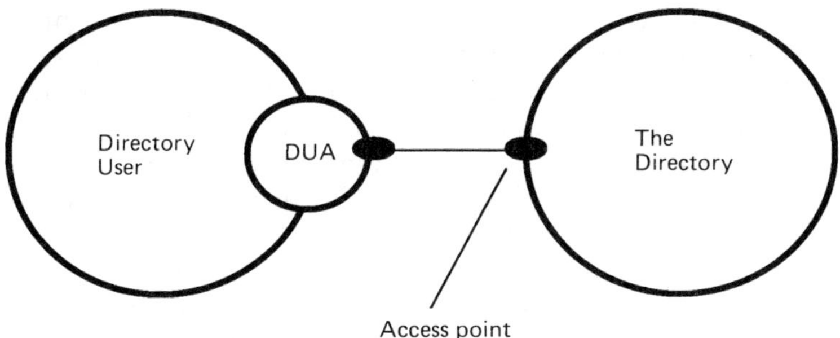

Fig. 11.1 — Access to the Directory.

The Directory itself is populated by a set of Directory Service Agents (DSAs). From the viewpoint of an external user, a DSA provides an access point which may be used by a DUA to exploit the services of the Directory (although, as Figure 11.2

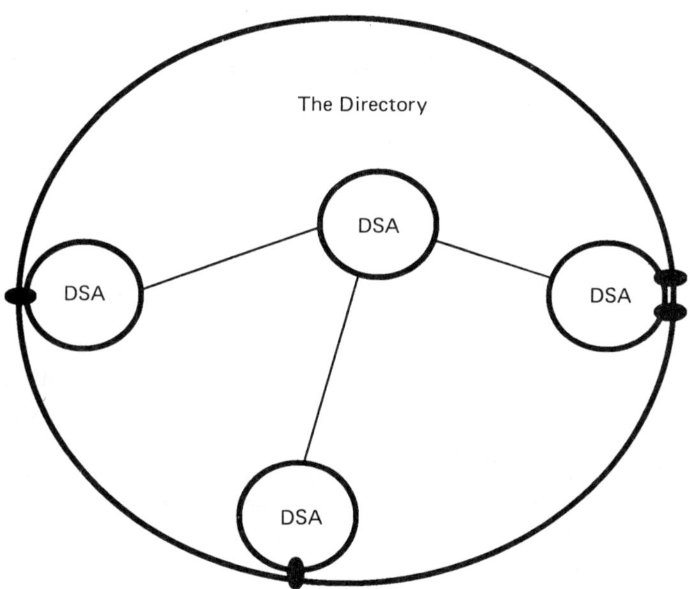

Fig. 11.2 — The distributed directory.

shows, some DSAs have no access points while others may have more than one). Internally, the DSAs cooperate in the provision of an integrated Directory service.

11.3 THE INFORMATION MODEL

The purpose of the Directory is to hold information about objects of interest in the outside world and make this information available to users. Each object is identified by a *name*, and is represented within the Directory by a single *entry*, which contains the information known about the object. The complete set of entries maintained by the Directory constitutes the Directory Information Base (DIB). Given the requirement that the Directory should be capable of supporting naming applications which are global in scope, possibly containing millions of entries, it is not practical to structure entries in a flat naming space. Consequently the entries of the DIB are partitioned according to the natural hierarchical structure of organizations, and ordered into a tree, the Directory Information Tree (DIT). Each vertex of the DIT (apart from the root vertex) corresponds to an entry (see Figure 11.3). The DIT

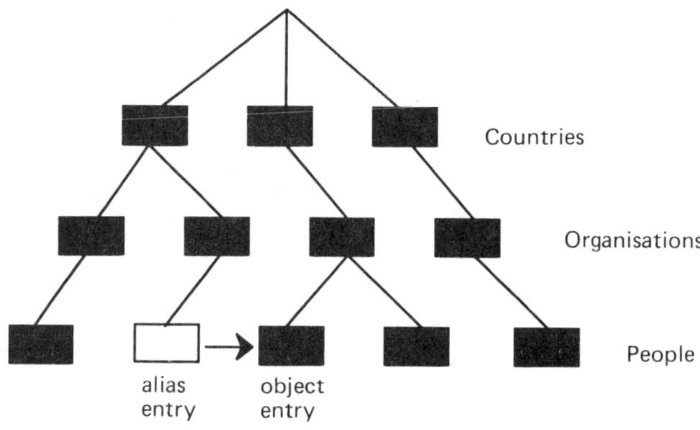

Fig. 11.3 — Entries in a DIT.

models a naming hierarchy, with major naming authorities such as country or organization associated with entries near to the root, and simple objects such as individual people or application processes represented by objects located lower in the tree.

As Figure 11.3 illustrates, there are two types of entry: *object entries* and *alias entries*. An object is always represented by a single object entry, but may also be referenced by one or more alias entries, which provide a mechanism to associate additional names with the object. Unlike object entries which appear throughout the DIT, alias entries are always leaf entries. An alias entry may reference any object entry in the DIT (including non-leaf entries), but may not reference another alias entry.

11.3.1 Directory entries

Each entry contains the collection of known information concerning the object which it represents. This information is made up of a collection of *attributes*, which are used both to construct the object's name and to hold further information about it. An attribute consists of an *attribute type* and one or more *attribute values* (see Figure

11.4). The attribute type identifies the class of information present in the attribute; the attribute value or values represent specific instances of the class. For example, an attribute of type 'Papers Published' may contain a set of attribute values, each specifying the title of a paper. Some attribute types have been defined in the international standards; others may be defined by national authorities or private organizations. The requirement that all assigned types within the Directory should be distinct is achieved by identifying each attribute type with an *object identifier*, which inherently possesses the property of uniqueness (see Appendix I). Within an entry, all attributes are required to have distinct types.

Two attribute types are used by the Directory to assist in its internal management. The *aliased object name* attribute appears in every alias entry and contains the name of the object entry to which the alias refers. The *object class* attribute is present in every entry (including alias entries) and identifies the set of rules defined for all entries which belong to that class. Among the rules which apply to the members of an object class is a definition of the attributes which must appear and those which may optionally appear in an entry.

The data types of the values which may be present in the attribute are constrained to conform to the syntax prescribed for the attribute type with which they are associated.

11.3.2 Names

The concept of naming has been introduced in an earlier section. This section describes how objects are named within the Directory. The mechanism used by the Directory to construct names is based upon the selection of certain attribute values as components of an object's Directory name which is defined below.

The standards refer to the pairing of an attribute type with a specific attribute value as an *attribute value assertion*; essentially, this is a proposition concerning the values contained in an entry. Informally, this can be expressed using the notation *type=value*, e.g. *Country=France*. At most, one of the values of an attribute may be singled out as its *distinguished value*. The set of one or more attribute value assertions which are true for the distinguished values of an entry constitute the entry's *relative distinguished name* (RDN). The RDN distinguishes each of the 'child' entries directly attached to a given object entry; each child possesses a distinct RDN.

If only one of the attributes of an entry possesses a distinguished value, then the RDN will comprise that single attribute value assertion; in other cases, an entry's RDN will contain several attribute value assertions where this is necessary to differentiate entries at that particular level within the DIT. Those attributes of an entry which possess a distinguished value (and therefore form part of the entry's RDN) will typically contain naming information, such as personal name or organizational role. Attributes which lack a distinguished value are concerned with secondary characteristics of the entry, such as telephone number or room number.

The RDN is intended to embody those characteristics of an entry which are persistent and unlikely to become obsolete. The attribute of 'Surname' would appear to belong to this category, yet even this can change where a woman decides to adopt her husband's surname when she marries. Unfortunately, truly invariant attributes such as 'City of Birth' do not fulfil the general requirement, that names (or components of names) should be easy to deduce, remember and discover.

One step remains in exploring the structure of names: the *distinguished name* of

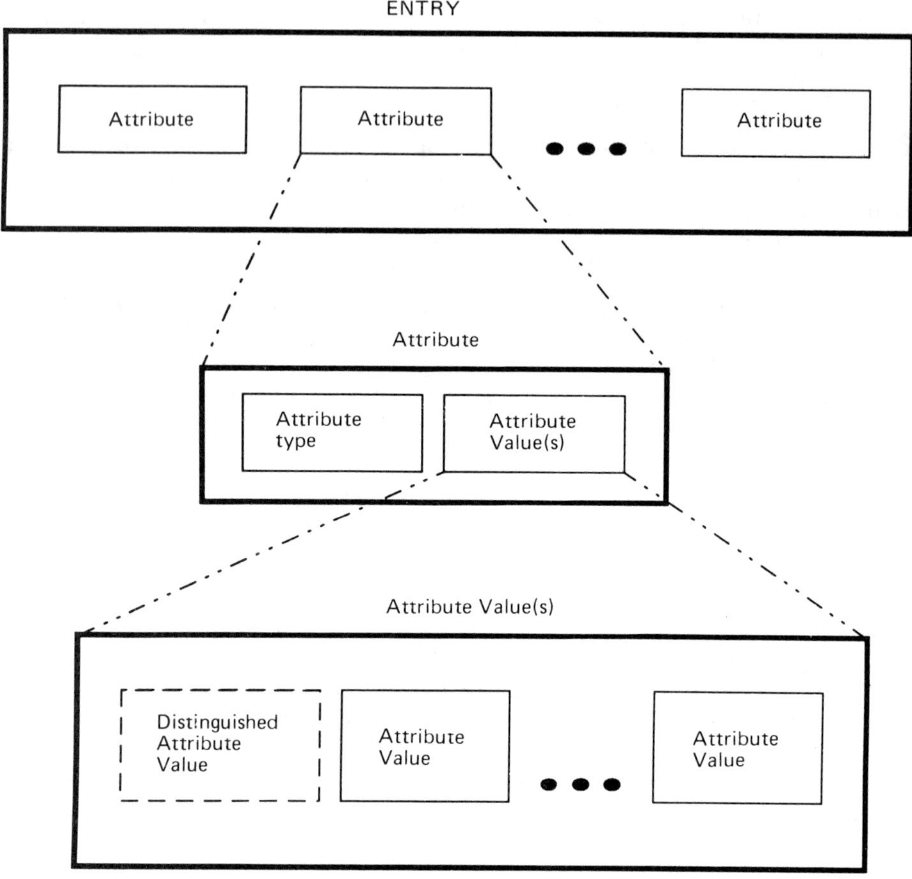

Fig. 11.4 — The components of an entry.

an object is composed of the sequence of RDNs traversed on the path from the root, through the intermediate vertices, to the entry which represents the object (see Figure 11.5). The distinguished name of an alias entry is clearly not the distinguished name of an object; while the purpose of an alias is to reference an object entry, it does possess its own distinguished name.

Finally, the term *Directory name* (or simply *name*) can be defined as a construct which singles out an object from all other objects named by the Directory. The name of an object has the property that it is unambiguous (denotes just one object), but is not necessarily unique (need not be the only name which denotes the object). An object many have several names, one of which is the distinguished name of the object entry, while the others identify alias entries which reference the object entry.

11.3.3 Directory schema

The Directory will be called on to support many different naming requirements; for example, to provide information on the addresses of individuals in business or

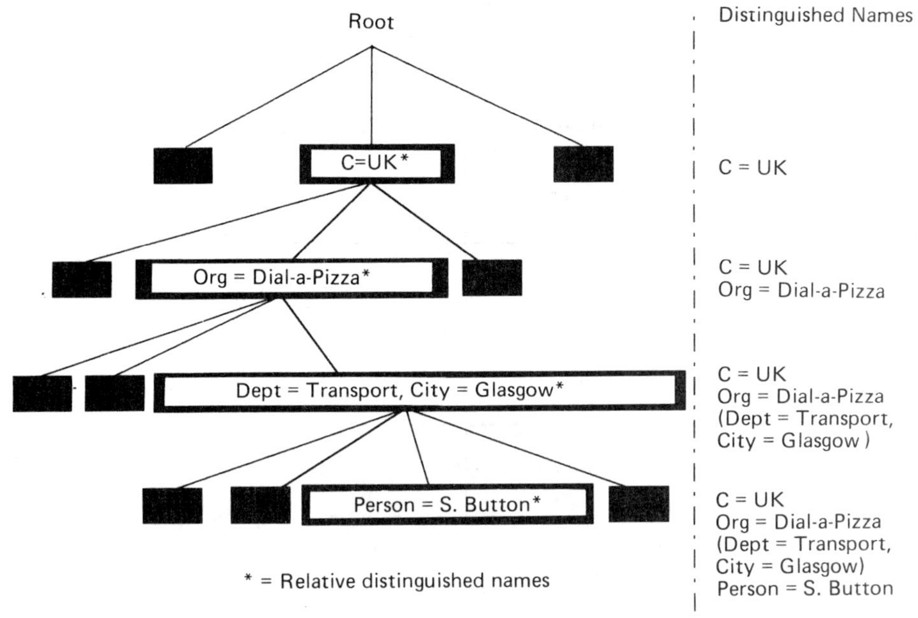

Fig. 11.5 — Distinguished names of object entries.

government contexts, or to provide the PSAP addresses of application processes. While the design of the Directory enables all these naming regimes to be accommodated within the model of a single, integrated Directory, the rules and constraints which apply to each naming application might differ. For each of these naming applications a *Directory schema* is required, to define the DIT structure, the relationships between entries, the attribute types which are permitted to appear at each level of the hierarchy, and additional rules which ensure that the Directory remains self-consistent while being subjected to continual modification. Figure 11.6 indicates how components of the schema relate to components of the DIT. The components of the schema are described below.

The *DIT structure* definitions determine the object classes of entries which may be present at each level of the DIT. Each arc in the DIT represents a relationship between an entry and its immediate subordinate. For such a link to exist, there must be a corresponding structure rule specifying the object class of the superior and that of the subordinate entry. In this way, the Directory can prevent the creation of inappropriate links in the DIT, for example a country as the subordinate of a city. The schema is likely to contain many structure rules. These rules also determine the attribute types permitted in the entry's RDN and therefore prescribe the distinguished name that each entry may possess.

The *object class* definitions specify the mandatory attribute types which an entry of that object class must contain and the optional attribute types which it may contain. This enables the Directory to prevent the addition of inappropriate attribute types to an entry: for example, adding a surname to the entry for an application

Schema	DIT elements
DIT structure	DIT
Object class	Entries
Attribute type	Attributes
Attribute syntax	Values

Fig. 11.6 — Directory schema components.

process. It also allows the Directory to prevent the creation of an entry with one of the mandatory attribute types for that object class missing: for example a person's entry without a surname.

When a new object class is required, it is often possible to define it as a subclass of one or more existing, standardized object classes. The new object class inherits the definitions of mandatory and optional attributes which apply to its superclasses. When an object class is intended for general use by more than one naming authority it is identified by assigning an object identifier to it.

A further element of the Directory schema is the definition of *attribute types* which may appear in object class definitions. An attribute type is defined by the assignment of an object identifier, the nomination of an attribute syntax, and an indication of whether the type holds a single value or more than one value. The definition of an *attribute syntax* specifies the data type; this may be a simple integer or character string, or may be a more complex ASN.1 construct.

11.4 DIRECTORY OPERATIONS

As indicated in section 11.2, the DUA gains access to the services of the Directory via one of its access points. An access point can be regarded as supporting one or more *ports*, each of which provides access to a group of related services. The Directory supplies services through three types of port: the **read port, search port**, and **modify port**. The DUA is regarded as having three corresponding ports which behave as consumers of the services supplied by these DSA ports (see Figure 11.7).

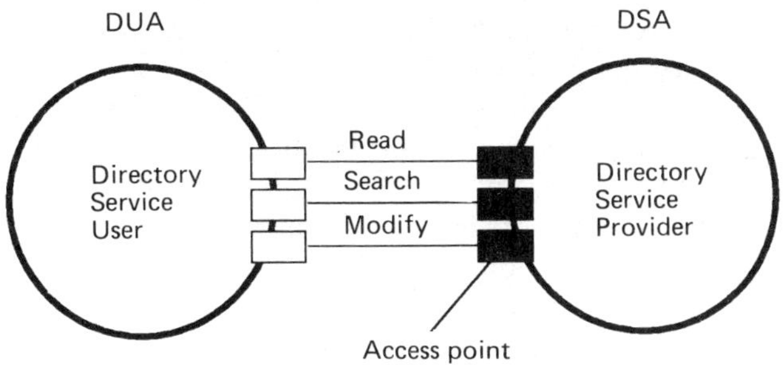

Fig. 11.7 — Service model for Directory access.

The *Directory Bind* operation is used to bind the two sets of ports in order to establish access to the Directory. As part of this operation the parties can exchange credentials, which allows each party to verify the identity of the other. The *Directory Unbind* operation is used at the end of the period of access to release the association. These operations are mapped directly to the A-ASSOCIATE and A-RELEASE services provided by ACSE.

The **read port** provides two operations for retrieval. The *Read* operation extracts information about an entry identified by name. The attributes to be returned are specified as part of the argument. This operation is also used to verify that the name supplied (the purported name) is indeed the distinguished name of a Directory entry. The *Compare* operation is used to check whether a supplied value matches the value of a particular attribute for a given object entry. One use of this operation is in password checking, where the Directory allows a stored password to be accessed by Compare, but not by Read.

A further operation is included, for convenience, in the read port. The *Abandon* operation enables the DUA to inform the Directory that it is no longer interested in the outcome of an outstanding interrogation. Some operations may cause a DSA to invoke corresponding operations on other DSAs; while the DSA can abandon an operation locally, it may be unable to abandon one propagated to other DSAs.

The **search port** provides two operations for exploration of the Directory. The *List* operation causes the Directory to return the set of entries which are immediate subordinates of a specified entry (i.e. those entries one level below, and directly attached to the given entry in the DIT). Since the quantity of information returned is potentially very large, the operation allows for the return of an incomplete result, rather than an outright failure on the grounds that some limit was exceeded. The operation also provides for the situation where a complete result can be obtained only by consulting other DSAs, in which case it returns reference information which the DUA can use to resume the enquiry elsewhere by accessing another DSA.

The *Search* operation causes the Directory to return specified attributes from all entries which lie within a given portion of the DIT and satisfy some selection criteria. The selection criteria are contained in a **filter** parameter, which expresses conditions (in the form of attribute value assertions) which an entry must satisfy in order to be selected. By testing each candidate entry against the filter, information can be returned concerning relevant entries only. In common with the List operation, Search anticipates the return of an incomplete result, and provides hooks to enable the DUA to resume the enquiry elsewhere.

The **modify port** provides four operations for modifying entries in the DIT. The *Add-entry* operation causes a new leaf entry to be added to the DIT. This may be either an object entry or an alias entry. The argument specifies the RDN of the new entry, the distinguished name of its immediate superior, and the other attributes to be placed in the entry. The Directory will ensure that the operation is consistent with the schema rules. The *Remove-entry* operation removes a leaf entry from the DIT.

The *Modify-entry* operation allows a sequence of changes to be applied to a specified entry. The performance of the operation is atomic: either all changes are made or the entry is left as it was before the operation. The types of modifications allowed include the addition or removal of complete attributes, and the addition, removal, or replacement of individual attribute values. Attempts to modify attributes which would change an entry's RDN are rejected. The *modify-RDN* operation allows an entry's RDN to be changed by specifying a new set of distinguished attribute values. The scope of this operation is limited to leaf entries.

A number of *service controls* can be applied to the operations described above. These allow the user to set limits on the use of resources which the Directory must not exceed. Limits may be set on the elapsed time allowed for the completion of the operation, the size of the results, the scope of a search, and the priority to be attached to the request. Another element common to the operations is the use of *security parameters*. These provide a variety of mechanisms for protecting the Directory information and enable either party to verify the identity of the other.

Where an operation cannot be performed successfully an error is returned indicating the reason for failure. Frequently this will occur because incorrect parameters have been supplied, such as the use of an invalid name for an entry, but may also result from violations of the security policy, service controls, or schema rules. An operation may fail because the access point used by the DUA cannot conveniently access that part of the DIT which contains the relevant DIT entries. In these cases the Directory may return a *referral*, to redirect the user to an access point better equipped to process the requested operation.

11.5 DISTRIBUTED OPERATIONS

The previous section has described the Directory in terms of the services it offers to its users, but has not considered how DSAs should operate in practice, nor how the DIT should be stored and managed. This section examines the internal structure of the Directory and the manner in which the DIT is distributed, within the framework of the distributed Directory model.

The distributed Directory comprises one or more DSAs, each of which may hold a fragment of the DIT. DSAs cooperate in satisfying users' service requests, and ensure that the whole of the DIT is accessible from all DSAs that hold some part of it. The internal structure of the Directory can be defined by the services that DSAs offer at their ports. The *service-ports* of the DSA are identical to those of the Directory object, described in section 11.4, and provide a point of access to directory services for the external user via the DUA. These ports are the **read, modify** and **search** ports.

In addition, the DSA has a second set of ports, the *chained-service-ports*, which permit inter-DSA communication, and enable DSAs to interact in a cooperative manner to provide directory services in a distributed environment. The chain-service-ports support services which have a one-to-one correspondence with those provided by the similarly named service ports; these ports are the **chained-Read, chained-Search**, and **chained-Modify** ports (see Figure 11.8). In effect, the chained-

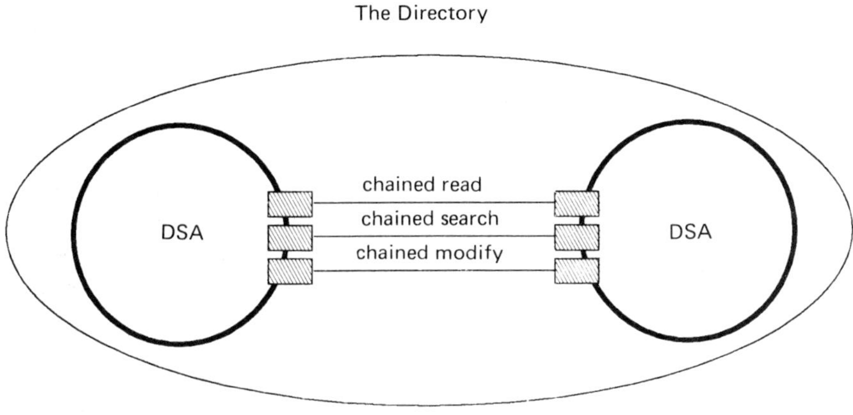

Fig. 11.8 — Distributed Directory model.

service-ports provide a means of propagating a user service request to other DSAs. (DSAs are not required to support the chained-service-ports, and may instead provide service via their service ports only when accessed directly by DUAs.)

Every entry in the DIT is the responsibility of some individual *naming authority*. However, a given entry may be replicated in other DSAs either through bilateral agreement between authorities or as the result of a DSA's cacheing the response to an earlier request. The originator of a request is always informed if a returned result is derived from cached information, since this is less authoritative than information obtained from a primary entry.

Each DSA holds a portion of the DIT, which is defined as consisting of one or more naming contexts. A *naming context* is a partial sub-tree of the DIT, identified by the distinguished name of its initial vertex (the *context prefix*), and extending downwards to include a collection of leaf and/or non-leaf vertices. A non-leaf vertex which lies at the boundary of a naming context marks the start of a subordinate naming context. This models the case where an authority devolves responsibility for a set of subordinate entries to another authority; devolution of authority begins at the root and continues downwards through the DIT. The naming contexts held by DSAs will reflect the administrative and operational requirements of the authority. Certain DSAs might hold only those entries which correspond to high-level domains, while others might hold only leaf entries. The naming contexts held need not share the same superior entry. Figure 11.9 illustrates a DIT with four naming contexts distributed over three DSAs.

An important property of the Directory is that a user may have a service request satisfied regardless of the location of the access point at which the request is made. To achieve this, each DSA must have some knowledge of the location of the requested information, and either return this information to the requestor (by referral), or make use of it directly to progress the service request within the Directory (using chaining or multicasting).

Chaining may be used when a DSA is unable to process a request itself. It is performed by transmitting the request to another DSA (using a chained-service-port) and reporting the outcome to the originator of the request. Chaining is appropriate where the DSA has specific knowledge concerning the naming contexts held by the other DSA. A request may be chained through successive DSAs before a response can be generated. The response retraces the path of the chained request.

Multicasting is also used where a DSA is unable to process a request itself. The DSA transmits the request to several other DSAs, either all at once, or by sending the request to each in turn until one is found able to continue processing the request. In either case, an identical remote operation is passed to each of the DSAs. Multicasting is used only when the DSA does not know the complete naming contexts held by the other DSAs.

A DSA may return a *referral* in its response to a service request from a DUA or DSA, consisting of a knowledge reference (see below) which may be used subsequently to progress the request by chaining or multicasting to other DSAs better placed to satisfy it. When a DUA receives a referral, it can use the information to bind to the DSA named in the referral. When a DSA receives a referral it may return this to the orginator of the request, or use it directly to chain the request to the DSA named. A variety of reasons may cause a DSA to return a referral rather than chain a request: the originator might have explicitly forbidden chaining when submitting the request; the knowledge reference might identify a DSA which does not support the chained-service-ports; for administrative reasons, perhaps concerning with charging, the DSA might be unable to bind to the DSA named.

11.5.1 Knowledge

Given that the DIT may be distributed over multiple DSAs, each of which holds a fragment of it, and that a DSA should attempt to deal with service requests concerning any entry (not just those held locally), there is an apparent need for each DSA to possess *knowledge information* to enable it to map a name to the location of its DIT entry. A DSA uses this information to identify and interact with another DSA which owns the fragment of the DIT relevant to the current service request.

Each DSA possesses knowledge information concerning the naming contexts which it itself owns and their location within the DIT hierarchy. For each naming context this information comprises the context prefix (which identifies the naming context), and two sets of *knowledge references*. The first set of references contains the names of all the entries held within the fragment of the DIT identified by the naming context; the second set contains the names of any subordinate naming contexts devolved from the current naming context, and identifies the DSAs to which authority for each subordinate naming context has been devolved.

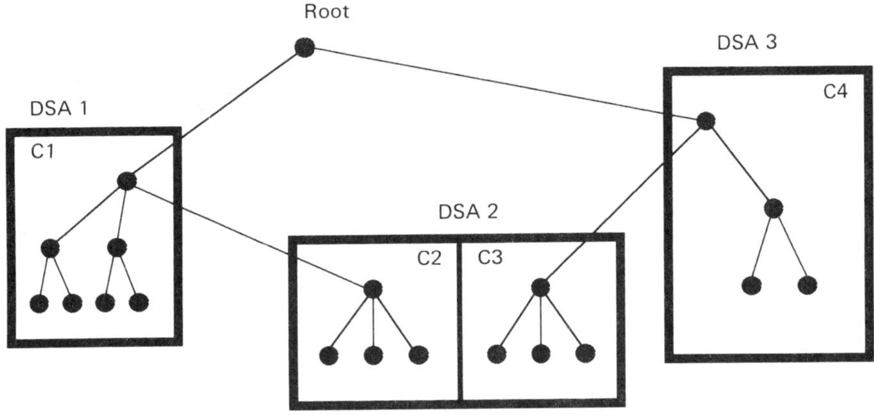

Fig. 11.9 — Naming contexts in an hypothetical DIT.

These rules ensure that there is a path of knowledge references from the root to every naming context in the DIT. However, to enable any DSA to locate any naming context, each must hold a further item of knowledge information: the identity of the DSA which holds the superior entry of this DSA's naming context. (Where a DSA has more than one naming context, the superior entry selected is the one with the fewest number of RDNs, i.e that which is 'highest' in the DIT).

This collection of knowledge information is the minimum required for the Directory to function at all, but many additional knowledge references are required to ensure that it performs acceptably. A DSA can optimize the process of name resolution by storing cross references which map naming contexts to DSA addresses, thus reducing the chain of remote DSAs which must be consulted to resolve a name. This information may be obtained simply by cacheing information discovered as a side-effect of ordinary directory operations. The current standards do not provide mechanisms for reporting changes in DIT structure to DSAs which hold knowledge references rendered invalid as a result of such changes.

No single DSA acts as the root-DSA and holds its naming context: the global scale of the Directory makes this impractical. Instead, the 'first-level' DSAs which have authority for the naming contexts which are immediately subordinate to the root must provide this functionality. Every first-level DSA must hold the full set of knowledge information logically possessed by the root. The autonomous first-level naming authorities will need to adopt suitable procedures to ensure the accuracy and consistency of the root naming context they hold in common.

11.6 DIRECTORY PROTOCOLS

This section considers the two application layer protocols defined for the Directory. The Directory Access Protocol (DAP) is used for communication between a DUA and DSA, and provides the services described in section 11.4. The Directory System

Protocol (DSP) supports interaction between a pair of DSAs, as described in section 11.5.

The familiar model for application layer communication applies to both protocols: each protocol defines how communication takes place between two application processes. This view is refined by regarding the activity as occurring between two application entities over the presentation service. The functionality of an application entity is factored into one or more application service elements.

In addition to the service elements specific to the Direcdtory protocols, two other application service elements are common to both. The remote operations service element (ROSE) supplies the concrete mechanism for realizing the model of request/response interaction between pairs of application entities. The operations available at the ports of the service model map directly onto ROSE services. The association control service element (ACSE) supports the establishment and release of an application association betwen two application entities, and provides a mapping for the Bind and Unbind operations.

The DAP contains three application-specific service elements corresponding to the three service-ports: the *readASE*, *searchASE*, and *modifyASE*. Together with ROSE and ACSE, these constitute the Directory Access application context (see Figure 11.10). An association which uses this application context can be initiated only by a DUA.

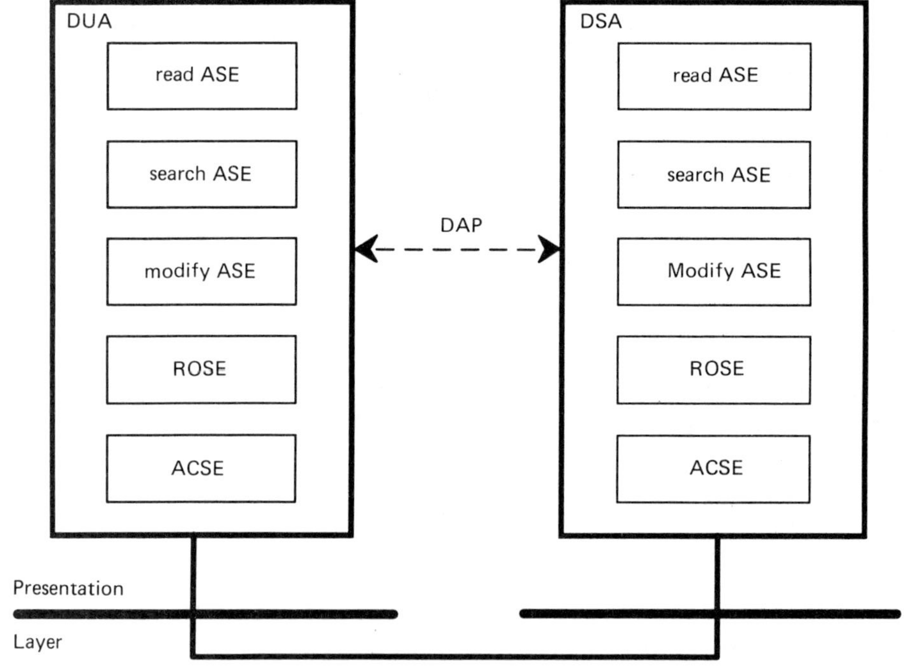

Fig. 11.10 — Directory access protocol model.

The DSP supports the services defined for the operation of the distributed Directory. There are three application-specific service elements which correspond to the three chained-service-ports: the *chained-readASE*, *chained-searchASE*, and *chained-modifyASE*. ROSE and ACSE are added to these three to form the Directory System application context (see Figure 11.11).

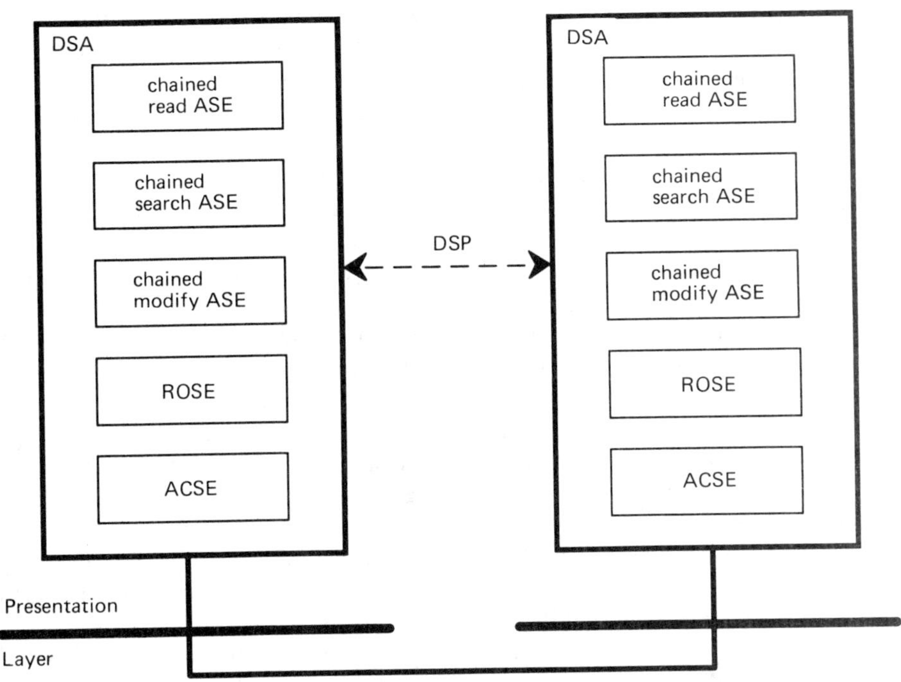

Fig. 11.11 — Directory system protocol model.

11.7 USING THE DIRECTORY

The Directory has been described in terms of its ports, operations, and internal structure. However, it is also useful to consider how it will actually be exploited in real applications. This section outlines some of the patterns of use which are likely to arise in many applications.

The most common use of the Directory is the straightforward look-up. In this activity, the DUA passes a name and an attribute type to the Directory. If the name is a valid distinguished name, the Directory returns the value or values of the attribute associated with the object entry. Variations of this include the look-up of an object identified by an alias, and the retrieval of values of several attribute types. These activities are supported by the Read operation.

In many cases, the human user of the Directory will be unable to supply sufficient information to name the object about which information is sought. However, if presented with a list of possible candidates, the user may well recognize the one he is looking for. This *browsing* activity allows the user to selectively explore the DIB as a means of locating required entries. Browsing is supported by the List and Search operations.

A simple 'Yellow Pages' facility is supported by the Search operation and its *filter* parameter. This allows entries to be selected based upon assertions about the values of relevant attributes (e.g. 'Business Category'). This imposes no additional requirements on the Directory other than to ensure that these attributes are present in the appropriate entries. However, this approach is likely to be expensive in a large DIT, since every entry present must be tested against the filter. An alternative approach is to create additional subtrees, structured to assist Yellow Pages look up. In effect, these subtrees are inversions of the DIT, and embody a naming hierarchy which places RDNs that include attributes such as 'Business Category' and 'Locality' near to the root, and 'Organization' towards the edges of the DIT.

A number of requirements exist for the support of communication between groups of individuals. The membership of a group can change over time by the addition and removal of individual members. Both a group itself and the members it contains can be represented by Directory entries. The Directory can be asked to enumerate the members of a group (using the Read operation), or asked whether a particular name is a member of a group (using the Compare operation). To support these activities, the entry representing a group will contain the multi-valued attribute 'Member'. A group member may itself be a group, but the recursive expansion of nested groups is performed as a DUA function rather than within the Directory. This use of the Directory is required by the MHS standards to support its distribution list services: the transmission of a message to a group of recipients by naming the group rather than enumerating each of its members.

Many applications require protection against threats to the security of the information conveyed. Threats take many forms, including masquerade (the pretence by a user to be a different user in order to gain access to information), repudiation (the denial of having participated in a communication), data interception (the observation by an unauthorized user of the data transferred in a communication). Most of the security services which protect against these threats depend upon *authentication*, where each party can be assured of the identity of the other. Authentication is based upon knowledge of a user's *credentials*, (which take different forms according to the mechanism employed). The Directory is a natural place to store credentials since communicating parties already consult the Directory to obtain addressing information. Retrieving the credentials of another party from the Directory is an activity broadly similar to retrieving its address.

The Directory supports two levels of authentication. The first is known as 'simple authentication', and is provided by storing a Password attribute in the entry of a user who requires the ability to authenticate himself to a Service. When the Service is called by the user, it can ask the Directory to verify that the password supplied by the user matches the stored password. Since any Service can consult the Directory in this way, the user needs only one password to access all the Services to which he subscribes. As the transmission of passwords in 'clear' (i.e. unencrypted form) is an inherently insecure practice, the Directory provides mechanisms to protect against the interception and reuse of password data. These employ simple one-way encryption techniques.

Where a higher level of security is necessary, requiring security capabilities which extend beyond the prevention of unauthorized access, then 'strong authentication' may be used. This is based upon public key cryptography, where two keys, one public and one secret, are used in the encryption and decryption operations. The Directory supports this approach by acting as the repository of users' public encryption keys, stored in a manner which ensures their integrity. Communicating partners may obtain each other's public key and use this to support services such as mutual authentication, access control, data confidentiality, data integrity and non-repudiation.

Since the Directory will become widely established as a support for communications activities, it is likely that the authentication framework it provides will be used by many OSI applications.

12

Functional standards

Throughout this book we have identified a feature common to all layers — options. In application layer standards we have seen how some application services are regarded as optional and negotiable between peer application entities. During an application association between two application processes, the set of application services available for use will necessarily be restricted to the intersection of the set of services *implemented* on the initiating end-system and that on the responding end-system — i.e. to the lowest common denominator.

Options themselves can be seen as falling into two groups:

(a) Those whose availability is dictated only by the implementation of the application standard on the end-system.
(b) Those whose availability is dictated by the implementation of the application standard on the end-system and, additionally, by the availability of an option in a lower layer entity implementation on which the application layer option is dependant.

An example of type (a) is F-CHANGE-ATTRIBUTE of FTAM; an example of (b) is F-CHECK of FTAM, as this requires the optional minor synchronize FU of the session layer.

The level of service available from an implementation of an application standard on an end-system is thus a statement of the options of both types, (a) and (b), that are available in that implementation. This statement is in effect a profile.

In instances of application association establishment, success depends on the result of negotiation of a common profile. This can be achieved even if the individual profiles of the implementations on the end-systems are very different — but only if they are flexible. For instance, two end-systems with implementations of an application standard may fail to establish an association, simply because the implementation of a layer entity on one of the systems insists upon an option unavailable in its peer.

In effect we have introduced two types of profile. The first type describes the potential capability of an application implementation on an end-system — a capability profile. It is static in nature and changes only if the implementation of the application entity (or any lower layer entity on whose options it depends) is upgraded or downgraded. The second type is that resulting from the establishment of an association. It is a negotiated common profile which lies within the capability profile of both of the end-systems involved in the association.

Reaching a middle ground profile by negotiation is potentially uncertain, and as such is against the fundamental 'open' objective of OSI. However, there are two ways of ensuring that an association can be established between two end-systems that claim to support an application standard. The first is to insist that an implementation should support, but not necessarily use, all optional features. Of course this is unreasonable; indeed one purpose of allowing options is to permit the implementation of minimal application entities for use in 'dumb' systems (such as point of sale devices) with specialized tasks to perform over OSI, and which never require full blown implementations. By the nature of their restricted implementation these systems may not be able to establish an association with many end-systems, but they do conform to the ISO standards and so are able to exist in the ISO/OSI environment. The second solution is to define some profile of an application standard that is accepted as a minimum over the OSI environment. If this profile is available on all end-systems then there is a guarantee of a common profile being reached in negotiation of an association. This 'minimum' profile is known as a *functional standard*.

Functional standards are not specified by ISO and are not part of the standards. Conformance to the ISO standards and to a particular functional standard are different issues. The functional standards are agreements amongst the OSI community, which comprises manufacturers, software houses, end-users and government procurement agencies.

Three bodies are making considerable progress towards the specification of functional standards:

— NIST in the USA
— CEN / CENELEC, the European body
— POSI, Japan

12.1 AN EXAMPLE OF FUNCTIONAL STANDARDIZATION

We shall use FTAM in order to give an example of the sort of things that you might expect in a functional standard. In particular we shall be looking at a hypothetical functional standard (based upon a developing European functional standard) for the transfer of files between the real filestores of two end-systems. As you would expect, such a functional standard makes recommendations covering all aspects of FTAM; in this case it specifies implementation of FTAM that will be capable of:

— reading a complete file;
— writing, i.e. replacing or extending a file, or inserting into a file;
— *optionally* creating and deleting a file;
— *optionally* reading the attributes of a file.

It also specifies how implementations of session, presentation, and other application ASEs (in the case ACSE) must be used to facilitate the FTAM functions defined above.

Notice that the functional standard does not place a constraint on the extent of implementation of the lower layer standards such as session — it simply makes a statement of the minimum level of implementation required to provide support for this FTAM profile.

When a supplier claims that his FTAM 'stack' product is *conformant* with a functional standard (a necessary statement when tendering for, say, government contracts) then he must, in addition, make a statement of support or otherwise of the aspects of the functional standard that are stated as *optional*.

There are a considerable number of sections to a functional standard of this kind; here we shall examine those which relate to the aspects of FTAM that we have covered in some depth earlier in the book — virtual filestore, file service and file protocol, and also to the lower layer standards.

12.1.1 Virtual filestore

This functional standard is concerned with files and not with structure of the filestore in which they reside. And so, under this heading, we concentrate on file-related issues. This functional standard, both in order to satisfy the majority of basic 'user' demands of file transfer and to encourage conformance, limits the scope of the file structures it handles to the *unstructured* and *flat* types discussed in section 8.3. It also restricts activity on these files to read, insert, replace and extend (where appropriate to file structure in question) in performing the transfer of whole files or identified FADUs.

The functional standard assigns levels of support to file-related aspects such as file (object) attributes. With respect to the virtual filestore four *support levels* are recognized:

m:	mandatory	This feature is mandatory in the ISO 8571 standard and shall therefore be implemented by all implementations claiming conformance to this functional standard.
s:	supported	This feature shall be implemented by all implementations claiming conformance to this functional standard.
os:	optionally supported	Implementations claiming conformance to this functional standard may or may not implement this feature. Conformant responder implementations are free to support 'os' features and to use them to control access by an initiator. If initiators do not support the corresponding features, interworking will be impossible. It is therefore recommended for conformant initiator implementations to support all the 'os' access control features.
—:	not supported	This feature is outside the scope of this functional standard.

Table 12.1 gives an example of how the functional standard constrains the virtual filestore for this flavour of FTAM by making use of the above support levels.

12.1.2 File service

The three support levels for this aspect of function standardization are much simpler:

s:	supported	This feature must be supported.
os:	optionally supported	It is left to the implementations as to whether the feature is supported or not.
—:	not supported	This feature is outside the scope of this functional standard.

The table looks like Table 12.2.

Table 12.1

Feature	Support level	Additional specifications
File actions		
on complete files:		
create file	os	
select file	m	
change attribute	—	
read attribute	os	
open file	m	
close file	m	
delete file	os	
deselect file	m	
on parts of files:		
locate	—	
read	s	
insert	s	
replace	s	
extend	s	
erase	—	
File attributes		
filename	m	Apart from minimum conformance requirements in ISO 8571 part 2, filenames shall be specified in the naming convention of the responding FTAM implementation. It is a local implementation matter of the FTAM responder whether or not an additional mapping onto the real filestore's filename convention is supported.
permitted actions	m	
contents type	m	
storage acount	os	
date and time of:		
creation	os	
last modification	os	
last read access	os	
last attribute modify	os	
identity of:		
creator	os	
last modifier	os	
last reader	os	
last attribute modifier	os	
file availability	s	
filesize	s	
future filesize	os	
access control	s	
permitted actions	m	
file availability	os	
legal qualification	os	
private use	—	

Table 12.2

Feature	Support level	Additional specifications
Service classes:		Conformant initiator implementations shall include the 'transfer class' in the request. Conformant responder implementations shall be able to respond with the 'transfer class'
file transfer	s	
file access	—	
file management	—	
transfer and management	os	
unconstrained	—	

12.1.3 File protocol

This section of the functional standard specifies the file protocol machine necessary to service the file service level specified. It defines the basic file protocol and the basic bulk data protocol by making support level statements about the implementation of FTAM FUs. It makes support level statements about each FADU, and for each places appropriate bounds on parameters.

12.1.4 ACSE and the lower layers

In each case this functional standard specifies the minimum implementation required by making service level statements about both service and protocol aspects of each standard, e.g. FUs, PDUs and PDU parameters.

12.2 FINALLY

Finally, as a warning to implementors and those who commission them:

Power dive

He spent a fortune on architects and builders.
He signed tickertapes of cheques for furniture,
carpets, paintings, filmstar beds. He surrounded the house
with plantations and parterres, hahas and gazebos.
And in the right place, the properest place
at last he saw completed a swimmingpool
that glittered like ancient Rome.

It was just before he hit the water
in his first dive that he glimpsed
the triangular fin cutting the surface.

Norman MacCaig

Appendix I — Abstract syntax notation one

ASN.1 has become the primary tool for the specification of international standards. Its antecedent, the X.409 part of the CCITT X.400 standard, had a more limited role. This was to provide a notation which allowed for the specification of arbitrarily complex data structures, coupled with a set of rules (in effect a transfer syntax), which defined the concrete representation of any instance of the data structure which could then be exchanged between open systems.

This approach was developed within ISO and resulted in the publication of two standards in 1987: ISO 8824 'Specification of ASN.1', and ISO 8825 'Specification of Basic Encoding Rules for ASN.1'. The main refinement to the X.409 standard introduced by ISO was to make manifest the distinction between the two roles of ASN.1. The first and more important role is to provide a specification notation which can be used to describe elements of a standard in a precise fashion. The second function of ASN.1 is to provide encoding rules which define the manner in which data structures are represented when transported between open systems. For example, where a PDU consisting of an integer value, followed by a character string, followed by a real value is to be transported between systems, ASN.1 supplies rules for the encoding of these data values down to the level of the order of bits in each byte, and the sequence in which the bytes are transmitted. The second of the ISO standards named above specifies these basic encoding rules for the encoding of values of the types defined in the ASN.1 notation. The establishment of these rules has removed a considerable burden from standards developers and implementors: where previously every standard had devised its own mechanism for encoding, by adopting ASN.1 the encoding rules employed by every standard could be confined to a single document.

Further developments in the exploitation of ASN.1 have occurred since the ISO standards were produced. The ASN.1 standards reflect the presentation requirement to divorce the *specification* of the values of complex data types from the concrete *representation* of these values in their exchange between open systems. The next step has been to extend the specification role of ASN.1 to contexts where no intention exists that the information elements described will be rendered as a concrete representation. This use of ASN.1 exploits the properties of the *notation* in areas where there is no requirement for *representation*.

In recent application standards, ASN.1 has been used to define every component element of the standard: model, ports, services, operations, applications contexts, application service elements. None of these elements is conveyed as a represented object between open systems.

AI.1 HIGH-LEVEL SPECIFICATION

The following examples show the use of ASN.1 in defining some of the information elements which appear in the Message Store standard. These are intended to illustrate the scope of ASN.1 as a specification tool rather than explain its detailed structure. See Chapters 10 and 11 for details of how these elements fit into a complete application standard.

```
--Definition of the MS-user object (UA)
  msUser OBJECT
     PORTS { retrieval [C],
             indirectSubmission [C],
             administration [C] }
     ::= id-ot-ms-user
```

This definition indicates that the MS-user (the UA) possesses three ports, all of which consume services supplied by the MS (retrieval is provided directly, and the others indirectly). An object identifier is associated with the MS-user object. The structure of the retrieval port is shown in the following definition:

```
--Definition of the Retrieval Port
   retrieval PORT
      CONSUMER INVOKES {
          Summarize,
          List,
          Fetch,
          Delete,
          Register-MS }
      SUPPLIER INVOKES {
          Alert }
      ::= id-pt-retrieval
```

This definition shows that the port is asymmetrical, as two objects may only bind their retrieval ports where one acts as consumer of the services (the UA) and the other as supplier (the MS). Details of the Fetch operation are shown in the following ASN.1 definition:

```
--Definition of the Fetch abstract-operation
   Fetch ::= ABSTRACT-OPERATION
      ARGUMENT  FetchArgument
      RESULT    FetchResult
      ERRORS    {
          Attribute errors,
          --various errors-- }
```

This definition follows the model of interaction defined in the ROS standard (and therefore allows for a direct realization of this abstract-operation as a ROS operation). If the Fetch request succeeds, the Fetch-result is returned; otherwise one of the prescribed list of errors is returned.

All of the examples shown above are complex, in that they use ASN.1's *macro* facility, which permits the standard notation to be extended to support new specification requirements. In none of these examples is there the implication that a concrete representation (a PDU) of the information element defined will ever be generated. The following example does show an information element which is intended for exchange between open systems:

```
--Definition of the Fetch argument
  FetchArgument ::= SET {
      information-base-type  [0]  InformationBase DEFAULT stored-messages,
      item                        CHOICE {
              search                [1]  Selector,
              precise               [2]  SequenceNumber },
      requested-attributes   [3]  EntryInformationSelection OPTIONAL }
```

AI.2 ASN.1 STRUCTURES

These examples have given a flavour of ASN.1 notation and illustrate its use from a top-down perspective. In this section, the components of ASN.1 notation are discussed.

ASN.1 is built from a small number of basic datatypes (or, more simply, *types*) which can be combined in various ways to construct new types. For example, an ordered list of existing types can be collected into a *sequence*, and an unordered list into a *set*. Certain components of a sequence or set may be allowed to be absent, or may be defaulted to a specified value if omitted. Given a list of types, a new type may be defined as the selection of any one of the values in a *choice* list. New types constructed in any of these ways are known as *structured types*. The following examples show some of the built-in types of ASN.1.

```
-- A Boolean type models a two-state variable.

        ClubMember  ::=  BOOLEAN

-- An Integer type models an integer variable, and may
-- be given upper and lower bounds.

        SubscriptionsPaid  ::=  INTEGER (1..max-members)

-- A Real type models a real number.

        StandardDeviation  ::=  REAL
```

```
--An Enumerated type models an integer whose values are given
-- distinct identifiers.

        PassCard  ::=  ENUMERATED { member(0), spouse(1),
                            associate(2), guest(3) }


-- A Bit String type models binary data, either a bitmap or a
-- collection of related logical variables.

        G3FacsimilePage  ::=  BIT STRING
        PeriodsOpen  ::=  BIT STRING {morning(0), afternoon(1),
                                      evening(2) }


-- An Octet String models binary data whose length is a multiple of 8 bits.

        MessageContent  ::=  OCTET STRING

-- A Null type indicates the absence of an element of a Sequence.

        MemberDetails  ::=  SEQUENCE {
             name               VisibleString,
             locker             CHOICE {
                  key-number         INTEGER,
                  non-player         NULL }   }

-- A Sequence may be used to model an ordered collection of variables of
-- the same type, possibly large in number.

        SeniorOfficers  ::=  SEQUENCE OF VisibleString
        -- in order of seniority

-- A Sequence is also used to model an ordered collection of variables
-- whose types may differ, and whose number is modest.

        FileHistory  ::=  SEQUENCE {
             creation-date       UTCTime,
             last-change         UTCTime,
             changed-by          VisibleString }

-- A Set is used to model a collection of variables whose types are
-- the same and whose order is insignificant.

        CommitteeMembers  ::= SET OF VisibleString

-- A Set is also used to model a collection of variables whose order is
-- insignificant, and whose number is known.  Each variable is identified
-- by a context-specific tag (see below).

        Applicant  ::=  SET {
            surname         [0]  PrintableString,
            given-name      [1]  PrintableString,
            phone-no        [2]  NumericString }
```

```
-- A Choice is used to model a variable that is selected from a group of
-- candidates. Each of these is identified by a context-specific tag.

        UpperLimit  ::=  CHOICE {
           latest        [0]  UTCTime,
           largest       [1]  INTEGER }
```

AI.3 TAGGING

Some of the examples shown above make use of *context-specific tagging* to distinguish elements of a Set or Choice. In fact all types possess a tag, such that an Integer can always be distinguished from a Bit String, but for the built-in types the tag-number is 'understood', and the notation does not show it explicitly. For other types, tagging allows further semantic and syntactic constraints to be attached to values of otherwise identical type (e.g. NumberOfChildren and RoomNumber are both Integers). Four classes of tag are defined: Universal tags are confined to types defined in the ASN.1 standard; Application tags define types which have scope throughout a particular Application standard; Private tags are intended for use within proprietory products and do not appear in international standards; Context-specific tags, as we have seen, are used freely within a Set or Choice to distinguish its members, and are limited in scope to that Set or Choice construct.

One aspect of ASN.1 which has fallen out of favour is the use of *implicit tagging*. This allows the type of a value to be implied by the value of its context-specific tag, rather than shown explicitly by its standard tag. This gives an encoding which is a few bytes shorter than that produced by explicit tagging, at the expense of some robustness. Consider the following definitions:

```
TypeA  ::=  VisibleString
TypeB  ::=  [0] IMPLICIT TypeA
TypeC  ::=  [0] TypeA
```

The representation of TypeB differs from that of TypeC in that the former omits the identifier (tag) which explicitly indicates that the value contains a VisibleString (i.e. TypeB contains the tag [0] followed by the octets of the string). In TypeC, this item of information is included (i.e. tag [0] is followed by the tag VisibleString, then the octets). While implicit tagging does give a more compact encoding, problems of ambiguity have arisen where attempts have been made to extend existing standards which use it. Consequently, the use of implicit tagging has diminished. Further, in the most recently published standards, context-specific tagging is employed in almost every Sequence, Set, and Choice, even where this introduces apparent redundancy. Given the unpredictability of requirements which may arise in the future, this approach is calculated to eliminate unnecessary constraints on the development of extensions.

The difficulties in extending an existing standard have been recognized in MHS, and an EXTENSIONS macro has been developed in that standard which enables an implementation to cope with encodings it does not recognize. The method allows an implementation to determine whether an extension component within a PDU may be safely ignored, or whether it is of critical importance, and gives grounds for failing the associated service request.

AI.4 ADDITIONAL TYPES

A number of types are defined in ASN.1 which are expected to be of use in many applications. Universal time (UTCTime) defines values which represent a calendar date and time, and may optionally include a local time differential factor.

A variety of character string types are defined, which correspond to existing character set definitions; these can be regarded as refinements of the Octet String type. These character string types include NumericString, PrintableString, TeletexString and IA5String.

Standards contain many elements which require identification, such as objects, ports, operations, application contexts, ASEs, attribute types, abstract syntaxes, and modules. This naming requirement is satisfied by the use of the *object identifier* type (OID). Object identifiers are constructed as an ordered series of components. The first component identifies the standards authority (ISO, CCITT, or joint-ISO-CCITT) responsible for the OID definition. The second component may identify an ISO standard, an ISO Registration Authority, an ISO national member body, or an organization otherwise authorized to issue OIDs for its own proprietary purposes. Subsequent components are allocated according to the naming requirements of each of these authorities. In effect, this structure constitutes a naming tree, the *object identifier tree*, which has the property that no two information objects may be allocated the same vertex of the tree. Consequently, an information object is unambiguously and uniquely identified by the sequence of OID components which constitute its OID. It is stressed that OIDs identify classes of object rather than specific instances of that class (hence an abstract syntax OID identifies a type of PDU rather than a specific PDU encoded according to the abstract syntax definition).

AI.5 BASIC ENCODING RULES

The description of ASN.1 is completed by considering the encoding rules which determine the representation of a value when exchanged between open systems (the transfer syntax). Given the distinction drawn between specification, and a method of concrete representation, it is clear that more than one set of encoding rules could be devised capable of producing a transfer syntax for values of a specified type. ISO 8825 defines one particular set of encoding rules, called the *basic encoding rules* for ASN.1.

The encoding of a data value contains four components: identifier, length, contents, and end-of-contents. The *identifier octets* encode the tag of the data value. A tag consists of two parts, class and number. The four classes of tag have already been introduced, Universal, Application, Private, and Context-specific. The built-in types described in this Appendix all have Universal tags and are distinguished by number.

The *length octets* indicate the number of octets occupied by the contents. There are two forms of length encoding: in the definite form, the length is represented directly; in the indefinite form, the overall length is not known. In this latter case, the content is constructed as a series of component data values, each with its own identifier, length, and content octets. The end of the series of component data values is marked by a special end-of-contents value. Thus in the indefinite case, the content length can be discovered only by traversing each of the component data values.

The *content octets* contain the primary information of the data value. Its length is variable, but always a multiple of eight bits. As indicated above, content may be simple in form, or *constructed*, where it comprises a series of component data values. End-of-contents octets are present only where the length is encoded in the indefinite form.

The basic encoding rules (and, implicitly, decoding rules) are suitable for automatic machine processing. Indeed a number of ASN.1 compilers have been developed which take ASN.1 specification text as input, and generate programming language output. When compiled, these programs are capable of encoding and parsing PDUs constructed according to the ASN.1 specification. Difficulties have arisen in this approach, notably in cases where macros are used extensively, and revisions to ASN.1 designed to ease these problems may be the subject of future standardization.

Appendix II — Acronyms

ACSE association control service elements
ADMD administration management domain
ASCII USA standard code for information interchange
ASE application service element
ASN.1 abstract syntax notation 1
AU access unit
AVA attribute value assertion
CCITT International Telegraph and Telephone Consultative Committee
CBMS computer based messaging system
CCR commitment, concurrency and recovery
DAP directory access protocol
DCS defined context set
DIB directory information base
DIS draft international standard
DIT directory information tree
DL distribution list
DP draft proposal
DSA directory system agent
DSP directory system protocol
DU data unit
DUA directory user agent
EBCDIC extended binary coded decimal interchange code
EDI electronic data interchange
EIT encoded information type
FADU file access data unit
FTAM file transfer access and management
FU functional unit
IFIP International Federation for Information Processing
IP interpersonal
IPM interpersonal message
IPMS interpersonal messaging system
IPN interpersonal notification
IS international standard
ISO International Standards Organization

ISORM	ISO reference model
JTM	job transfer and manipulation
LAN	local area network
MAP	manufacturing automation protocol
MD	management domain
MHS	message handling system
MS	message store
MTA	message transfer agent
MTS	message transfer system
MTSE	message transfer service element
NC	network connection
OID	object identifier
O/R	originator/recipient
OSI	open systems interconnection
PCDL	presentation context definition list
PCI	protocol control information
PDU	protocol data unit
PM	protocol machine
PRMD	private management domain
PTT	postal telegraphique telephonique
QOS	quality of service
RDN	relative distinguished name
ROS	remote operations
ROSE	remote operations service element
RTSE	reliable transfer service element
SAO	single association object
SAP	service access point
SDE	submission and delivery entity
SDU	service data unit
SPSN	synchronization point serial number
TC	transport connection
UA	user agent
VT	virtual terminal
WAN	wide area network

Appendix III — Glossary

Abstract syntax A formal definition of the contents of an information unit. It does not specify any encoding technique for the representation of such information.

Application Layer seven of the ISORM. It is concerned with the provision of system-independent application services, such as file transfer and electronic messaging.

Application agent The partner to an application entity in an application process, often indivisible from its partner in a real implementation. It represents the union of the system-independent nature of the application to the system-dependent resources that are manipulated by the application (e.g. a filestore).

Application context A named context which specifies, for a particular application, how the association between the systems is established, which ASEs are then used, and how the association is released. In effect this detailed specification constitutes a protocol.

Application process A process available on an end-system that embodies both an application entity and an application agent. It provides OSI application services to end-users (human users or programs).

Application service element These are the building blocks within the modular architecture of the application layer. An ASE is a generic grouping of service elements within the application layer that together offer a service profile covering a specific area of application functionality.

Association A cooperative environment that must be established between peer application processes before application-specific activity can commence.

Association control service element ACSE is a generic grouping of the service elements within the application layer that together offer services related to the establishment and management of a cooperative relationship between peer application processes.

Commitment, concurrency and recovery An ASE concerned with providing a reliable environment over an association.

Connection A logical relationship established by peer (data communication-related) layer entities defining a data path of agreed quality between the peer service users of that layer.

Connection-oriented A mode of operation which requires that a connection be established before data transfer can occur between peers.

Connectionless A mode of operation in which each data exchange carries with it a full description of its destination peer, so that a connection is not required.

Data Notionally a stream of octets handled transparently by the data communication-related layers (session and below). It normally contains application information in a commonly understood encoding (ensured by the presentation layer).

Data link Layer two of the ISORM. It is concerned with the organization of data transmission over a physical medium.

Defined context set A set of presentation contexts negotiated between peer presentation entities.

End-system A computer system capable of initiating, or responding to, an application association request. Also known as an 'open system'.

End-to-end Concerned with activity which occurs directly between peers on end-systems.

Entity An implementation of a layer protocol specification on an end-system providing the system-independent services defined in the service definition. It supports one or many concurrent connections.

Full-duplex A data transfer mode permitting data transmission between peers in both directions at the same time.

Functional unit Within a layer, a grouping of related service elements into a single unit. The definition of subsets of a layer, for implementation and negotiation purposes, is expressed in terms of functional units.

Half-duplex A data transfer mode permitting data transmission between peers in either direction, but in only one direction at any time.

Initiator A service user or layer entity on the end-system which initiated an activity.

Information The object of exchange between application processes during an application association, such exchange representing the purpose of the application activity; e.g. the transfer of a record of a file.

Information unit The basic unit of exchange between application processes. An information unit is defined by an abstract syntax.

Interpersonal messaging system Acting as a 'higher layer' MHS, the IPMS provides for the end-to-end exchange of information between the IPM class of user agents.

Jobmill If an an end-system normally functions in an interactive manner, i.e. with activity controlled by a human user via a terminal, then a jobmill service may be provided where programs can be submitted to run without the need for an interactive terminal. This form of activity is often referred to as 'background' or 'batch'.

Layer A component of the ISORM, which is made up of seven layers.

Message transfer agent The type of entity which populates the message transfer system. MTAs use a store and forward method to relay messages from originator to recipient. They interact with UAs when a message is submitted, and upon delivery.

Message transfer system The basic carrier service for MHS. It conveys messages as transparent data, without regard to content and without alteration.

Network Layer three of the ISORM. It is responsible for coordinating data transmission over a sub-network, and in general for achieving the relaying of data over multiple sub-networks traversed between end-systems involved in a cooperative application association.

Peer An entity of the same layer as that under discussion in the current context.

Physical Layer one of the ISORM. It is concerned with the attachment of an end-system to a real physical medium, and with the mechanics of data bit transmission over that medium.

Presentation Layer six of the ISORM. It is concerned with the representation of application information in transit between peer application processes.

Presentation context — The association of an appropriate transfer syntax with an abstract syntax.

Presentation data value — A logically indivisible part of an information unit. An abstract syntax defines a set of one or more presentation data values.

Protocol — The private language and procedures of a layer.

Protocol control information — That part of a protocol data unit which conveys specific, layer-dependent, instructions between peer layer entities. The remainder of the protocol data unit, if present, contains user data (a service data unit).

Protocol data unit — A message exchanged between peer layer entities which helps to coordinate cooperative activity within the layer. It is made up of protocol control information and, optionally, user data. The format of such messages is defined in the protocol specification.

Protocol machine — The part of a layer entity that is an implementation of the layer protocol specification.

Protocol specification — The precise specification of the protocol of a layer in an ISO document.

Release — An activity that closes a connection or association between cooperating peers.

Remote — The other end-system involved in an OSI activity; e.g. 'remote application process' is a reference to an application process on some end-system other than that which, in the current context, is local.

Remote operations service element — An ASE concerned with providing a basis for remote requests for operations to be submitted to an end-system, and for that end-system to be able to issue a reply to the initiating end-system.

Responder — The peer of the service user or layer entity defined under 'initiator'.

Resynchronization — A service provided by the session layer to support controlled restarting of an information exchange between peer application processes, usually after some failure in the lower layers.

Service — A facility provided by a layer to its (superior) user — layer entity or application agent — by use of which it in turn performs its functions.

Service access point — The notional point at which a service user and a layer entity can meet so that services can be offered by the layer entity to the particular user. The interface through a service access point is the set of service primitives defined in the service definition.

Service access point address A label which uniquely identifies a point of contact between a layer entity and a service user (a superior layer entity). Service access point addresses effectively tie together a 'stack' of entities for a particular application association.

Service data unit A unit of data that is transparently transferred between superior peer service users by the cooperation of peer entities of that layer.

Service definition An ISO document defining the services provided by a layer to its (superior) users.

Service element That part of a layer protocol concerned with the realization of a particular service.

Service primitive The interface, defined in the service definition, between a layer entity and a service user. There are four types: request, indication, response and confirm.

Service provider The whole of the subordinate OSI communications environment as seen by cooperating peer service users.

Service user A user (generally a superior layer entity) of services provided by the cooperation of peer layer entities. Access to these services is provided by service primitives.

Session Layer five of the ISORM. It provides high-level management of data communication.

Single association object A component of an application entity that is composed of a single instance of ACSE, together with any meaningful combination of ASEs.

Standard A formal description of a layer to which ISO/OSI products must conform in full or in part; legal subsets are defined in terms of functional units.

Sub-network The combination of a real physical medium and a method of organization of data transmission over that medium which forms a data transmission capability between two computer systems.

Synchronization A set of services provided by the session layer to support the coordination of the exchange of information between peer application processes.

Token A mechanism of the session layer used to determine which end-system is currently in control of some aspect of session activity. A token is available for use only if the functional unit with which it is associated is selected in the particular connection.

Transfer syntax A specification for the encoding of information of a given abstract syntax that will be applied to such information whilst it is in transit between peer application processes.

Transport Layer four of the ISORM. It provides a reliable data transfer service to the session layer, irrespective of the reliability of the underlying sub-network(s).

User agent The user agent provides access to MHS for its end-user. The minimum functions which the UA must provide is the ability to perform the submission and delivery interactions with the MTA.

Virtual filestore An abstract model for describing files and filestores and possible actions on them.

Appendix IV — The ISO standards

ISO set up a sub-committee (SC16) to develop OSI in 1977 and the first fundamental document to emerge from this was the Basic Reference Model, the ISORM (1979). Since then standards for individual layers have been developed with those for the lower layers appearing first. This was simply because the lower layers modelled an environment that was well understood and for which there were already working 'de facto' international standards. The standards for the upper layers have been longer in the melting pot and are only now beginning to solidify into International Standards (IS). There are a number of stages in the standardization process and progression between each is achieved by international consensus. Basically these stages are: Draft Proposal (DP), Draft International Standard (DIS) and International Standard (IS). Only on reaching IS can a standard be regarded as totally 'stable' although many manufacturers will, in anticipation of stability, begin to implement standards when they reach the DIS stage. Once a standard reaches IS, it can be 'enhanced' or 'clarified' by the addition of addendums which go through a similar 'staging' procedure before becoming a part of an IS.

Listed below, in numerical order, are the ISO documents to which the reader can refer for detailed presentation of all aspects of OSI covered in this book. These documents are available from National Standards Institutions, for example, in Great Britain from: British Standards Institute, Linford Wood, Milton Keynes, MK14 6LE.

ISO 7498 Information Processing Systems — Open Systems Interconnection — Basic Reference Model

ISO 8072 Information Processing Systems — Open Systems Interconnection — Transport Service Definition

ISO 8073 Information Processing Systems — Open Systems Interconnection — Transport Protocol Specification

ISO 8326 Information Processing Systems — Open Systems Interconnection — Connection Oriented Session Service Definition

ISO 8327 Information Processing Systems — Open Systems Interconnection — Connection Oriented Session Protocol Specification

ISO 8348 Information Processing Systems — Open Systems Interconnection — Network Service Definition

ISO 8509 Information Processing Systems — Open Systems Interconnection — Service Conventions

ISO 8571 Information Processing Systems — Open Systems Interconnection — File Transfer, Access and Management
Part 1: General Introduction
Part 2: The Virtual Filestore
Part 3: File Service Definition
Part 4: File Protocol Specification
Part 5: Protocol Implementation Conformance Statement Proforma

ISO 8649 Information Processing Systems — Open Systems Interconnection — Association Control: Service definition

ISO 8650 Information Processing Systems — Open Systems Interconnection — Association Control: Protocol specification

ISO 8822 Information Processing Systems — Open Systems Interconnection — Connection Oriented Presentation Service Definition

ISO 8823 Information Processing Systems — Open Systems Interconnection — Connection Oriented Presentation Protocol Specification

ISO 8824 Information Processing Systems — Open Systems Interconnection — Specification of Abstract Syntax Notation One (ASN.1)

ISO 8825 Information Processing Systems — Open Systems Interconnection — Specification of Basic Encoding Rules for Abstract Syntax Notation One

ISO 8831 Information Processing Systems — Open Systems Interconnection — Job Transfer and Manipulation Concepts and Services

ISO 9040 Information Processing Systems — Open Systems Interconnection — Virtual Terminal Services

ISO 9066-1 Information processing systems — Text communication — Reliable transfer part 1: Model and Service Definition

ISO 9066-2 Information processing systems — Text communication — Reliable transfer part 2: Protocol specification

ISO 9072-1 Information processing systems — Text communication — Remote operations part 1: Model, notation and service definition

ISO 9072-2 Information processing systems — Text communication — Remote operations part 2: Protocol specification

ISO 9594-1 Information processing systems — The directory — Overview of Concepts, Models and Services

ISO 9594-2 Information processing systems — The directory — Models

ISO 9594-3 Information processing systems — The directory — Abstract service definition

ISO 9594-4 Information processing systems — The directory — Procedures for distributed operation

ISO 9594-5 Information processing systems — The directory — Protocol specifications

ISO 9594-6 Information processing systems — The directory — Selected attribute types.

ISO 9594-7 Information processing systems — The directory — Selected object classes.

ISO 9594-8 Information processing systems — The directory — Authentication framework.

ISO 10021-1 Information processing systems — Text communication — MOTIS — Service and system overview.

ISO 10021-2 Information processing systems — Text communication — MOTIS — Overall architecture.

ISO 10021-3 Information processing systems — Text communication — MOTIS — Abstract service definition conventions.

ISO 10021-4 Information processing systems — Text communication — MOTIS — Message transfer system: Abstract service definition and procedures.

ISO 10021-5 Information processing systems — Text communication — MOTIS — Message store: Abstract service definition.

ISO 10021-6 Information processing systems — Text communication — MOTIS — Protocol specifications.

ISO 10021-7 Information processing systems — Text communication — MOTIS — Interpersonal messaging system.

Appendix V — References

Adams, D. (1979) *The Hitch-hikers Guide to the Galaxy*. Pan Books, London.
Currie, S. (1988) *LANs Explained*. Ellis Horwood, Chichester.
Deasington, R. (1986) *X.25 Explained*. Second Edition. Ellis Horwood, Chichester.
Tanenbaum, A. S. (1988) *Computer Networks*. Second Edition. Prentice Hall.

Index

ELLIS HORWOOD SERIES IN COMPUTERS AND THEIR APPLICATIONS

Series Editor: IAN CHIVERS, Senior Analyst, The Computer Centre, King's College, London, and formerly Senior Programmer and Analyst, Imperial College of Science and Technology, University of London

Matthews, J.L.	FORTH
Millington, D.	SYSTEMS ANALYSIS AND DESIGN FOR COMPUTER APPLICATIONS
Moseley, L.G., Sharp, J.A. & Salenieks, P.	PASCAL IN PRACTICE
Moylan, P.	ASSEMBLY LANGUAGE FOR ENGINEERS
Narayanan, A. & Sharkey, N.E.	AN INTRODUCTION TO LISP
Parrington, N. & Roper, M.	UNDERSTANDING SOFTWARE TESTING
Paterson, A.	OFFICE SYSTEMS
Phillips, C. & Cornelius, B.J.	COMPUTATIONAL NUMERICAL METHODS
Rahtz, S.P.Q.	INFORMATION TECHNOLOGY IN THE HUMANITIES
Ramsden, E.	MICROCOMPUTERS IN EDUCATION 2
Rubin, T.	USER INTERFACE DESIGN FOR COMPUTER SYSTEMS
Rudd, A.S.	PRACTICAL USAGE OF ISPF DIALOG MANAGER
de Saram, H.	PROGRAMMING IN MICRO-PROLOG
Savic, D.	OBJECT ORIENTED PROGRAMMING WITH SMALLTALK/V
Schirmer, C.	PROGRAMMING IN C FOR UNIX
Schofield, C.F.	OPTIMIZING FORTRAN PROGRAMS
Sharp, J.A.	DATA FLOW COMPUTING
Sherif, M.A.	DATABASE PROJECTS
Smith & Sage	EDUCATION AND THE INFORMATION SOCIETY
Smith, J.M & Stutely, R.	SGML
Späth, H.	CLUSTER ANALYSIS ALGORITHMS
Späth, H.	CLUSTER DISSECTION AND ANALYSIS
Stratford-Collins, P.	ADA
Tizzard, K.	C FOR PROFESSIONAL PROGRAMMERS
Turner, S.J.	AN INTRODUCTION TO COMPILER DESIGN
Wexler, J.	CONCURRENT PROGRAMMING IN OCCAM 2
Whiddett, R.J.	CONCURRENT PROGRAMMING FOR SOFTWARE ENGINEERS
Whiddett, R.J., Berry, R.E., Blair, G.S., Hurley, P.N., Nicol, P.J., Muir, S.J.	UNIX
Yannakoudakis, E.J. & Hutton, P.J.	SPEECH SYNTHESIS AND RECOGNITION SYSTEMS
Zech, R.	FORTH